NONVIOLENCE

"Considering the hostile and violent state of our world, Christians cannot afford to be ignorant on this issue. We need to know ahead of time how Christ wants us to respond so that we don't make tragic mistakes when unexpected events come our way. While so many argue from clever human logic, Preston has taken the time to make a solid biblical argument. I highly recommend that every believer examine the truths in this book. You may discover that much of your current belief system has been influenced by sources other than Scripture."

Francis Chan, *New York Times*
bestselling author of *Crazy Love,*
Letters to the Church, and *Forgotten God*

"We need Preston Sprinkle's book because there are too many Christians who haven't given a moment's thought to their own violent use of our glorious Scripture's message of peace by approving and applauding the use of violence to accomplish peace. The contradictions at work are baffling. Bravo to Preston Sprinkle!"

Scot McKnight, professor of New
Testament at Northern Seminary

"When I was in college a student had the sense that between the Old Testament and the New Testament God either had a conversion experience or went through an anger management seminar. What Preston Sprinkle does in this book is show how erroneous such thinking is. He lays out a strong biblical case that the God of Moses and Joshua is the same God incarnated in Jesus. This is a God who calls us to nonviolence in our confrontations with evil and the agents of war. For those who take the Bible seriously this book will do much to move us beyond sentimental pacifism to a scriptural basis for nonviolent resistances."

Tony Campolo, professor emeritus of
Sociology at Eastern University

"Evangelical Christians often think they know what the 'biblical position' is on matters of war and supporting 'our troops.' Preston Sprinkle reads the Bible through the same evangelical lenses but comes to radically different conclusions: that the Bible opposes militarism and promotes nonviolence from Genesis to Revelation. Those who read this book with an open mind will be forced to do what the author himself did: rethink what it means to be Christian, especially in the most militarily powerful nation on earth."

Michael J. Gorman, Raymond E. Brown
Professor of Biblical Studies and Theology at St.
Mary's Seminary and University in Baltimore

"Preston Sprinkle's *Nonviolence* is timely and compelling, in our culture where peace is the great lacking commodity. Sprinkle explains how Jesus Christ was deeply passionate about peace and ending violence. His solution was never weapons or war. His answer was always peace. Because His kingdom is a kingdom of peace. Sometimes Christians pursue inner personal peace and live ambivalent to a world that has no peace. Sprinkle is spot-on when he explains that the peace of God is *not* something we only experience on the inside, nor is His peace only for a kingdom after we die. The peace of God is for this world today. Sprinkle's powerful challenge is for Christ-followers everywhere, to become promoters of peace, teach peace, model peace, and lead the way to peace on earth—as it is in heaven."

Palmer Chinchen, PhD, cultural artist, speaker,
and author of *True Religion* and *Barefoot Tribe*

"I served the kingdom of America in three wars: World War II, Korea, and Vietnam. But then I became a Christian and my view of war radically changed. I now believe that Christians should serve the kingdom of Christ. There are many ways in which Christians can honor their country—one could be a conscientious objector and serve in the military in that way. Preston Sprinkle has written a compelling book that examines what the whole Bible says about warfare and violence. *Nonviolence* will steer your gaze away from a nationalistic worldview and force you to look upon Jesus, the One who conquered the enemy by suffering."

Robert Armstrong, Master Sergeant in the
US Marine Corps (Ret.) and veteran of World
War II, Korea (Purple Heart), and Vietnam.

"*Nonviolence* will challenge you as it did me. Sprinkle goes after the most difficult biblical issues involving Christian nonviolence. The book speaks passionately to the 'problem,' especially within the conservative side of evangelicalism, of nonviolence. More specifically, it seems that the more conservative one's Christian position, the more hawkish they tend to be. This should not be so. Those who want to be peacemakers will be empowered by the freshness and vigor Sprinkle brings to the subject. As a war veteran and now as a Christian, I recommend reading this new effort to reconcile the problem of violence with the peaceable kingdom to which Jesus seems to repeatedly allude."

Steve Watkins, adjunct professor of Religious Studies and Humanities at Northern Kentucky University and Lieutenant Commander in the Chaplain Corps of the US Navy (SEAL).

NONVIOLENCE

NONVIOLENCE
THE REVOLUTIONARY WAY OF JESUS

PRESTON SPRINKLE

with
ANDREW RILLERA

DAVID C COOK

transforming lives together

NONVIOLENCE
Published by David C Cook
4050 Lee Vance Drive
Colorado Springs, CO 80918 U.S.A.

Integrity Music Limited, a Division of David C Cook
Brighton, East Sussex BN1 2RE, England

The graphic circle C logo is a registered trademark of David C Cook.

The website addresses recommended throughout this book are offered as a
resource to you. These websites are not intended in any way to be or imply an
endorsement on the part of David C Cook, nor do we vouch for their content.

All Scripture quotations, unless otherwise noted, are taken from The Holy
Bible, English Standard Version® (ESV®), copyright © 2001 by Crossway, a
publishing ministry of Good News Publishers. Used by permission. All rights
reserved. Scripture quotations marked NASB are taken from the New American
Standard Bible®, Copyright © 1960, 1995 by The Lockman Foundation.
Used by permission. (www.Lockman.org.); NIV are taken from the Holy
Bible, New International Version®, NIV®. Copyright © 1973, 1984 by Biblica,
Inc. ® Used by permission of Zondervan. All rights reserved worldwide.
www.zondervan.com; NLT are taken from the Holy Bible, New Living Translation,
copyright © 1996, 2007 by Tyndale House Foundation. Used by permission
of Tyndale House Publishers, Inc., Carol Stream, Illinois 60188. All rights
reserved; NEB are taken from the New English Bible, copyright © Cambridge
University Press and Oxford University Press 1961, 1970. All rights reserved.
The author has added italics to quotations for emphasis.

Library of Congress Control Number 2013940870
ISBN 978-0-8307-8177-5
eISBN 978-0-8307-8251-2

The Team: Alex Field, Michael Covington, Karen Lee-Thorp,
Amy Konyndyk, Caitlyn Carlson, Karen Athen
Cover Design: James Hershberger
Cover Illustrator: Zach Richert

Printed in the United States of America
First Edition 2013

1 2 3 4 5 6 7 8 9 10

011521

CONTENTS

ACKNOWLEDGMENTS

Since the topic of warfare and violence is furiously debated, I wanted to go out of my way to have my view critiqued before I published it. Therefore, during the writing process, I had dozens of scholars, pastors, professionals, and laypeople read parts (or all) of this manuscript.

At the top of the list is my friend and former student Andrew Rillera. Andrew is one of the brightest students I've ever had, and therefore he was an easy choice as I sought help to write this book. He devoted countless hours to research, editing, and helping craft and recraft arguments in several chapters.

I'm very thankful and honored to have Greg Boyd write a new foreword to this book. As many will know, Greg has been passionate about this topic for many years, and I personally have learned so much from him. While we don't agree on everything when it comes to Christian nonviolence (in particular, how to understand violent commands in the Old Testament), Greg has been a trustworthy guide in my own journey, and I'm honored to call him a friend.

Many other biblical scholars and historians took precious time to read through chunks of this book. Thanks to Benjamin Foreman, Ron Sider, Peter Leithart, Joey Dodson, Scott Duvall, Paul Larson, Andrew Pitts, George Kalantzis, Ben Reynolds, Jason Hood, Joel Willitts, and Richard Hess.

Special thanks to Tremper Longman for carefully reading through the Old Testament chapters and walking me through his improvements as we threw down some killer Mexican food in Santa Barbara.

Many thanks also to Scot McKnight, who not only read the New Testament section and offered many helpful comments, but who also encouraged me throughout the writing process.

I also chatted with several ex- (and current) military friends about the contents of this book. Thanks to Steve Watson, Bob Armstrong, and Parker Armstrong (no relation).

Several philosophers and ethicists picked apart my last couple chapters and offered invaluable feedback. Thanks to Jeff Steele, Jeff Cook, and especially Justin Bronson, whose extensive comments on several drafts of chapters 11 and 12 exceeded my own word count in those chapters. I also thank that group of professors at Ouachita Baptist University, mostly philosophers, who went around and around with me about using violence as a last resort in defense of the innocent. Tully, Matt, Eric, Big Dread, and several others whose names have escaped me. That was a fun night. Though I'm glad a fight didn't break out. I would have lost.

Several pastors and laypeople read some or all of my earlier drafts and offered very helpful comments, especially when it came to communicating to the "normal" person. Thanks to Matt Halsted, Gregg Lennox, Grant Pedersen, Ryan Hinkle, Matt Larson, Dalton Sprinkle, and Todd Nighswonger. Most of all, my wife, Christine, combed through several chapters and saved me from saying some pretty stupid things. Thanks, hunny, for your invaluable feedback, but most of all for being the best wife a guy could ask for.

Thanks to my four kids, Kaylea, Aubrey, Josie, and Cody, for loving me and always asking, "Are you done with your book yet, Daddy?" Yes, kids, I'm done with my book!

Mark Beuving—my friend, colleague, and faithful editor—read through the entire manuscript with a fine-toothed comb. I can't imagine ever publishing a book without it first passing by your eyes.

And thanks to the folks at David C Cook for your commitment to me and this project: Alex Field, Caitlyn Carlson, Don Pape, and Karen Lee-Thorp.

Most of all, thank You, Jesus, for sustaining me and forgiving me for mistakes I've made in this book. I hope that it's still a pleasing aroma in Your sight and brings much glory to Your name. If it doesn't, then please raise up someone else to write a response that corrects my error. May Your truth, not mine, be magnified.

FOREWORD

Have you ever found yourself reading a familiar passage of Scripture, but for whatever reason, this time it felt like you were reading the passage for the very first time? Perhaps you see something you hadn't noticed before, or perhaps you feel the gravitas of the passage more profoundly than you had previously.

Both happened to me in 2003 as I was reading Jesus' Sermon on the Mount. I came to Matthew 5:44–45, where Jesus instructed His audience to "love your enemies and pray for those who persecute you, that you may be children of your Father in heaven." Jesus then explained that the Father "causes his sun to rise on the evil and the good, and sends rain on the righteous and the unrighteous." I had at this point been a Bible-reading Christian for almost thirty years and had read this passage numerous times. But this time, for some reason, the passage rocked my world!

Among other things, I had never before appreciated the unqualified nature of Jesus' instruction. Love and pray for enemies, full stop. No qualifications, no exceptions, no conditions. In fact, as I contemplated this remarkable teaching, it occurred to me that there *couldn't* be any exceptions to Jesus' command to love enemies since Jesus based His teaching not on the relative merits of our enemy's character but on the unconditionally loving character of our heavenly Father. The Father's love is reflected in the fact that He "causes his sun to rise on the evil and the good" and "sends rain on the righteous and the unrighteous." In other words, the Father loves the way the rain falls and the sun shines. God's love, then, is an indiscriminating kind of love.

Moreover, I noticed for the first time that Jesus instructed His followers to love like this *"that you may be* children of your Father in heaven."	Jesus makes our willingness to unconditionally love enemies and to pray for persecutors the benchmark criteria for being considered a child of the Father! When we love the indiscriminating way our Father loves, we reflect the truth that we are "born from above" (see John 3:3) and have our Father's "DNA," as it were. Once I gained this insight, I discovered over time that, in one form or another, this teaching permeates the New Testament and is even anticipated throughout the Old Testament, as will become abundantly clear as you read this book.

As eye-opening as my new reading of Matthew 5:44–45 was, it also raised a number of difficult questions. Given that unqualified enemy love is the benchmark for being considered a child of the heavenly Father, how is it that so few Christians throughout history, at least since the fourth century, have grasped this? Even more puzzling, how is it that the church often seemed to practice the opposite of this teaching? One thinks of the Crusades, the Inquisition, the many wars Christians waged against other Christians throughout Europe and in the American Revolution, as well as the manner in which the church to a large degree condoned the violent enslavement of Africans and the unjust treatment of the natives in America. How did a people who were called to never forcefully resist an evil person (Matt. 5:39), to always turn the other cheek (Matt. 5:39), and to be "peacemakers" (Matt. 5:9) develop such an appetite for violence?

While killing for religious purposes was thankfully outlawed in Western countries since the mid-seventeenth century, it's not like the Western church, and especially the church in America, has lost its taste for violence. Evangelical American Christians tend to be more supportive of the US military, of capital punishment, and of gun-ownership rights than the general population—which is saying *a lot* given the love this country has always had for guns. How have we so consistently minimized, if not completely overlooked, Jesus' benchmark teaching?

However we might answer that question, the good news is that the Spirit is currently removing the blindfolds from many people's eyes. Since 2003, when I first embraced Jesus' benchmark instruction, I have become aware of the growing multitude of people all over the globe—and Preston Sprinkle is certainly one of them—who have had experiences similar to mine. Their eyes have been opened to the importance, truth, and beauty of the New Testament's call to enemy-love and nonviolence.

On that note, I would like to challenge you to read *Nonviolence: The Revolutionary Way of Jesus* carefully and with an open mind and heart. For if you do, you might very well consider yourself part of this Spirit-led movement by the time you finish it.

My 2003 discovery also raised a number of important and challenging biblical questions. How, for example, are we to reconcile Jesus' revelation of a nonviolent God with the Old Testament's several depictions of God commanding the Israelites to "show no mercy" as they slaughtered "anything that breathes" in certain regions of "the promised land"? And how does Jesus' revelation square with the Old Testament's depiction of God almost wiping out the entire human race in a flood or of God drowning Pharaoh's army in the Red Sea or of God incinerating Sodom and Gomorrah?

Finally, when I grasped Jesus' benchmark for being considered a child of the Father, it raised a host of practical questions. For example, does Jesus really expect His followers to "not resist an evil person" when that evil person intends to harm and perhaps kill them or their loved ones? And how does the New Testament's teaching on loving enemies apply in the face of monstrous leaders like Adolf Hitler? Wasn't it a good thing that a multitude of brave US and Allied soldiers were willing to take up arms against Nazism?

In the pages that follow, Preston spells out the biblical case for nonviolence in a clear, concise, fair, and compelling manner. Just as importantly, he boldly addresses the sorts of questions I just raised. Readers may not agree with every aspect of Preston's responses (I don't), but I doubt any sympathetic reader will be able to deny the overall force of the excellent case he puts forth.

I would like to close with a brief prayer.

"Gracious Lord, use this work to teach all who profess faith in Christ what it really means to love like the Father loves, which is to say, what it means to walk as a child of our heavenly Father."

—*Greg Boyd*
Pastor, teacher, speaker,
and author of 18 books

MOUNTAIN OF SKULLS

TREE OF LIFE

The strange-looking tree on the cover of this book depicts a "tree of life"—the rich symbol of peace that envelopes the biblical story. We see it in Eden. We see it in the New Jerusalem. But the one on the cover can be seen in Mozambique. It stands as a beacon of hope on a mountain of skulls.

Like many countries in Africa, Mozambique has a history of violence. Two years after the country was decolonized in 1975, a civil war erupted—a war that one anthropologist described as "among the worst in contemporary times."[1] For the next fifteen years, Mozambicans hacked each other to pieces as they fought for control, and the blood flowed wide and deep. Over one million people died in the war, half of whom were children. Nearly half of its sixteen million citizens were affected by the war on some level. They were raped, abused, tortured, blinded, dismembered, kidnapped, starved, enslaved, and exiled. Children saw parents slaughtered. Parents saw children boiled. Farmers were nailed to trees. Heads were used as footstools to give rest to weary killers. Those who survived were forever crushed by the psychological effects of violence. "Our life has been taken from us," said one survivor. "The life here, the life in the world, is no good now, it has been broken by war. We eat suffering for dinner."[2]

Though the war ended in 1992, its horrid memory will never end. Reversing the psychological impact of the war seemed to be an insurmountable hurdle. But there was another problem. After the 1992 peace agreement, more than seven million guns remained buried in caches across Mozambique. This posed a real threat to the volatile situation. Though there was peace, violence could erupt at any moment. So with international support, the government of Mozambique initiated several disarmament projects aimed at weeding out the hidden weapons. One of these initiatives was the Christian-backed "Tools for Arms" project, otherwise known as "Swords into Plowshares."[3]

The project got its name from the book of Isaiah, which predicts a time of peace when warring nations will "beat their swords into plowshares, and their spears into pruning hooks," and they will not "learn war anymore" (Isa. 2:4). Instruments of violence will be turned into instruments of productivity. And this was the logic behind the Mozambican initiative. In order to draw out the weapons from the bush, people were given an instrument of agriculture in exchange for every weapon turned in. A shovel for a rifle, a plow for a machine gun. One village turned in a whole cache of weapons and received a tractor in return. The initiative wasn't perfect. Mozambique still has many problems. But it hasn't seen anything like the unspeakable bloodshed that soaked the dust for those fifteen brutal years.

So what did they do with all those weapons? They turned them into symbols of peace. They hammered them into trees of life.

One of the ways to reverse the effects of war is to take the very tools of violence and forge them into symbols of hope. As part of the "Swords into Plowshares" project, Mozambican sculptors decommissioned the guns and used the parts to create works of art—sculptures that symbolize peace. Isaiah's prophecy provided a soothing balm for the incurable wound of a country ripped apart by warfare. And these sculpted trees of life capture an aspect of Jesus's vision for the world—a vision of peace and harmony secured by His own blood and guaranteed through His resurrection.

VIOLENCE AND WARFARE IN THE TWENTIETH CENTURY

Mozambique is only one of many countries longing for peace. The last hundred years have been called the most violent century in history.[4] Over 187 million people, most of whom were civilians, have been killed in war. Around 170 million have been killed by their own governments. We've witnessed at least seven different genocides, including the Rwandan bloodbath in 1994 when eight hundred thousand people were slaughtered in just ninety days. And Rwanda was a Christian country, one of the most Christianized places in the world. Still, mothers with babies on their backs hacked to pieces next-door neighbors with babies on their backs, and Rwanda—a largely unknown country—became infamous.

Then there's the threat of nuclear warfare. One nuclear warhead could decimate Los Angeles. Fifty could take out California. A thousand could erase America from the globe. Currently, there are twenty-six thousand nuclear warheads in the world, each of them eight times more powerful than the one America dropped on Hiroshima, which killed over one hundred thousand people. We could literally blow up the entire planet tomorrow.

Then there's the escalation of violent crimes: homicide, rape, and torture, not to mention the multibillion-dollar industry of human trafficking. Movies and music are much more violent than they were just fifty years ago, and video games have been added to the mix. The world's passion for violence is growing, and its callousness toward it is thickening.

We long to see millions of sculpted trees of life strung across the globe.

CHRISTIANS AND WARFARE

So what is the Christian response to warfare and violence? Is it ever necessary to wage war to confront evil? Or can you use violence toward an enemy who is attacking your family? And what about capital punishment? Should Christians celebrate the death of a mass murderer? Or a suicide bomber? How about killing to save a life? Self-defense? Serving in the military? Killing in the military? Do we pray that dictators meet Jesus or meet a sniper? Surely Hitler could have used a bullet to the head! And how should the church view its relationship to the state? When our country goes to war, demands our patriotism, promotes itself as the hope of the world, how should the church respond? Total allegiance? Qualified allegiance? Indifference? Protest?

Christians can't seem to find a common answer to any of these questions. This is natural, of course, since Christians disagree over many things. But what has shocked me—what has led me to write this book—is how outraged Christians get toward those who disagree with them on these issues. If you ever want to stir up your Bible study, ask the other people if it'd be okay to join the military, kill an intruder, or assassinate Hitler if you had the chance. Ask them if they wept or cheered when bin Laden was killed. The questions themselves make people angry. I've dealt with many issues over the years—free will and election, spiritual gifts, the end times—but I have never seen such heated discussions erupt as when issues of war, violence, and nationalism come up. Never. Disagreement over these issues pricks something deep in the heart of us.

All the more need to open God's Word to see what *He* thinks about these issues.

So let me ease the tension. This book is not intended to be the last word on the subject, and it's certainly not the first. I'm writing this book to help contribute to the ongoing discussion of how Christians should think about warfare, violence, and their close cousin, nationalism. I'm not going to answer all the questions, mostly because I don't have all of the answers! I have spent much time researching this topic, and the one thing I've seen is that the Bible doesn't always give straightforward answers to all of our questions. But in order to address these issues from a Christian perspective, we need to dig into Scripture to see what God does say about them. So often in heated debates, the Bible is rarely consulted. Or if it is, it's done haphazardly or with blatant bias. Oftentimes we start with a view we are convinced is right; *then* we go to Scripture to find verses that support it. We're all guilty of this on some level. But we should at least work hard at laying aside our preconceived beliefs about warfare and violence and invite God to critique our view in light of His precious Word.

MY RELUCTANT JOURNEY TOWARD NONVIOLENCE

Now, as the title of this book suggests, I have come to a working conclusion about Christians and violence. I believe that the Bible advocates nonviolence. I do not believe that Jesus wants Christians to use violence. And if I can be so blunt: I think that a large portion of the American evangelical church has been seduced, whether knowingly or not, by nationalistic militarism. Yet our inspired Word of God aggressively critiques this very thing, as we will see.

But you should know, I wasn't handed this view growing up. It doesn't come from hippie parents or a Mennonite pastor. I didn't grow up a "pacifist," and I don't have a natural aversion to violence and bloodshed. In fact, everything in my upbringing cuts against the grain of what I'm going to argue in this book. I grew up in a Christian home, and like many evangelicals, I was enamored with war. I played with toy tanks and soldiers, loved watching old war films, and cheered with all my might when America fought against the Iraqis in Desert Storm. My immediate reaction after 9/11 was, *Let's just nuke the Middle East and get rid of those terrorists!* My favorite movies growing up were *Rocky III, Top Gun,* and *Gladiator.* (At the risk of sounding hypocritical, they still are.) Throughout high school and college, I hunted, fished, voted Republican, and chewed tobacco. I even dated a girl who chewed tobacco. I pretty much *was* the guy on the cover of Springsteen's *Born in the USA* album. The idea that someone could be a Christian *and not* think that war and military might were the best way to fight evil was weird and confusing. *Could someone actually read the Bible and still endorse nonviolence? That person must be biblically illiterate or anti-American,* is what I thought.

As I matured in my faith, none of this changed. *Gladiator* came out when I was in seminary, and I was first in line! It wasn't until I taught an ethics course at Cedarville University in Ohio in the spring of 2008 that I began to wrestle with these issues, and for the first time I was forced to consider what the Bible actually says about violence. I was shocked at how many passages in the New Testament discuss violence (and patriotism) and how few of them (if any) support the use of violence by a Christian. Admittedly, the Old Testament is a bit trickier. But my worldview was sent into a tailspin as I searched long and hard to find New Testament support for the so-called just war position. I didn't find any.

And so by the fall of 2009, I became what many people would call (though I don't like the term) a pacifist. In short, I didn't believe that the Bible endorsed the use of violence by the church or individual Christians. Over the last few years, I've spent a lot of time and energy studying this topic, reading opposing views, and looking into Scripture. I've talked to Christians who endorse war and Christians who protest war. I've discussed these issues with Army vets, Marines, Navy SEALs, cops, pacifists, pastors, laypeople, men, women, and people of all ethnicities. I've tried my hardest to understand God's Word and the diverse perspectives of those who read it. And the more I study, the more I discuss, the more I have become convinced of this general position. Christians shouldn't kill or use violence— not even in war.

I'm still an evangelical Christian. And I'm not Amish, Quaker, or Mennonite. I own several guns and still believe that the smell of a recently fired shotgun on a crisp fall morning comes darn near close to paradise. The Christian subculture in which I was raised and still worship is nondenominational conservative Reformed. I've been influenced over the years by John Piper, John MacArthur, R. C. Sproul, and many others who swim in that pond. Shockingly, most within this tradition disagree with my position, some with relentless passion.

All the more need—again—to open God's Word to see what *He* thinks about these issues.

AMERICAN MILITARISM AND THE EVANGELICAL CHURCH

Militarism refers to the "belief or desire … that a country should maintain a strong military capability and be prepared to use it aggressively to defend or promote national interests."[5] By *militarism*, therefore, I do not mean the people participating in the military (I myself come from a long line of Marines) but the overarching "belief or desire" of having a strong military to protect or advance national interests. It's undeniable that America is becoming more and more militarized.[6] And many people—military folks and others—have questioned America's relentless attraction to military prowess. Evangelicals, however, are quick to celebrate it—the bigger the better.

Throughout the twentieth century, American Christians have shown a varied reaction toward military might. But beginning in the late 1970s and through the early twenty-first century, the dominant view among evangelicals has been that militarism is the key to religious freedom and the hope for peace in the world.[7]

For instance, one of Christianity's bestselling authors, Hal Lindsey, located the moral demise of America in the "crisis of military weakness." He believed that "the Bible supports building a powerful military force." Lindsey went on to say that "the Bible is telling the US to become strong again" and "to use our vast and superior technology to create the world's strongest military power."[8] And many evangelicals agree. Jerry Falwell, a widely influential evangelical from the 1970s through the 1990s, called America back to biblical values, which included patriotism and a strong military to ward off the threat of atheistic communism.[9] Military general and fellow evangelical William Boykin said that "Satan wants to destroy this nation … and he wants to destroy us as a Christian army."[10] He therefore saw America's military as an extension of God's fight against evil. Other Christian conservatives, such as G. Russell Evans and C. Greg Singer, argued that only liberals promoted "pacifism, disarmament [of the US military], and abortion on demand."[11] One of evangelicalism's most-read theologians, Wayne Grudem, saw America's "superior military weaponry" as "a good thing for the world." After all, "genuine peace in the world comes through the strength of the United States"[12]—CIA drone strikes notwithstanding.[13]

Being an evangelical has become synonymous with being pro-family, anti-abortion, pro-Republican, and pro-war. All protesting voices are declared liberal or anti-Christian. In fact, when America went to war in Iraq, a flurry of protest arose. Even though the Iraq war was the most opposed war in America's history—even more than Vietnam—"churchgoers were more supportive than non-church-goers and evangelicals were the most supportive of all."[14] Military historian and Vietnam vet Andrew Bacevich wrote, "Were it not for the support offered by several tens of millions of evangelicals, militarism in this deeply and genuinely religious country becomes inconceivable."[15]

Now, this is not the place to argue whether the war in Iraq was just. I only want to point out that evangelicals have a strange affection for military power and an odd history of being pro-war. Perhaps that is why the very thought of nonviolence ignites a near-violent reaction within the church. It's become closely associated with cowardly weakness fit for communists and liberals. We live in a strange scene of redemptive history when opposition to war, violence, and militarism is deemed unchristian.

But we must leave aside all this clutter and read the Bible afresh. We must invite God to challenge our presuppositions, and this is my challenge to all of us: despite your upbringing; despite what you've always been taught; despite what you already think about violence, self-defense, serving in the military, or capital punishment; despite whether you are Republican, Democrat, Libertarian, or Socialist; despite whether you come from a military family—as I do—or are in the military yourself, I ask you to consider with fresh eyes what the whole Bible has to say about this crucial topic. I don't claim to have solved all the issues, nor do I arrogantly believe that everyone who disagrees with me is therefore disagreeing with the Bible. Because I am a human interpreter, my words are fallible. At the same time, I invite you to follow my journey through Scripture and submit to what God says about violence in His infallible Word.

DEFINITION: PACIFISM VERSUS NONVIOLENCE

There are two important words I need to explain up front. First, the word *pacifist* (or *pacifism*). I mentioned above that I don't like this term. Here's why. There are over twenty different types of pacifism, many of which I would not associate with. The term is too broad to be helpful and greatly misunderstood. When people ask me if I'm a pacifist, I ask them to define what they mean. They usually don't know what they mean, or they will define the term in a way that does not describe what I believe. The very term *pacifism* is often thought to mean *passive-ness*. It's assumed that pacifists just sit around and let wicked people wreak havoc on the world. But this is a gross misunderstanding of what I'll argue in this book.

Moreover, there's nothing distinctively Christian about the term *pacifist*. There have been plenty of well-known pacifists who weren't Christian. They believe that it's wrong to use violence, but Jesus is largely irrelevant in their view other than being a good role model. I don't endorse this type of pacifism. In fact, I find it offensive, and I think Jesus does too. Were it not for the life, teaching, death, resurrection, and universal lordship of King Jesus, I would not advocate nonviolence. No way. It doesn't make any human sense to me to let somebody beat me up. Apart from Jesus and the good news of His atoning death and life-giving resurrection, nonviolence seems ridiculous.

Then there is all the cultural baggage that comes with the word *pacifism*. For old Vietnam vets, the term conjures up memories of protestors cursing them when they returned home, or pot-smoking hippies making love, not war at Woodstock. For many evangelicals the term is associated with letting your family be killed, allowing evil to run rampant, or being a liberal Democrat. Or the term is associated with effeminate males who couldn't win a fight anyway, or who have a natural disdain for shooting guns or watching football. None of this describes me at all. I love sports. I love red meat. I've never voted Democrat. I own several guns, and I love to shoot them—just not at people. I don't have any natural aversion to violence. I enjoy watching UFC fights and violent movies, even though I probably shouldn't. The point is, there's nothing emotional, cultural, or political that's driving my view. I know I sound like a fundamentalist, but the only reason I endorse Christian nonviolence is because I believe the Bible tells me to.

For these reasons, I will not use the term *pacifist/ism* to describe what I think the Bible teaches about violence. I'll stick to the less loaded term *nonviolence*.

DEFINITION: VIOLENCE

But this brings up another question: What do I mean by *violence*? If you search the web or read a few books on violence, you'll see that no two people agree on a definition. So let's start with how the dictionary defines violence:

> The exercise of physical force so as to inflict injury on, or cause damage to, persons or property; action or conduct characterized by this; treatment or usage tending to cause bodily injury or forcibly interfering with personal freedom.[16]

This definition is pretty good, but if you start toying with it you will see that it's not perfect. For instance, is violence limited to just physical *force*? If I slip some poison into my neighbor's tea, did I commit violence? Yes, of course. And if I use physical force that causes an injury, does this necessarily mean that I was violent? Maybe. But if I push a person out of the way of a moving car, I don't think anyone would accuse me of acting violently, even if the poor elderly woman broke her hip when I knocked her to the ground. And what about psychological or verbal violence? You can do a whole lot of destruction to someone by simply lashing out with your words.[17]

As you can see, defining *violence* isn't all that easy. I like the way ethicists Glen Stassen and Michael Westmoreland-White defined the term:

> Violence is destruction to a victim by means that overpower the victim's consent.[18]

Concise. To the point. Yet captures the necessary ingredients. By *destruction* they don't mean total annihilation, but rather some sort of harm done to the person. So even if the elderly woman may not have consented to being shoved across the street, once she saw the car blaze by, she would realize that I wasn't trying to destroy her. Therefore, if you do some sort of harm to someone else, whether it's bodily, emotional, or mental harm without his or her consent, then you have violated that person. You have committed an act of *violence*.

Of all the definitions I've read, I like this one the most. I want to tweak it only a bit to fit with the purpose of my book. In what follows, I will focus particularly on *physical* violence. Verbal and psychological violence are important topics—and the Bible has much to say about them. But those aspects of violence would demand a much longer book. I also want to modify the previous definition ever so slightly by adding a statement of intent. In other words, an act of violence may not actually destroy the victim but is *trying to* destroy him or her. There are various activities, therefore, that *could be violent*—corporal punishment, mixed martial arts, etc.—but don't necessarily have to be. It depends on the intent.

So, for the sake of this book, I will use the term *violence* to refer to: *a physical act that is intended to destroy (i.e., injure) a victim by means that overpower the victim's consent.*[19]

NONVIOLENCE: A BIRD'S-EYE VIEW

I've written this book for a general audience. I'll try to avoid technical jargon, and I'll keep the tone conversational. However, given the importance of the topic, and given the fact that Scripture has much to say about it, we'll have to thoroughly study the Bible to figure out what God says about warfare and violence. And I make no apologies about this! I know that most books written for a general audience don't study technical details in Scripture—they often don't need to. But for this topic, we need to. Think about it. Eight hundred thousand churchgoers were slaughtered by fellow churchgoers in Rwanda two decades ago. Children continue to be gunned down by sociopaths in Connecticut and by drones in Pakistan. Wars continue to rage around the world. This is not an issue that we should take lightly. It demands nothing less than in-depth study and painstaking precision.

When I first started this book, I wanted to keep the endnotes to a minimum. But I found this to be unhelpful. I know that many readers will want to know where I'm getting my information from or will want further proof for my arguments, so I've included a healthy dose of information in the endnotes for you. I could have included much more, actually. This book could have included five hundred pages of endnotes! (And in previous drafts, it nearly did.) But I had to trim a lot of stuff out to make the book more readable. I tried to find the balance between showing all my research and being clear and concise in my argument. So I ask the average reader to please excuse all the endnotes, and I ask the scholars to please excuse their frequent absence. I'm trying to bridge an unbridgeable gap between scholars and "ordinary" people.

So here's how we're going to tackle the subject. My purpose is to summarize what the entire Bible says about warfare and violence. I'm sure you already have many questions about whether I'd kill Hitler or the psycho trying to hurt my family. We'll get to these questions (and others) in chapters 11 and 12. But Bible-believing Christians cannot—or should not—approach these questions without first studying what the Bible says about violence. Surprisingly, there are few books written about this topic that actually take a thorough look at what the Bible says. So this is the gap I'm trying to fill. I want to focus primarily on what the Bible says about the topic. Then—and *only* then—will I wrestle with the various moral issues related to violence.

We'll begin with four chapters on the Old Testament. I've purposefully devoted so much space to the Old Testament because this is where most questions arise. Many people assume that the New Testament doesn't endorse violence, while the Old Testament does. And many Christians don't know what to do with this. Some simply dismiss the Old Testament as *old* and therefore irrelevant. Others assume that since the Old Testament allows for violence, it must be allowed today. As we'll see, both of these assumptions are wrong.

We'll then spend four chapters on the New Testament—two on the Gospels, one on the Epistles, and one on Revelation. I'll focus on passages and themes that are most pertinent for the discussion. This is why I spend an entire chapter on the book of Revelation, which is often taken to endorse excessive violence. Spoiler alert—it doesn't.

After the New Testament, I'll spend one chapter on the early church (pre-AD 313). The importance of this chapter will be addressed when we get there. Finally, I'll deal with some of the "what about" questions that surround the topic. Again, I cannot stress enough how important it will be for us to saturate ourselves in the Bible before we address those questions. If you skip to chapters 11 and 12, nothing I say there will make sense. We must come at the "killing Hitler" questions after we have first inhabited the world of the Bible.

I've also included an appendix on just war theory. I left this outside the main body of the book since it's not directly related to my purpose. However, in the last few years I've often heard Christians frame the discussion in terms of pacifism versus just war theory. Few Christians, however, actually know what just war theory is, so I wanted to take time to explain it. Moreover, I actually don't think that my position is all that far from just war theory. But you'll have to look at the appendix to see why.

As we journey through Scripture, you may notice that I'll be following the Bible as it unfolds—Genesis through Revelation. This is intentional. Some call this *biblical* theology; others call it *narrative* theology or a *redemptive historical* hermeneutic. Whatever jargon you want to slap on it, I call this approach common sense. God didn't give us a dictionary on religious thought. He gave us a story. Yet too often, Christians treat the Bible as a handbook of dos and don'ts that fell from heaven. It's not, and it didn't. Scripture contains a rich, multifaceted true story about how God created the world, how sin corrupted it, how God sought to restore His corrupted world, and how God will finish the job. All the dos and don'ts—including whether God's people should kill—are wrapped up in this beautiful, dynamic story. But to understand these commands, we have to follow the story.

THREE GOALS

My hope for this book is threefold. First, I want everyone who reads this book to rethink what the Bible—and only the Bible—says about warfare and violence. There are too many nonbiblical worldviews that have controlled this discussion, even within "Bible-believing" churches. I'm not saying that you must land on my view, although I hope you do. I would consider this book a mild success if you at least reconsidered your view in light of the Bible.

Second, I hope that this book will help snuff out the militaristic spirit that has crept into the American church over the last few decades. As I will show, Scripture protests against militaristic zeal. Specific questions about military service or violence as a last resort are more difficult to sort out. But such unchecked allegiance to military might, eager vengeance toward America's enemies, or warfare as the *only* way to confront evil are all serious aberrations from biblical Christianity. The church's blind endorsement of war has become one of the most gaping holes in evangelical thought. I hope to expose this.

Third, I pray that this book will help evangelical Christians to *fight*. Fight against evil. Fight against the schemes of the Devil. Fight against sin. Fight against injustice. As good soldiers of Christ who are members of the blood-bought church, I pray that we would *fight* the good fight. But in light of what the Bible teaches, I pray that citizens of God's kingdom would emulate their King and fight without using violence.

WAS ISRAEL A VIOLENT, GENOCIDAL, BLOODTHIRSTY NATION?

THE PROBLEM

Richard Dawkins, the well-known atheistic philosopher, has famously stated:

> The God of the Old Testament is arguably the most unpleasant character in all fiction: jealous and proud of it; a petty, unjust, unforgiving control-freak; a vindictive, bloodthirsty ethnic cleanser; a misogynistic, homophobic, racist, infanticidal, genocidal, filicidal, pestilential, megalomaniacal, sadomasochistic, capriciously malevolent bully.[1]

Even if you don't know what some of those words mean, you can tell they're bad. If Dawkins's view of our "God of the Old Testament" contains even an ounce of truth, then we've got a real problem on our hands. Is the God of the Old Testament really a bloodthirsty, vindictive bully? An infanticidal racist? Or more specific to our topic: Does God command a bloodthirsty genocide in the Old Testament but enemy-loving forgiveness in the New? And if so, what do we do with the contradiction?

It's not just atheistic philosophers who recognize the problem. Many Christians who love the Bible are troubled with the widespread carnage in the Old Testament. Biblical scholar C. S. Cowles described the Old Testament as "a bloody history saturated with violence," and God is depicted as "full of fury against sinners"—quite unlike Jesus, who loved His enemies. Moses must have misunderstood what God meant, said Cowles, when He gave Israel such "genocidal commands."[2]

There seems to be a lot of blood and guts in the Old Testament, while the New Testament is much more peaceful. So does God endorse killing in the Old Testament but not in the New? We'll spend this chapter and the next three trying to answer that question. We will see that killing is sometimes sanctioned by God in the Old Testament, but that killing is not the ideal way God wants His people to deal with their enemies—not even the really bad ones. God's *original intention for humanity* is *shalom*—peace—and not violence. And the Old Testament moves toward this goal.

VIOLENCE AND PEACE IN THE FIRST CHAPTERS OF GENESIS

Shalom (peace) is a rich and multifaceted Hebrew term that refers to the absence of war or conflict, but the word encompasses much more: wholeness, completeness, fullness, abundance, joy, and harmony. All of these words color in various facets of the Hebrew concept of *shalom*. According to one Hebrew scholar, *shalom*

> signifies the well-being of a human in all imaginable aspects. It stretches from the well-being of

satisfaction and contentment about one's welfare, to security, to being unharmed including keeping healthy, to getting along with each other in every form of relationship.[3]

From the beginning, God wanted *shalom* to permeate His creation on every level. And in the end, God will achieve this goal.

Genesis 1–2 paints a picture of *shalom*, God's original intention for creation. Here, we see nothing but perfect peace, harmony, and beauty—the way God intended things to be. Seven times in Genesis 1 God says that His creation is "good." When He concludes His work, He considers it "very good" (1:31). There is perfect harmony between the Creator and His creation, and there is perfect harmony among all created things. Adam and Eve submit to God; the animals and vegetation submit to the human pair. When Adam stuffs a tomato seed into the soil, the earth obeys by popping out weed-free, luscious tomato plants. When Eve calls for an animal, it comes right to her. Everything in God's good creation lives in perfect harmony. Humans with humans, animals with animals, creation with animals and humans. There is no violence. Just *shalom*.

But sin invades God's good creation, and all harmony is shattered: harmony between God and humans, between humans and humans, and between humans and creation. Enmity, strife, and violence take the place of *shalom*, as we see with Cain, who rises up and kills his brother (Gen. 4). Interestingly, God responds not by killing Cain—meeting violence with violence—but by placing a mark on Cain so that no one else will take vengeance on him. God responds to the first murderer with grace—a visible preservation of *shalom*.

Yet sin continues to manifest itself in violent ways. Cain's descendant Lamech shows up in the story with blood dripping from his hands. Cain slew his brother and knew the shame of his violence, but Lamech *boasts* in killing a *teenager*: "I have killed a man for wounding me, a young man for striking me" (Gen. 4:23). Now, seven generations after Cain, people aren't just violent. They're celebrating violence.

Sin devastates humanity. It gets so bad that, years later, God decides to send a flood to (nearly) wipe out the evil human race and start over: "Now the earth was corrupt in God's sight, and the earth was filled with *violence*" (Gen. 6:11). It's not just random evil that God punishes, but specifically *violence*, which is understood as a form of *corruption*.[4] Widespread aggression among humanity engulfs the earth, prompting God to punish the world by a flood.

Put simply: the early chapters of Genesis celebrate peace while showing disdain for violence among humans—even as "just" punishment for a killer.

VIOLENCE AND PEACE AMONG THE PATRIARCHS

You may think this changes once we get to Abraham and the patriarchs. But actually, the rest of Genesis continues to promote peace and discourage violence, even when it seems like people deserve the latter. For instance, when Abram and his nephew Lot arrive in the Promised Land, Abram gives Lot first dibs on the land so that there will be no strife between the two clans (13:8). Abram could take by force what is rightfully his, but peace takes priority.

Years later, Abraham's son Isaac digs a bunch of wells that are now rightfully his, but he ends up giving them to Abimelech, the Philistine king. Why? So that there will be peace between the two (Gen. 26:1–33). In other words, Isaac forfeits what is duly his to prevent strife and maintain *shalom*. Isaac, in fact, is much stronger than Abimelech in terms of financial and physical power. According to Abimelech's own confession, "you are much mightier than we" (Gen. 26:16). So if they fought over the wells, Isaac probably would pummel him. But Isaac chooses the Edenic ideal over the way of Cain. He chooses peace, not war, even if it means being wronged. Sometimes peace demands sacrifice—a truth broadcasted in the New Testament.

The stories of Jacob and Esau also celebrate nonviolent peace as the ideal. Jacob's gets pretty messy, especially when he ventures to the land of Uncle Laban (Gen. 29–31). Still, Jacob has numerous opportunities to respond with vengeful violence toward evildoers, yet he never does. For instance, to prevent the potential clash with his brother, Esau, Jacob assumes the posture of a servant to his lord.[5] Instead of meeting force with force, Jacob humbles himself as a servant in order to preserve peace. He then goes above and beyond by offering a massive gift to stave off any potential strife.[6]

Another story where violence is condemned is the incident with Levi, Simeon, and their sister Dinah. As the story goes, a Canaanite named Shechem rapes Dinah and then has the nerve to ask her father, Jacob, for her hand in marriage. Jacob agrees on one condition: Shechem and his people must get circumcised. Shechem (who must *really* have a thing for Dinah) agrees. So after he and his people go under the knife and are "sore" (Gen. 34:25),

Levi and Simeon slaughter the entire city for what Shechem did to their sister.

Are their actions justified? It's not altogether clear. Genesis 34 doesn't clearly say that Levi and Simeon are wrong. Neither does the chapter say they are right. It just tells the story. Personally, everything in me wants to cheer for these two brothers. I mean, the guy *raped their sister*! But later in Genesis, their violence seems to be *condemned*, not *celebrated*: "Simeon and Levi are brothers; weapons of violence are their swords.... For in their anger they killed men.... Cursed be their anger, for it is fierce, and their wrath, for it is cruel" (Gen. 49:5–7). Even though I want to applaud their killing, Jacob condemns it. And it's likely that the inspired author of Genesis agrees with Jacob.[7]

The Old Testament does not offer a blank check toward violence. Genesis shows that the patriarchs are not far from Eden. God's desire for nonviolent peace remains the ideal—even when confronting injustice and enmity.

There are two main exceptions to this nonviolent *shalom* in the book: Genesis 9 and 14. In Genesis 9:5, God seems to allow the death penalty for murders.

> Whoever sheds the blood of man,
> > by man shall his blood be shed,
> for God made man in his own image. (v. 6)

This verse elevates the sanctity of human life and therefore condemns murder by giving the strictest of penalties: death. However, several questions surround this verse. Is Genesis 9:6 a proverb or a command? In other words, does Genesis 9:6 give a general principle or an absolute command? You may assume the latter, but it's interesting that even God didn't kill Cain for murdering Abel. The same goes for Moses, David, and other murderers in the Old Testament. And does this verse give humans authority to administer the death penalty, or does it say that God will punish the murderer?[8] The Hebrew is not as clear as our English translations imply. These questions should caution us against racing to Genesis 9:6 to show that God wants all societies to institute the death penalty. In any case, know that God will later institute the death penalty in the law of Moses, so Genesis 9:6 probably anticipates that law. But let us not ignore the plain meaning of this verse: God fiercely condemns murder, because all people are made in His image.

In Genesis 14, a bunch of kings take Lot captive, and Abram goes to get him back. The text says that Abram "led forth his trained men" and "divided his forces against them by night, he and his servants, and defeated them and pursued them to Hobah, north of Damascus" (Gen. 14:14–15). Though it's probable that Abram's militia used violence, the text leaves out the details. Most importantly, Genesis 14 doesn't say that God commanded Abram to do this, nor does it sanction his actions. All is says is what Abram did without commenting on whether it was good or bad. The Bible often describes what a person did but doesn't say that we should imitate him or her. We need to sort out whether the story is *described* or *prescribed*, or what I will call later the "is" and the "ought." Abram fought against the kings to get his nephew back (the "is"), but this doesn't mean that we "ought" to do the same.

In the end, Genesis 14 doesn't clearly endorse violence, and it doesn't celebrate violence in any explicit way.[9]

VIOLENCE IN OLD TESTAMENT LAW

Such aversion toward violence begins to change when we get to the law of Moses. By *law of Moses* I'm referring to all the commandments God gave Israel through Moses on Mount Sinai. These commandments are the dos and don'ts recorded in Exodus through Deuteronomy. And there are many commandments that sanction some sort of violence among the people of Israel. Much of the violence is punishment for crimes, including the death penalty for murdering someone (Exod. 21:12–14, 19; Lev. 24:17, 21), hitting one's parents (Exod. 21:15, 17; Lev. 20:9), kidnapping (Exod. 21:16; Deut. 24:7), sacrificing a child to the god Molech (Lev. 20:3), or committing a whole range of other offenses. These laws may or may not seem problematic to you. After all, they only allow violence as punishment for wrongdoing, even if some of the wrongs (such as hitting your parents) don't seem to merit such stringent penalties. I should point out, however, that in fifteen of the sixteen cases where the death penalty is sanctioned, other penalties such as a stiff monetary fine are allowed. The criminal doesn't have to go to the chopping block.[10] And some crimes, such as theft or damage to someone else's property, receive a rather light penalty compared to other cultures in the world at that time.[11] The Bible doesn't sanction mutilation as punishment, but other cultures would hack off hands, ears, noses, and other body parts for a whole range of offenses.[12]

So the perceived strictness or violent nature of these biblical laws must be understood in light of other ancient cultures rather than our own.

The most glaring concern comes when the Old Testament sanctions wholesale slaughter of the Canaanites. Israel's "warfare policy"

has raised an ageless ethical problem for anyone who looks to the
Old Testament for moral guidance. For instance, God commands
Israel to

> save alive nothing that breathes, but you shall
> devote them to complete destruction, the Hittites
> and the Amorites, the Canaanites and the Perizzites,
> the Hivites and the Jebusites, as the LORD your God
> has commanded. (Deut. 20:16–17; cf. 7:1–2)

God tells Israel to slaughter everyone living within the borders
of the Promised Land. We have a term for this sort of thing. We call
it genocide.

So what does an enemy-loving, peacemaking, cheek-turning
follower of Jesus do with this seemingly bloodthirsty God who con-
dones violence in the Old Testament but not in the New?

One way to solve the tension is to recognize that the old and new
covenants are different. Please note: I didn't say that the *God* of the old
and the *God* of the new are different. God is the same yesterday, today,
and forever. But sometimes His rules change because His relationship
to humanity is taken to a new level. The same is true for us. I don't let
my five-year-old drive my car, but when she's sixteen, I just might let
her. And I don't let my nine-year-old daughter date boys, but when
she turns … thirty-five, I might entertain the thought. You get the
point. Just because something is commanded under the old covenant
doesn't mean it'll be the same in the new. So I could save both you
and me a lot of time by just skipping to the New Testament and
ignoring the Old, *not* because it's authored by a different God, but

because God's rules in the Old Testament are different from those in the New. God's relationship with Israel was different from God's relationship with the church.

There is a good deal of truth to this, but I'm uncomfortable driving such a thick wedge between the old and new covenants. They're not the same, certainly. But didn't Jesus say that He came not to abolish the Law and the Prophets but to fulfill them (Matt. 5:17)? Therefore, instead of writing off the violence in the Old Testament as a thing of the past, I'm going to explore a more cohesive way of understanding the Old Testament's relation to the New. Yes, there is much *discontinuity* between the two. That's undeniable. But there's a good deal of *continuity* as well. And this is where our narrative approach will help us.

In short, the law was *not* God's ideal moral code for all people of all time. Rather, God met the Israelites where they were and began to take "incremental steps" toward His moral ideal.[13] Nonviolence—it's not just a New Testament invention. It's the capstone of the Old.

THE INTENTION OF THE LAW

Not everything in the law was intended to embody God's ideal ethic—His perfect way of doing things for all people of every age. The law, rather, was intended to meet the Israelites where they were and set them on the right path toward the ideal. Many laws given in Exodus through Deuteronomy, in fact, were not God's ideal moral code—His Edenic ethic, if you will. Rather, they were glimpses of God's ideal that would be revealed fully in Christ. In other words, the law of Moses was designed to guide a particular nation, living in a particular land, for a specific time and in a specific culture.[14]

What we have in the law of Moses is a moral code that both *accommodates to* and *improves upon* the ethical systems of the surrounding nations. Here's what I mean.[15]

The law of Moses *accommodates to* some of the moral norms of the ancient Near East (i.e., the cultures and nations that existed during Israel's time). Some of these moral norms include polygamy, slavery, and divorce, as we'll discuss. This is the world Israel lived in. To exist, they had to take part in these structures while at the same time critiquing them. And this is what the law of Moses did. It didn't outlaw every less-than-perfect cultural practice; rather, the law took the practice as it was and improved it.

Take polygamy, for example. A classic example of God tolerating this less-than-perfect practice is seen when Abram takes Hagar to be his second wife (Gen. 16:3). As the story goes, Abram's first wife, Sarai, is barren, so she tells Abram to marry Hagar in order to produce offspring. This was a common practice of the day and was tolerated by God.[16] Now, God does rebuke Abram for failing to trust Him to give Sarai a son, but He doesn't condemn Abram for taking a second wife. Polygamy, especially when one wife was barren, was tolerated by God but was not the moral ideal.

It's clear from Genesis 1–2 that God's Edenic ideal was monogamy, not polygamy. But by the time Israel came on the scene, polygamy was a common part of the culture, and God didn't do away with polygamy overnight. Instead, He worked within this non-ideal form of marriage and improved it. For instance, Deuteronomy 21 says that "if a man has two wives, the one loved and the other unloved … he may not treat the son of the loved as the firstborn in preference to the son of the unloved, who is the firstborn" (vv. 15–16). Now you may think: *What's the guy doing with two wives? And why doesn't God nip the problem in the bud and condemn polygamy right then and there?* Because again: God *accommodates to* this less-than-ideal practice, while at the same time improving it. In Deuteronomy 21, God improves upon the way polygamy was typically played out in the ancient world, where the sons of the unloved wife had no rights. Here, God works within a broken system to gradually improve it until it's eventually done away with. Polygamy in Israel was much more humane than it was in the surrounding cultures.

The same goes for slavery. The Old Testament law doesn't condemn slavery outright, even though slavery falls short of the Edenic ideal. Slavery was part of the ancient societal structures, yet God doesn't crush these structures immediately. Rather, He takes incremental steps toward the ideal moral code in which there is no slavery. As part of these incremental steps, God improves upon the nature of slavery. Slaves were treated brutally in the ancient world. They weren't considered human and didn't have any rights. But in the Mosaic law there is a "humanized attitude toward servants/slaves" as Israel moves toward an "ultimate ethic" where slavery will be banished altogether.[17]

For instance, the law of Moses forbids a master from physically abusing his slave, but in other ancient cultures, the master could do whatever he wanted to his slave.[18] According to other nations, slaves were nothing more than living tools, pieces of property. But in the Bible, slaves are treated with more human dignity. Israel is also commanded to offer refuge for slaves who ran away from a foreign nation (Deut. 23:15–16). Such laws, though, were foreign to— and *a moral improvement upon*—the laws of other nations, where harboring runaway slaves was punishable by huge fines or sometimes death, while the returned slave would be mutilated![19] Yes, Israel *accommodated to* the cultural practices of the day (slavery), but God made incremental improvements upon such practices (a much more humane treatment of slaves).

Perhaps the clearest example of this incremental improvement comes with the law's perspective on divorce. The Old Testament law appears more lenient on divorce than the New Testament. Jesus Himself affirms: "Because of your hardness of heart Moses allowed you to divorce your wives, but from the beginning it was not so" (Matt. 19:8). In other words, God *accommodated to* their hard hearts by allowing divorce in some circumstances. And yet, Jesus affirms that Moses's allowance was not the Edenic ideal: "From the beginning it was not so." Jesus sought to restore that Genesis 1–2 ideal, and He'll do the same with violence. Stay tuned.

These three examples (polygamy, slavery, and divorce) show that God both *accommodates to* and *improves upon* the ethical systems of the surrounding nations.

Paul's writings in the New Testament offer a fitting commentary on this temporary nature of the law. Paul recognizes that the law served the purpose of guiding Israel for a period of time but was not intended to give us never-ending moral absolutes. In Galatians 3, he says that the law was Israel's "guardian until Christ came," but after He came "we are no longer under a guardian" (vv. 24–25).[20] The law was the ethical authority for those living under the old covenant but not for those in the new covenant.[21] This doesn't mean that the law is totally irrelevant for Christians. Indeed, Paul himself finds underlying *principles* in the law that are relevant for today, and Jesus Himself sought to draw out the true *intention* of the law.[22] But the specific application of all the culturally bound laws given to Israel—what to do when your ox gores your neighbor, or how to build an altar to sacrifice your goat[23]—was designed to guide Israel for a specific time. God never intended the law to be binding on all people of all time. Jesus, not Moses, reveals God's ideal ethic.[24]

To sum it up, the law of Moses reveals God's progression toward an ideal moral code but isn't in itself the ideal moral code. Paul Copan expressed this well:

> Mosaic times were indeed "crude" and "uncultured" in many ways. So Sinai legislation makes a number of moral improvements without completely over-hauling ancient Near Eastern social structures and assumptions. God "works with" Israel as he finds her. He meets his people where they are while seek-ing to show them a higher ideal in the context of ancient Near Eastern life.[25]

So what does this have to do with violence and warfare? As with polygamy, slavery, and divorce, the law of Moses *accommodates to* and offers *moral improvements upon* ancient Near Eastern warfare policy and violence. From our perspective, the Old Testament seems like an ongoing bloodbath. Compared to the laws of other nations, however, the Old Testament's laws regarding war and violence are quite tame, and in some cases absurd. To understand violence in the Old Testament, therefore, we must view it within the "redemptive movement" of God's plan. God meets Israel in its brutally violent world and takes incremental steps away from such violence and toward peace and nonviolence.

We'll see this play out in the next chapter more clearly. Israel had a policy of warfare that not only accommodated to the warfare policy of the surrounding nations, but also improved upon it to pave the way back to Eden—the place where trees of life are nourished.

ISRAEL'S BIZARRE WARFARE POLICY

GOD AND MILITARISM

The law of Moses was not a cul-de-sac but an on-ramp toward God's ideal ethic. Though it sanctions warfare and violence in some cases, this doesn't *in itself* mean that God will always authorize the same sort of warfare and violence for all people of all time. As with other laws—polygamy, slavery, etc.—God *accommodated to* the ancient Near Eastern way of life by allowing violence in certain circumstances. However, when we look at Israel's violence in light of other ancient warfare practices, we see that God's law (and other parts of the Old Testament) offers a *moral improvement upon* the ways of the other nations.

One important feature we will see in this chapter is that God never sanctions *militarism*—even when He allows warfare. Israel may have wielded a sword, but it was blunt and short compared to those of neighboring countries, and much of the time it was kept in storage.

The best way to witness Israel's "moral improvement" upon ancient Near Eastern warfare is by looking at other nations. Israel was less violent and had a stripped-down—almost absurd—warfare policy compared to the nations around it. Israel's distinct warfare policy can be seen from four different angles.

1. Israel and Canaan: A Clash of Societies

The first angle has to do with how Israel's society was structured. Not all societies are organized in the same way. America is a democracy in which the people possess a good deal of power. Other societies are monarchical (ruled by a king), where the people have little power. Still others are run by firm distinctions in social class, such as the caste system in India. During the Middle Ages, Europe was run by a feudal system, where a few nobles owned the land while the peasants worked it.

The ancient world also had different societal structures, though most were monarchical and feudal. Feudal societies were organized like a social pyramid, where a few nobles held the power. At the top of the pyramid sat the king.[1] In Egypt, for instance, the king (or pharaoh) was a divine-like ruler who had absolute power. Under him were a few nobles who owned land and had a measure of delegated power. And under them was everyone else. Now, what Egypt was on a large scale, Canaan was on a smaller scale.[2] While Egypt was an empire, Canaan was a collection of city-states—mini empires spread throughout the land. Both Egypt and Canaan were structured along the same hierarchical paradigm. The king and his posse owned it all.

But Israel was different. Israel, quite shockingly, was an *egalitarian* (think "equal") society, meaning that all families were entitled to own land. Everyone had equal access to gain wealth.[3] It was not a monarchy (originally),[4] where the king owned it all. And it was not a feudal system, where a few elite nobles controlled the land while the rest lived as peasants. This is shocking, because no other society in the ancient world operated this way. Every other society was hierarchical. They were ruled by kings and nobles who pretty much did whatever they wanted.

You may wonder how this relates to our topic of war in the Old Testament. Here's how. The point is actually crucial, so read carefully.

In Canaan, the kings and nobles were able to maintain control over the land through a professional army—a highly trained group of warriors who stockpiled many weapons: swords, spears, chariots, and horses. They were paid a good salary through taxation and were honored with land that the peasants cultivated for them. Such an army would cost a lot of money (something Americans can certainly appreciate), but a professional army was essential for the king and nobles to maintain power and secure their space in the land. The stronger the military, the better the "homeland security." External attacks were halted by a strong military; internal revolts were kept at bay by the same force. The very existence of the king-centered feudal system depended upon the strength of the army. Without it, the king would not maintain ownership over the land for very long. Having a king meant having a warrior who wielded absolute power through his military.[5]

But Israel is different. Yahweh is their King who *owns all the land* (Lev. 25:23), and *He* will be their army. God doesn't need a human army to protect His land. He is quite capable of defending the land Himself, as He demonstrates time and time again.[6] Later on, in fact, Israel is condemned for wanting a militaristic king who will fight its battles, as the other nations have (1 Sam. 8:20). Such misplaced trust befits pagans, not God's people.

To ensure Israel's trust in Him rather than in a human king, God gives Israel an economic system that can't support a professional army. After all, somebody has to fund the army. But not in Israel. No taxes are supposed to be collected to support a military—God wants excess money to be given to the poor, not to fund a military (e.g., Deut. 14:29). And when Israel does end up choosing a king, God does not allow him to have the financial means to support an army (Deut. 17).[7] Israel's economic system, therefore, is set up *so that* the nation can't sustain a standing army without violating the system itself. Israel's "army"—if we can even call it an army—is a group of weekend warriors whose skills, or lack thereof, testify to the power of God, who alone ensures victory.[8]

Israel's egalitarian society, then, is different from and *critical of* the Canaanite society it is to drive out. The Canaanite hierarchical system, held together by the power of the king and his military might, is to be abolished. While the other nations place much faith in their king and the power of his army, Israel is called to have faith in its King and His power. All other forms of "homeland security"—professional army, superior weapons, alliances with other nations—are considered idolatry.[9]

2. Israel's Nonmilitaristic Warfare

Israel's lack of, and inability to sustain, a professional army is one of the most bizarre aspects of its society. None of this would make sense to modern or ancient military tactics. Against all human logic, intuition, and desire to secure oneself by military might, Israel flaunts its weak and outdated military regime.

Consider the Bible's most descriptive passage about Israel's "army." Though it's lengthy, I'll quote it in full:

When you go out to war against your enemies, and see horses and chariots and an army larger than your own, you shall not be afraid of them, for the LORD your God is with you, who brought you up out of the land of Egypt. And when you draw near to the battle, the priest shall come forward and speak to the people and shall say to them, "Hear, O Israel, today you are drawing near for battle against your enemies: let not your heart faint. Do not fear or panic or be in dread of them, for the LORD your God is he who goes with you to fight for you against your enemies, to give you the victory." Then the officers shall speak to the people, saying, "Is there any man who has built a new house and has not dedicated it? Let him go back to his house, lest he die in the battle and another man dedicate it. And is there any man who has planted a vineyard and has not enjoyed its fruit? Let him go back to his house, lest he die in the battle and another man enjoy its fruit. And is there any man who has betrothed a wife and has not taken her? Let him go back to his house, lest he die in the battle and another man take her." And the officers shall speak further to the people, and say, "Is there any man who is fearful and faint-hearted? Let him go back to his house, lest he make the heart of his fellows melt like his own." And when the officers have finished speaking to the people, then commanders shall be appointed at the head of the people.

When you draw near to a city to fight against it, offer terms of peace to it. And if it responds to you peaceably and it opens to you, then all the people who are found in it shall do forced labor for you and shall serve you. But if it makes no peace with you, but makes war against you, then you shall besiege it. And when the LORD your God gives it into your hand, you shall put all its males to the sword, but the women and the little ones, the livestock, and everything else in the city, all its spoil, you shall take as plunder for yourselves. And you shall enjoy the spoil of your enemies, which the LORD your God has given you. …

When you besiege a city for a long time, making war against it in order to take it, you shall not destroy its trees by wielding an axe against them. You may eat from them, but you shall not cut them down. Are the trees in the field human, that they should be besieged by you? Only the trees that you know are not trees for food you may destroy and cut down, that you may build siegeworks against the city that makes war with you, until it falls. (Deut. 20:1–14, 19–20)

Let's sum up the main points of this passage. First, God—not military might—determines the victory (v. 4). Second, Israel's army is made up of volunteers at the time of battle. In other words, there isn't to be a professional standing army.[10] If anyone has recently built a house, planted a vineyard, betrothed a wife, or is simply "fearful and fainthearted," he doesn't have to go to war (vv. 5–9). Third, if the Israelites do go to war, they are to first offer peace to the city (vv. 10–11) before they fight against it. Fourth, only if the city rejects peace is Israel sanctioned to go to war (v. 12). Fifth, noncombatants are not to be killed during war (vv. 13–15). Lastly, even fruit trees aren't to be destroyed (vv. 19–20).[11] Talk about limited objectives! If you read Deuteronomy 20:16–18, you will see that Israel has a different war policy for those living in Canaan, and we'll discuss that in the next chapter. For now it's important to underscore the point: Israel's "army" is deliberately weak so that God will be shown to be unquestionably strong.[12]

The intentional weakness of Israel's army is put on bold display in Deuteronomy 17. As we mentioned in the last section, God is Israel's King. However, God will allow Israel to have a human king under certain conditions, and Deuteronomy 17 spells out those conditions—one of which is stripping the king of all military might. Namely, the king is not allowed to build a professional army ("he must not acquire many horses for himself") nor can he make military alliances with other nations (Deut. 17:16–17).[13] God will shed the king of all military strength so that his faith will be in God, not in military power. Other nations will therefore see that Israel marches to the beat of a different military drum. They have a God in the heavens who guides and protects, who defends and delivers. They don't need to supplement God with a human army. And when they do actually fight, God wants them to remain a ragtag group of weekend warriors. This way, when they win (if they have faith in God) it will be clear to them and everyone else that victory belongs to Israel's God, not to Israel's military.

This is why in several instances Israel was commanded to hamstring their enemies' horses and burn their chariots.[14] Horses and chariots were the ancient version of tanks. They were superior weapons. The army with the most horses and chariots was bound to win the war. So when Joshua (and others) hamstrings horses and burns chariots, he destroys their potential usefulness to Israel in further battles. It's like killing an enemy with a knife and *not* taking his gun. And the reason is clear: "Superior weaponry was rejected, in order to demonstrate trust in Yahweh as warrior."[15]

When chariots are mentioned in a positive light, they are God's chariots, not Israel's. God rides on the chariots of the clouds (Hab. 3:8; Deut. 32:13), surrounds His people with angelic chariots (2 Kings 7:6), and takes His prophet home in a chariot of fire (2 Kings 2:11). Who needs earthly chariots when God fights with heavenly ones? The prophets *themselves* are even called "the chariots of Israel and its horsemen" (2 Kings 13:14; cf. 2:12)—they are bearers of the word of God, who alone secures Israel's existence.[16]

In contrast to Israel's comical military policy, the surrounding nations stockpiled horses, chariots, and other superior weapons. Such military strength was essential for their survival and domination. The Assyrians boasted about their enemies being "afraid in the face of my terrible weapons."[17] Egypt was known for having many chariots, as were the Hittites.[18] As we discussed before, the king's military power was what kept him on the throne. The surrounding nations relied upon military might for protection and imperial aggression.

Israel's deliberately weak military in a militaristic culture was one more incremental step away from war and violence toward an Edenic *shalom*.

3. God Fights While Israel Mops Up

As we mentioned above, Yahweh—the King of Israel—protects Israel. In fact, He often fights single-handedly. This is the reason Israel doesn't need a standing army. The clearest example of this "God-centered" warfare is in the Red Sea crossing (Exod. 14–15), where God miraculously divides the waters and defeats the Egyptian army. The entire "battle" is fought and won by God alone. Israel does nothing but stand on the sand and watch. No swords. No fighting. No human participation whatsoever.[19]

God's victory at the Red Sea sets the standard for Israel's subsequent battles: more than picking up arms to fight, Israel needs to have faith in God to win the war. In other instances, Israel will sometimes bear arms. But this "Red Sea principle" (God fighting alone) will characterize many future conflicts. When Israel trusts in its own military might—horses, weapons, and soldiers—it loses. When it trusts in God, it wins. "The king is not saved by his great army," sings the psalmist. "A warrior is not delivered by his great strength. The war horse is a false hope for salvation, and by its great might it cannot rescue" (Ps. 33:16–17).

The exodus from Egypt isn't the only time when God fights alone. Israel's history is loaded with many examples. In 2 Chronicles 20, the Moabites and Ammonites invade Israel, so King Jehoshaphat leads out an Israelite force to meet them in battle.[20] But instead of sharpening their swords and strapping on armor, the Israelites pray,

fast, and sing a bunch of worship songs to prepare for battle. "You will
not need to fight in this battle," shouts the priest. "Stand firm, hold
your position, and see the salvation of the LORD on your behalf" (v.
17). When they go to fight, they find their enemies *already defeated*
by God (v. 22). Sounds a lot like the Red Sea crossing. Again, God
fights and wins the war by Himself. The Israelites return with their
hands free from blood.

We could look at many other examples of such God-centered
wars,[21] but suffice it to say that the Israelites aren't given a green
light to go out and kill whomever they want whenever they feel
threatened. Nor are they ever allowed to invade a country to
dismantle an unjust government or preemptively strike a nation
building chariots of mass destruction. Warfare comes with strin-
gently limited objectives. In some cases Israel never swings a sword.
Such vengeance left in God's hands is one incremental step toward
His ethical ideal, where all forms of violence and war would be
banned.

There are other wars, however, where Israel wields the sword.
But even in these, the Bible emphasizes God's action far more
than Israel's. Take Deborah and Barak's defeat of the Canaanites,
for example. Barak draws out the enemy, but it is the Lord who
"routed Sisera and all his chariots and all his army before Barak by
the edge of the sword" (Judg. 4:15). Jael, an Israelite woman, ends
up killing the leader by driving a tent peg through his skull, but
this is the only description of an Israelite killing another person
(and it isn't even in battle). At the end of the day, "God subdued
Jabin the king of Canaan before the people of Israel" (v. 23). And
when the Israelites sing a song to celebrate, they highlight God's

miracle as the decisive event in the battle (5:19–21). Even though humans fight, the emphasis lies on God, who gives the victory.

Other wars in the Old Testament emphasize God's agency, while minimizing human participation. Gideon's "battle" with the *whole of Bible...* Midianites is probably the best known, where God deliberately trims down his militia from thirty-two thousand to three hundred. When the Israelites go to battle, they sneak up on the enemy at night, blow a trumpet, smash some pots, and watch as the enemy *kills each other*. Divinely orchestrated friendly fire! The only mention of Israelite violence is at the end when the "two princes of Midian" are killed (Judg. 7:25). Other than that, God sovereignly wins the war. Israel does next to nothing.

In some cases, then, God alone fights while Israel stands and watches. In other cases, Israel participates, but it doesn't take center stage. God's intervention decides the victory. Almost all of the divinely sanctioned wars in the Old Testament highlight the same theme.[22]

How does such a Yahweh-centered view of warfare *improve upon* Israel's ancient Near East neighbors?

Other nations believed that their god (or gods) helped them in battle. But in most cases these gods played only a supporting role, rather than a leading one. In many other Near Eastern war records, the king might give lip service to his god's involvement in the battle, but at the end of the day, he believed—contrary to the psalmist— that the king *was* saved by his great army and a warrior *was* delivered by his great strength.[23]

Here's one example. An Assyrian king named Assurnasirpal II (883–859 BC) recorded a highly descriptive account of a war. He

began by acknowledging the help of his god, Assur: "With the assis-
tance of Assur my lord, I departed from Tushan. ... With the exalted
strength of Assur my lord (and) with a fierce battle I fought with
them." But then he went on to recount all of his great strength and
skill as a military leader:

> I rained down flames upon them ... I conquered
> the city. I felled with the sword 800 of their com-
> bat troops (and) I cut off their heads. I captured
> many troops alive. I carried off valuable booty. I
> piled up a heap of live (men and) of heads before
> his gate ... I carried off much booty. I conquered
> 50 cities ... I massacred them. I carried off their
> booty. I captured 50 soldiers alive.[24]

That's a lot of I's. The Assyrian king was quite impressed with his
military might. Unlike Israel, other nations didn't normally celebrate
their weakness to emphasize the strength of their god.[25] The Israelites
are to trust in God as their Warrior. Trusting in their military strength
or kingly power amounts to idolatry.[26]

But you may wonder: How does highlighting God as warrior
solve the moral problem of violence? Doesn't this just make God out
to be a "moral monster"?[27]

It's all a matter of perspective. From the Bible's perspective, God
is the author of life, and as the author of life, He also has the right
to take life away. This right belongs exclusively to the Creator.[28]
Whenever God allows humans to take life, it's an extension of His
own judgment on sin. God never kills haphazardly or without

= death

reason. However you slice it, there's a difference between the Creator killing rebellious humans as punishment for sin and an Assyrian king slaughtering peasants because they get in the way of his empire.

We should also point out that God doesn't gloat in His violent actions. When God punishes humanity, it's often accompanied with sadness or prefaced by a long period of grace.[29] When He does get angry, it's seen as retributive punishment—a just sentence for wicked behavior—not as hotheaded madness.

In brief, the emphasis on God as the primary agent in warfare sets Israel apart from the surrounding nations. Such emphasis offers a moral improvement upon the unchecked and arbitrary violence practiced by the surrounding nations—a violence reveled in by bloodthirsty gods.

4. Glorifying Violence

Another clear difference between Israel and its neighbors is that Israel did not glory in violence the way other nations did. Again, from our perspective, the Old Testament looks like it was written by Quentin Tarantino with all its brutal scenes. But in light of other ancient war accounts, the Old Testament looks much less gruesome.[30]

We can see the contrast in violence by looking at the different criminal laws. For instance, Babylonian law insisted that hand, ear, breast, or foot be cut off for minor infractions. Egyptians also practiced mutilation for certain crimes: cutting off hands, feet, and even noses. Many times the punishment far outweighed the crime by most standards—death for stealing or for plowing a field freshly sown with seed. And while the Old Testament allowed criminals to be beaten with no more than forty strokes (Deut. 25:1–3), it was far less harsh that Egyptian law, where a hundred lashes was the mildest form of punishment and criminals could be beaten up to two hundred times with rods. Moses's laws of punishment, while seemingly harsh from our perspective, were much more humane in light of ancient Near Eastern systems of law.[31]

Violence in judicial courts, however, was nothing compared to the unchecked barbarism relished on the battlefield. Egyptians, Babylonians, Hittites, and Canaanites all gloated not only in victory but also in the brutality of their sadistic violence. And their written accounts savor the gore. The Canaanite goddess Anath was believed to revel joyfully in butchering humanity. According to one ancient text, after Anath slaughtered a bunch of people and waded in their blood, her "liver swelled with laughter, her heart was full of joy, the liver of Anath (was full of) exultation."[32] When the Egyptians went to war, they chopped off heads and hands, delighted in their enemies' lying "prostrate in their blood," and piled "a great heap of corpses" in the aftermath.[33] All wars are brutal. But there's a difference between documenting that a war happened, as the Old Testament usually does, and reveling in the gruesome details to reinforce one's military might. God scathingly rebukes those nations that displayed such "shock and awe" power, as He consigns them to the pit of hell for "spread[ing] terror in the land of the living" (Ezek. 32:23).[34] Flaunting your military strength before almighty God is a dangerous thing to do.

None of Israel's neighbors, however, were as violent as the Assyrians, who left behind many written records of their savage torture techniques. The Assyrians were notorious for practicing "psychological warfare," where they would carve up their enemy in order to scare future foes into giving up without a fight. To induce such fear, Assyrian warriors would cut out tongues, impale people with stakes, tear out intestines as food for birds, and flay people alive, plastering their skins on city walls to advertise the gore. Victims had their eyes carved out, tongues torn out, lips cut off, and testicles ripped off "like seeds of a cucumber in June," as one Assyrian author put it.[35] The Assyrians weren't just violent. They glorified violence in a way that far surpasses anything in Bible. If you can handle it, here's how the Assyrian king Sennacherib describes the aftermath of his victory:

> I cut their throats like lambs. I cut off their previous lives (as one cuts) a string. Like the many waters of a storm, I made (the contents of) their gullets and entrails run down upon the wide earth. My prancing steeds harnessed for my riding, plunged into the streams of their blood as (into) a river. The wheels of my war chariot, which brings low the wicked and the evil, were bespattered with blood and filth. With the bodies of their warriors I filled the plain, like grass. (Their) testicles I cut off, and tore out their privates like the seeds of cucumbers.[36]

I could give many other examples, but you might lose your lunch. The war policies of Israel's neighbors horrified their enemies with bloodthirsty accounts of torture and mutilation. They didn't just condone violence. They delighted in violence and publicized it for all to see.

How does this compare with the Old Testament? While there are many accounts of violence and warfare in the Old Testament, it is significantly toned down compared to their neighbors. Many Old Testament war accounts sum up the fight in a single statement: "Joshua overwhelmed Amalek and his people with the sword" (Exod. 17:13); "Then Horam king of Gezer came up to help Lachish, and Joshua defeated him and his people until he had left him no survivor" (Josh. 10:33 NASB). These are a far cry from cutting off testicles and tearing out intestines. There is simply no text in the Old Testament that comes close to the horrifically detailed accounts of violence in some ancient Near Eastern accounts.[37]

Compared to other nations, Israel did not glorify violence. While God allowed Israel to participate in some wars, He never allowed His people to revel in the carnage the way their neighbors did. Again, God met Israel where it was but took incremental steps toward a more ideal way of life shaped by *shalom*. Israel's warfare policy was paving the way for Israel's journey back to Eden.

SHOULD AMERICA FOLLOW ISRAEL'S WAR POLICY?

We just walked through a lot of information. But the points we noted are important for understanding how the Old Testament ultimately supports Christian nonviolence. So let's summarize what we've learned so far.

Building on the previous chapter, we've seen that Israel's warfare policy both *accommodated to* and morally *improved upon* the policy of the surrounding nations. We've seen this in four main areas. First, in contrast to Canaan's hierarchical society, Israel was egalitarian with God as its King. They didn't need—nor could their economic system sustain—a professional army. Second, Israel didn't have a standing military equipped with superior weapons. Contrary to the surrounding nations, Israel was to boast in its unprofessional militia and *therefore in God*, rather than in horses and chariots. Third, Israel's battles emphasized God's involvement, sometimes to the exclusion of Israel's involvement. Though war still happened, human violence was often downplayed. And fourth, Old Testament descriptions of warfare are far less violent than ancient Near Eastern texts, which revel in the gore. War is always "hell," as William Sherman famously said. But the Old Testament doesn't relish the brutality as the other nations did.

So what does God think of militarism? Does God think, with Hal Lindsey, that the moral downfall of America is due to a "crisis of military weakness"? Does "the Bible" really "support building a powerful military force" as Wayne Grudem says? Should we consider a strong national defense to be a biblical virtue?

No.

Not at all.

Quite the opposite, in fact.

However, as we saw in chapter one, America's excessive militarism is inconceivable apart from "the support offered by several tens of millions of evangelicals."[38] This is unbelievable. Most of all—as we've seen in this chapter—it's unbiblical.

If America, for instance, used the Bible to shape its warfare policy, that policy would look like this. Enlistment would be by volunteer only (which it is), and the military would not be funded by taxation. America would not stockpile superior weapons—no tanks, drones,

F-22s, and of course no nuclear weapons—and it would make sure its victories were determined by God's miraculous intervention, not by military might. Rather than outnumbering the enemy, America would deliberately fight outmanned and under-gunned. Perhaps soldiers would use muskets, or maybe just swords. There would be no training, no boot camp, no preparation other than fasting, praying, and singing worship songs. If America really is the "new Israel," God's holy nation as some believe, then it needs to take its cue from God and His inspired manual for military tactics. But as it stands, many Christians will be content to cut and paste selected verses that align with America's worldview to give the military some religious backing. Some call this bad hermeneutics; others call it syncretism. The Israelite prophets called it idolatry.

Idolatry. The Bible consistently—and quite explicitly—portrays waging war like the nations did as spiritual prostitution. Ezekiel considers military alliances as "play[ing] the whore with the Egyptians" (16:26) and "prostitut[ing] yourself with the Assyrians" (16:28 NLT). Brutal displays of military power are characteristic of those who belong in hell (32:23–32). Isaiah considers military might to be mere "flesh," a character trait of evildoers and workers of iniquity (Isa. 31:2–3; cf. Amos 1–2). Waging war like the surrounding nations—bigger, stronger, more powerful, more fearsome—is equivalent to prostituting yourself out to sex-hungry lovers while paying your clients for their addictive services. Crude language, I know, but that's just what the Bible says about such infatuation with military prowess.

But America is not God's nation. Let me make this clear: I do *not* think that America *should* use the Bible to construct or defend its military program, because America is not the new Israel, nor is it

Thank you for saying this?

a Christian nation. What the Old Testament does do is critique the massive wave of Christian support for America's unbridled militarism. Such allegiance is misplaced; such support is unbiblical. The nations—like Assyria—were ruled by militarism, but God's people should never celebrate military power, and we certainly shouldn't find our hope and security in it. If God warned Israel against having a strong military—and it *was* God's nation—how much more should God's people today *not* put stock in the military prowess of a secular country? Jesus said that the gates of hell will not prevail against God's kingdom, and no band of terrorists, fascist government, oppressive dictator, or disarmament program will trump Jesus's promise.

Seeing America's military strength as the hope of the world is an affront to God's rule over the world. It's idolatry.

4

KILL EVERYTHING THAT BREATHES

CRUSADES AND CONQUESTS

On April 3, 2003, America was two weeks into its invasion of Iraq. Donald Rumsfeld, the US defense secretary at the time, persuaded President Bush to deploy more troops, using these words:

> Have I not commanded you? Be strong and coura-
> geous. Do not be terrified; do not be discouraged,
> for the LORD your God will be with you wherever
> you go.

Rumsfeld's words were a quotation from Joshua 1:9 (NIV), which God spoke to Joshua just before he conquered Canaan. God's nation was told to wage a "holy war" on the pagan Canaanites. And Rumsfeld saw fit to use the same logic for America's own (holy?) war against Iraq. Christian leader Jack Graham agreed. "This is a war between Christians and the forces of evil," preached Graham. "The ultimate terrorist is Satan."[1] Another famous radio preacher was asked if America was justified in going to war in Iraq. "Yes. Maybe we need to go back to the Bible and see what the Bible actually says," the preacher suggested. "God told the children of Israel to go into the land, destroy the Canaanites."[2] Whether explicit or implied, the point seems clear: America is a holy nation, and the terrorists in Iraq, like the Canaanites, need to be annihilated.[3]

These leaders weren't the first to use Joshua's conquest to give religious backing to war. The crusaders of the Middle Ages mapped the book of Joshua onto their conquest of Palestine, as Arabs were massacred out of obedience to the Old Testament. Later, American colonists settled the "holy land" (America) but first had to exterminate the Canaanites (American Indians). Or at least, this was how they justified the slaughter. One preacher condemned Native Americans when he celebrated "the mercies of God in extirpating the enemies of Israel in Canaan." Benjamin Franklin viewed the carnage as "the design of Providence to extirpate these savages in order to make room for the cultivation of the earth."[4] I wonder how many people have been killed, tortured, and in some cases cannibalized, all because certain Christians (mis)applied the book of Joshua to their lives.

Needless to say, there is an ethical urgency to understand how—if at all—Joshua's conquest applies to us today. Does the conquest of Canaan justify a Christian's use of violence?

DID GOD REALLY COMMAND THE CONQUEST?

There are many different ways that people have understood Joshua's conquest.[5] Some think that Joshua (and Moses before him) misunderstood God, who never really meant that the Israelites should kill all the Canaanites. The Israelites merely "acted on what they believed to be God's will."[6] While this approach distances God from an apparent genocide, nowhere in the Bible does it say that the Israelites misunderstood God.[7] In fact, the Israelites are rebuked for *not* driving out all the Canaanites from the land. If God never commanded Israel to drive them out, then such a rebuke would be nonsensical.

Others—yes, even Christians—assume that the God of the Old Testament is quite different from the God of the New. The God of the Old is filled with wrath, judgment, and violence, and it fits His character to command an indiscriminate slaughter of the Canaanites. But the God of the New, revealed in Jesus Christ, shows us how to love, forgive, and live peaceably with all humanity. So when it comes to the Canaanite genocide, there's no problem. The God of the Old is a God of genocide. Let's just be thankful that we serve the God of the New.

I don't think either of these views does justice to what the Bible actually says. A basic reading of the Bible shows that God commanded the Israelites to drive out all the Canaanites.[8] "You shall devote them to complete destruction," God says (Deut. 20:17). And yes, throughout Joshua's conquest we see him carry out this command, at least on a few cities. And finally, yes, the command to kill all the Canaanites *seems* to include women and children. Let's start with this plain reading of Scripture and then move toward a solution for the ethical problems therein. But I cannot emphasize enough that any solutions we propose *must* come from the text. God doesn't need us to make excuses for Him, nor does He need us to give Him a lesson in morality. But perhaps there's more to the conquest than is often recognized.

SETTING THE CONTEXT

We should first understand two fundamental aspects of the conquest: the people and the land; namely, the *Canaanites* and *Canaan*.

Who were these Canaanites? Many critics such as Richard Dawkins will describe the conquest with a slanted view of these people. You would think that they were innocent peasants living peaceably with one another, when all of a sudden a sociopath named Joshua came in and slew all the women and children. But this is not the way the Bible presents the event. The Canaanites on the whole were a particularly wicked people by anyone's standard.[9] Incest, bestiality, orgiastic religious prostitution, and child sacrifice were a regular part of life. The Canaanite gods themselves were said to be engaged in shameless sexual feats, and the Canaanites joined in. Paul Copan said that the "sexual acts of the gods and goddesses were imitated by the Canaanites as a kind of magical act: the more sex on the Canaanite high places, the more this would stimulate the fertility god Baal to have sex with his consort, Anath, which meant more semen (rain) produced to water the earth."[10] Humans, therefore, were encouraged to participate in the wild orgies of their gods.

The Canaanites were not innocent peasants. But this doesn't mean that other nations were any better. In fact, God says that even *Israel* wasn't much better (Deut. 9:5). So why rain down judgment on the Canaanites while other nations are allowed to live? To answer this, we have to understand the uniqueness of the land of Canaan.

God didn't randomly pick on the Canaanites because they were the most wicked. Rather, He sought to drive them out of the land because *the land would become God's residence on earth.* This means the Canaanites were having sex with prostitutes and sacrificing babies to foreign gods right there in God's living room. Put simply:

the Promised Land would become God's new home on earth. Yes, God dwells in heaven. But biblically speaking, He also resides on earth—first in Eden, then in the tabernacle, and then in the temple. Since God is holy (set apart), His presence requires "sacred space," and God chose the land of Canaan to be that sacred space—the piece of earth where His holy presence would dwell.

But the land became defiled and therefore had to be cleansed, as God says: "The land became unclean, so that I punished its iniquity, and the land vomited out its inhabitants" (Lev. 18:25). The logic, again, is that the Promised Land is God's residence. "The land is mine," God says. "You are strangers and sojourners with me" (25:23). And if Israel lives a holy life, not defiling God's residence as the Canaanites did, then God says, "I will make my dwelling among you ... and ... walk among you" (26:11–12). But if the Israelites live like the Canaanites did, then the land too will "vomit you out when you make it unclean, as it vomited out the nation that was before you" (18:28).

So God didn't bully the Canaanites because of their ethnicity, nor did He coax Israel into a "bloodthirsty massacre" carried out with "xenophobic relish."[11] Rather, God's holiness demands sacred space for Him to dwell with human beings. This is why the Canaanites had to be driven out of God's new residence.

Although it's popular to call the conquest *genocide*, this term is not a fitting description of what happened in the Bible. While it is true that genocide involves the attempted killing of an entire population, and this is what God commanded in Deuteronomy, genocides are always fueled by a feeling of racial superiority that leads to an ethnic cleansing. But there was none of this in Joshua. In this sense,

Joshua's conquest cannot be called genocide. It was God's judgment on persistent evil, and no genocidal nation today can claim such authority.[12]

GRACE: GOD'S PREEMPTIVE STRIKE

So, God commanded Israel to drive out the Canaanites as an extension of divine justice in light of God's special claim on the land of Canaan. But they weren't eliminated without warning. This point is often missed—or ignored—by skeptics who highlight the immorality of the event. Way back in Genesis 15, God told Abram that he would have to wait 430 years before his people would take full ownership of the land. The reason is that "the iniquity of the Amorites [a people living in Canaan] is not yet complete" (Gen. 15:16). In other words, though the Canaanites were sinful (aren't we all?), they hadn't yet exhausted God's patience. They had 430 years to turn from their wickedness to the God of Israel.

But would such repentance have been realistic? After all, how would they know about this God of Israel?

Good question—and it's one that the Bible answers. After God wreaks havoc on Egypt and brings His people through the Red Sea, He broadcasts His divine power across the world.[13] All the nations *know* about this God of Israel, even those living in Canaan. The Canaanites living in the city of Gibeon are a case in point. After Israel enters the land, the citizens of Gibeon come to Joshua and say: "We have heard a report of him, and all that he did in Egypt" (Josh. 9:9). Therefore, "we are your servants. Come now, make a covenant with us" (v. 11). These Canaanites know about the God of Israel and are quite unwilling to oppose Him. God trumpets His reputation across the ancient world, and these particular Canaanites not only hear it but also turn to Him (albeit through espionage).

The most well-known example of someone accepting God's preemptive grace in Canaan is Rahab, the Canaanite prostitute living in Jericho. Like the Gibeonites, Rahab declares that all the people of Jericho "have heard how the LORD dried up the water of the Red Sea … and as soon as we heard it, our hearts melted, and there was no spirit left in any man because of you" (Josh. 2:10–11). Even though they all come face-to-face with God's grace and could have accepted it, only Rahab goes on to confess that "the LORD your God, he is God in the heavens above and on the earth beneath" (v. 11). Instantly, God removes her sins as far as the east is from the west. But the rest of the people of Jericho and many other Canaanite cities choose to remain in their wickedness and oppose the God of Israel.

But even if the rest of the people Jericho didn't believe the report they heard about the God of Israel, God intentionally has Israel march around the city for seven days. Think about it. Jericho probably contains only a few hundred people (a few thousand at best), and Israel numbers around six hundred thousand! The soldiers in Jericho have seven days to give in to what is clearly an inevitable victory for the Israelites. And yet they choose to reject the God of Israel and defend their city. The point is that the seven-day march around the city could be viewed as another offer of grace by the God of Israel, an offer already taken up by Rahab yet rejected by the rest of Jericho's inhabitants.

God persistently forewarns the Canaanites that He is coming as Savior and Judge. If they reject Him as Savior, they will face Him as Judge. God believes, therefore, in preventive wars—wars waged by the extension of grace.

In sum, the conquest is God's punishment for relentless wickedness among people living in God's special residence, who rejected God's offer of grace. Whatever you think about the conquest as a whole, you have to distinguish between arbitrary killing—genocide—and retributive punishment. Or as Old Testament scholar Christopher Wright said: "There is a huge moral difference between arbitrary violence and violence inflicted within the moral framework of punishment."[14] The conquest, like the flood, was divine capital punishment after many years of spurned grace.

TOTAL ANNIHILATION: NOT THE FULL PICTURE

We still need to dig deeper into what actually happened. Most people familiar with the biblical story assume that Israel went in and slaughtered every single Canaanite. However, a quick look at all the evidence shows that such "total annihilation" wasn't the case. After Joshua finished the conquest, there were many Canaanites left alive.[15] You may think, yes, that's because Israel disobeyed God, who commanded total annihilation. And maybe that's true. However, it's not altogether clear that God actually intended Israel to massacre every man, woman, and child—young and old, solider and civilian. The Bible itself suggests a more complex situation. Here's how.

If you look at all the passages where God commands the conquest, you will see that *most* of them say that God would "drive out" or "dispossess" the Canaanites.[16] Such language in itself means only that the Canaanites would be forced out of the land. "Drive out" doesn't mean "slaughter." For instance, Adam and Eve were driven out of Eden (see Gen. 3:24), and Cain was driven out into the wilderness (see 4:14). Later on, David would be "driven ... out" into the wilderness by King Saul (1 Sam 26:19).[17] Adam, Eve, Cain, and David were not annihilated. They were simply forced out of a particular location. And this is the most common language God uses when referring to the Canaanite conquest. After all, God's main concern was that there be no Canaanites living in His residence (unless they turn to Him, like Rahab). Any killing would be a result of their resistance, not Yahweh's insatiable thirst for blood.

The Bible also says that the conquest would happen "little by little," not all at once.[18] In fact, some of these "little by little" passages say that the Canaanites would be driven out by "hornets" (Exod. 23:27–30). Scholars debate the meaning of this, whether it was literal hornets or a figure of speech, but one thing is clear: a wholesale slaughter of all the Canaanites by an ancient *blitzkrieg* is not the uniform picture in the Bible.[19]

So what do we do when there is language of annihilation? Deuteronomy 20 clearly says that "you shall save alive *nothing that breathes*, but you shall devote them to complete destruction" (vv. 16–17). Several passages in Joshua describe Israel's obedience to Deuteronomy's command of total annihilation—the people left alive no breathing thing. Here are the passages in Joshua that describe the slaughter of particular cities in Canaan:

- Of Jericho: "They devoted all in the city to destruction, both men and women, young and

old, oxen, sheep, and donkeys, with the edge of
the sword" (6:21).

- Of Ai: "Israel had finished killing all the inhabitants of Ai. ... All who fell that day, both men and
women, were 12,000, all the people of Ai. ... He
had devoted all the inhabitants of Ai to destruction" (8:24–26).
- Of Makkedah: "He devoted to destruction every
person in it; he left none remaining" (10:28).
- Of Hazor: "They struck with the sword all who
were in it, devoting them to destruction; there
was none left that breathed" (11:11).
- Of Madon, Shimron, Achshaph, and other cities:
"Every person they struck with the edge of the
sword until they had destroyed them, and they
did not leave any who breathed" (11:14).[20]

All of these passages refer to Israel carrying out the Deuteronomy
20 command of total annihilation against specific Canaanite cities
and not necessarily the whole land. However, there is one verse in
Joshua that refers to Israel annihilating the entire population of
Canaan:

> So Joshua struck the whole land, the hill country
> and the Negeb and the lowland and the slopes, and
> all their kings. He left none remaining, but devoted
> to destruction *all that breathed*, just as the LORD
> God of Israel commanded. (10:40)

This seems rather clear. Joshua and his army killed every breathing Canaanite. If this were the only verse we had, we would have to conclude that annihilation was the goal and that this goal was achieved. But there's one glaring problem: the book of Joshua *itself* doesn't say that Israel annihilated the entire population. Several passages in Joshua say that "there remains yet very much land to possess" (13:1), and that "they did not drive out the Canaanites who lived in Gezer, so the Canaanites have lived in the midst of Ephraim to this day" (16:10), and that "the Canaanites persisted in dwelling in that land" (17:12). This is why Joshua would exhort Israel at the end of his life that "you may not mix *with these nations remaining among you* or make mention of the names of their gods" (23:7; cf. vv. 12–14). And when the book of Judges picks up where Joshua left off, it's clear that many Canaanites were not slaughtered but continued to live in the land.[21]

The point is that some passages suggest that all the Canaanites were annihilated, while others suggest that they were not. What do we do with this?

One option is that the Bible contradicts itself, and some take this view. But before we chalk up the problem to a hopeless contradiction—a big problem, of course, for those who believe that the Bible is inspired—let's consider another option. Perhaps there's a bit of *hyperbole* in the biblical account of the conquest.[22]

Last night, the Dodgers slaughtered the Yankees. I mean, they absolutely annihilated them!

Hyperbole refers to overstating something to make a point, and we do this all the time. (Just like my phrase "all the time.") The language of slaughtering and annihilating the Yankees is overstating something to make a point, even though the Dodgers really did beat them up pretty good. ("Beat them up," there I go again ...) That's hyperbole. It's when you make comprehensive and sometimes exaggerated statements to make a point. You may think that there's no way the *Bible* does that! But think again. Hyperbole is a common rhetorical device in Scripture. "If your right eye makes you stumble, *tear it out and throw it from you*," says Jesus (Matt. 5:29 NASB). Sounds painful, and it would be if taken literally, as would "swallowing a camel," which Jesus says the Pharisees are quite fond of doing (23:24).

The Bible sometimes overstates something to make a point. Since this is true, perhaps the biblical phrases that refer to total annihilation are *hyperbolic*—they are overstating the case to make a point. I know this may sound fishy, but our only other option is that the Bible contradicts itself: Joshua 10 says the Israelites annihilated all the Canaanites, while Joshua 13–24 says they didn't. So let's explore the hyperbole option a bit further.

How would we prove that the annihilation statements are hyperbolic and therefore not actually saying that everyone was killed? The fact that the Canaanites *weren't* all killed is one conclusive piece of evidence that the statements are hyperbolic. Outside the Bible, hyperbole appears frequently among ancient nations, especially in their warfare accounts.[23] For instance, the Egyptian pharaoh Thutmose III said that "the numerous army of Mitanni was overthrown within the hour, *annihilated totally*."[24] But historically speaking, many folks of Mitanni survived well after Thutmose had died. They weren't "*annihilated totally*." They were simply defeated. Thutmose was using hyperbole. Again, the Egyptian pharaoh Merneptah fought against Israel and said that "Israel is wasted, his seed is not," suggesting that Israel ceased to exist as a people. That's what "his seed is not" means. But this was in the thirteenth century BC, and Israel continued to live on. Clearly Merneptah overstated the case.

The book of Joshua itself reveals clear examples of hyperbolic war rhetoric. For instance, Joshua 11:22 says that "there were no Anakim left in the land" (NASB) after Joshua got through with them. Sounds like total annihilation. But later, Caleb asks permission to drive out the Anakites (same people) from the hill country.[25] Therefore, either the book of Joshua contradicts itself, or Joshua 11 ("there were no Anakim left in the land") is hyperbolic. I think there's a good biblical case for the latter.

The point is well-known and thoroughly documented by historians: hyperbolic language about comprehensive defeat was typical war rhetoric and wasn't intended to be taken literally. If this were true—and there's every reason to believe that it is—then Joshua didn't annihilate every single Canaanite.

Now, let's revisit Joshua 10:40, which sounds like Joshua killed every single Canaanite. Again, the text reads:

> He left none remaining, but devoted to destruction
> *all that breathed*, just as the LORD God of Israel
> commanded.

We have proved that Joshua didn't actually "[devote] to destruction all that breathed" in the whole land of Canaan. The phrase must be hyperbolic and simply means that Joshua took control of the land.

Now, I want to suggest that this hyperbolic phrase clarifies God's original command in Deuteronomy 20:16–17:

> You shall save alive nothing that breathes, but you
> shall devote them to complete destruction.

Compare Joshua 10:40 with Deuteronomy 20:16–17 cited above and think carefully about how they relate to each other. It seems clear that whatever Joshua 10 means—and it doesn't mean total annihilation—it is intended to describe Joshua's *fulfillment of God's command in Deuteronomy 20*. The language is the same. Also, Joshua says in Joshua 10:40 that his (hyperbolic) annihilation fulfilled God's command, which points back to God's command in Deuteronomy 20:16–17. Therefore, since the author of Joshua 10:40 describes the Canaanite defeat hyperbolically, then it seems likely that God's command in Deuteronomy 20 was also intended to be hyperbolic.

If this is true—and I'm only suggesting it as a legitimate possibility based on biblical evidence—then God never commanded a wholesale slaughter of "everything that breathes" in Canaan.[26] He intended Israel to kill only those who stubbornly resisted His offer of grace (unlike Rahab, who accepted it) and opposed Israel in war. But it's unlikely that Joshua would have chased after exiled Canaanite women and children to hack them to pieces.

This suggestion isn't bulletproof, but I think it carries some good merit. But even if God *did* actually command a wholesale slaughter, we do know without a doubt that no such slaughter actually happened.

There is one more sticky issue that we have to wrestle with. What about the references to woman and children who were killed? This issue is sobering to me, and it should be to you, too. If you believe that the Bible is historically accurate, then we are not just dealing with an interesting theological issue. We're dealing with real people, real blood, *actual babies* who were speared at God's command. Some Christians don't see this as a moral problem. They should.

WOMEN AND CHILDREN?

It's one thing to kill soldiers in combat, but to kill noncombatants seems to be unjustified. How much more horrific, then, is Joshua's extermination of Canaanite women and babies? Aren't children, in particular, exempt from the wickedness that blanketed the land of Canaan? They were simply born into a depraved society. So how do we reconcile Jesus, who had a special heart for children, with the God of the Old Testament, who commanded Israel to slaughter Canaanite babies?

Let's begin with God's reason for telling Israel to kill (or "dispossess"?) the children. Deuteronomy says that if Israel doesn't get rid of *all* the Canaanites, then the people of Canaan will end up leading Israel astray (20:18). And this is exactly what happens. Israel does not drive out all the Canaanites, and Israel ends up getting "Canaanized." In fact, Israel's dark history is littered with many Canaanite-like practices, including idolatry, child sacrifice, and male cult prostitution—all of which they learned from the Canaanites left in the land.[27]

Now, the killing of children still doesn't sit right with me. It still feels morally repulsive. And yet Israel's failure to dispose of *all the Canaanites* ends up biting God's people in the end. Their moral collapse, which elicited God's judgment, began when they failed to drive out *all* the Canaanites from the land. So when read from the perspective of the rest of the Old Testament, we can at least see the logic of the command. As morally difficult as it is, God was right. Failure to drive out all the Canaanites would lead to Israel's ruin.

But there's another option that I will throw out as a suggestion. Perhaps the phrase "men and women, young and old" is not to be taken literally. This may sound a bit shady, but hear me out. We have already shown that hyperbolic language is typical in the conquest account. So let's explore the possibility that God didn't actually intend for Israel to slaughter all the women and children.

The phrase "men and women, old and young" is first mentioned in Joshua 6:21 in the battle of Jericho, and then again in 8:25 in the battle of Ai. Both battles are part of the conquest. It appears, then, that Joshua and Israel slaughtered all the women and children in these cities. However, there is a possibility that the mention of "men and women, old and young" is a stock phrase that simply means "everyone" without necessarily specifying the age or gender of the people. A number of evangelical scholars argue for this.[28] First, these scholars say that both Jericho and Ai were probably military outposts and not vibrant cities filled with citizens of every age. They were therefore most likely stocked with soldiers, not civilians. Second, the only women or children mentioned are Rahab and her family (which probably included children), and they were rescued, not killed. Furthermore, Rahab was a prostitute and—how can I put it?—it would make sense that she would find much business in a city filled with Canaanite soldiers. Third, apart from Joshua 6 and 8, which mention women and children, all other accounts of Israel killing Canaanites in the conquest include—and *only* include—combatants, not civilians. There is no record of Israel actually killing a Canaanite woman or a child during the conquest apart from the two verses in Joshua 6 and 8.

None of these arguments are bulletproof in themselves. Taken cumulatively, though, they do offer some merit to the view that God didn't literally command Joshua to slaughter babies. But there's another argument that offers clear biblical support for this view. It comes from the book of 1 Samuel, where the phrase "man and woman, child and infant" *cannot* mean what it seems to say.[29]

In 1 Samuel 15, God tells Saul to slaughter all the Amalekites including "man and woman, child and infant, ox and sheep, camel and donkey" (v. 3). The text goes on to say that Saul killed "all the people," except he "spared Agag and the best of the sheep and of oxen and of the fattened calves and the lambs, and all that was good, and would not utterly destroy them" (15:8–9). Notice: Saul spared only the king and some animals; he *didn't* spare any other Amalekites. When Samuel rebukes Saul, it's not because he spared some *people*, but because he "pounce[d] on the spoil" (15:19; cf. 15:14, 21). So it seems that Saul did actually kill all the men and women, children and infants. However, when you read on in 1 Samuel, you still see plenty of Amalekites running around. David goes on to kill (again?) all the Amalekites in the land, "leaving neither man nor woman alive" (1 Sam. 27:9). But even David's annihilation can't be taken literally, since he continues to battle with the Amalekites again in 1 Samuel 30:16–20. Then in 2 Samuel

1:8 we read about an Amalekite who claims to have killed King Saul. No matter how often Israel annihilates the Amalekites, they just don't seem to go away.[30]

Here's the point: the phrase "man and woman, child and infant" is used in 1 Samuel 15:3 as a rhythmic description of total defeat and is not meant to include every breathing Amalekite baby. It can't. The text doesn't allow this. Please note: it's not my human sentiment that demands this, but the rest of 1 Samuel.

Perhaps the same phrase about women and children in Joshua 6 and 8 should be understood along the same lines: a rhythmic description of total defeat, without demanding the slaughter of children. So, even though it appears that women and children were killed, there's some evidence that may suggest a less barbaric picture. Israel's clash with the Canaanites resulted in killing other combatants and, perhaps, driving out its civilians who resisted God's new kind of society under His kingship.

PLEASE DON'T MISAPPLY JOSHUA TO YOUR DAILY LIFE

The Canaanites were horrifically wicked, and yet God gave them hundreds of years to repent. Some did, while most didn't. And since God chose Canaan to be His new residence on earth—and as Creator, He had every right to do so—He had to drive out all its wicked inhabitants. The ones who resisted God's grace faced the sword of Israel, God's tool of judgment.[31] While moral problems remain, such as the possibilities that women and children were actually slaughtered (though I have my doubts), the conquest was not a genocide at the hands of a bloodthirsty God.

But the one thing that must be noted about the conquest, the thing that is most relevant to the topic of this book, the point that will be essential for understanding the church's nonviolent posture, is this: nowhere in Scripture, Old or New Testament, is Joshua's conquest prescribed for future generations. It's only a description of what happened. There is nothing in the Bible that appeals to the conquest as justification to wage war or engage in violence. Nothing. The conquest, like the flood and the judgment on Sodom and Gomorrah, was a one-time, non-repeatable event whereby God judged a particularly wicked people.

To take the point further, all subsequent wars that God commanded Israel to wage focused on defending the land. Like the conquest, where Israel *took* the land, subsequent wars sanctioned by God had something to do with *keeping* the land. That is, the *Promised Land given to Israel*, and not any sort of land that belongs to any given nation. This is why Christians cannot appeal to the conquest to justify using violence today. This would be like burning a city to the ground because God once did it to Sodom and Gomorrah (something James and John tried to do and were rebuked for in Luke 9:51–56). Some things are *described* in the Bible that aren't meant to be *prescribed*.

The crusaders were therefore wrong. The colonialists were also wrong. Rumsfeld, Bush, and others who sanitize contemporary wars with verses from Joshua are not only wrong but marching down a dangerous path. After all, God warred against the militarized, chariot-stacked, well-fortified Canaanites, *not* the demilitarized, unprofessional Israelites who fought with trumpets and prayer. Before we apply Joshua to our lives, we need to make sure which side of the Jordan we are living on. Militarism invites God's wrath.

SWORDS INTO PLOWSHARES

A SEAL'S STORY

"War changed me permanently," said Steve Watkins. "The worst scenes I've ever seen were of what humans did to one another: charred and contorted corpses on the Highway of Death, naked bodies hanging from street posts, and stumbling upon Bengali slaves being raped by armed militia. War," he continued, "is the deconstruction of creation itself. It defaces God as it defaces the images created in His likeness."[1]

Steve was a Navy SEAL during Desert Storm. But not just any SEAL: Steve Watkins was one of the most ferocious fighters in his squad. After passing the rigorous selection process known as BUD/S (a feat in itself) Steve went on to advanced training in demolitions, weapons, and close-quarters battle. Steve later became skilled in Brazilian jujitsu under Rickson Gracie (older brother of Royce Gracie), arguably the best fighter the sport has ever seen. But it was in sniper school that Steve found his real niche. He became widely known as one of the sharpest shooters in SEAL Team Five. Whether up close or from a distance, in the water or on land, behind a rifle or bare-fisted, Steve is a trained killer—the embodiment of a militarized warrior. Needless to say, whenever Steve and I hang out, I feel safe.

Steve wasn't born a killing machine, however. As a kid, he had an impulse for peace, not violence. He hated to see even animals be killed. But in America, a desire to kill reinforces manliness. All aversion to death was smothered by his desire to be a man—culturally defined. But something happened while he was in the SEALs. Steve became a Christian. Immediately his perspective on violence changed: "The feeling of fighting no more just felt Christian to me, and I've never lost it. I want to be a voice for nonviolence."

Steve left the SEALs in 1993, and now he serves as a Navy chaplain. He's the only chaplain in the military who wears the SEAL insignia, the Trident. "I am a walking contradiction," Steve told me with a chuckle. "Now I can spare life, rather than take it." Steve's nonviolent stance is a direct outflow of his commitment to Christ. It's a sign of strength, not weakness, and it's certainly not based on any lack of fighting skills. Quite the opposite. For Steve, being a man means being a man of peace, and this isn't attained by simply renouncing violence: "Members of the kingdom are called to turn swords into plowshares"—to be active agents for peace. "And this pursuit is, I believe, important if we call ourselves followers of Jesus."

I love hearing about Steve's journey because he blows apart all stereotypes of what it means to be—in his own words—a pacifist. A trained killer with blood on his hands, Steve has wiped those hands clean with the blood of the Lamb. Steve's journey parallels Israel's own experience with war. God's original intention for creation was peace. And as we traverse the Bible's unfolding story, we see God working toward this goal.

However, Israel's dance with violence became an affair, much like Steve's. They drifted from fighting divinely-approved wars with limited objectives into becoming a warfare state like the surrounding nations. But God's plan to restore Eden will not fail. He will bring His people back to the garden. God sanctioned certain wars along the way, but this was never the ideal. Like Steve, Israel's own redemption would incite it to relinquish violence. They would hammer their swords into plowshares and lurch toward God's Edenic goal—worldwide *shalom* through the suffering Servant.

JUDGES: THE CANAANIZATION OF ISRAEL

Israel's digression into a warfare state begins in Judges—a book that drips with violence. One could wrongly use Judges to authorize warfare and militarism, as Wayne Grudem did when he said, "It is a good thing in God's sight," according to Judges, "when a government has enough military power to defeat the enemies who would bring armies to attack it."[2] This statement is bewildering. Never does Judges promote military power; it often celebrates military weakness.[3] And while the book contains violence on every page, we have to distinguish between the "is" and the "ought." The "is" describes what happened, while the "ought" describes what *should* happen. Just because the Bible records certain events—like the rape of Dinah and Judah's sexual affair with Tamar—doesn't mean that God approves of what happened.[4] Wars are everywhere in Judges (the "is"), but they don't all reflect God's desire (the "ought").

What we find in Judges is that God approves of wars that are part of the ongoing conquest; for instance, taking or defending the land. Even still, militarism is condemned. Victory comes from Yahweh, not swords and spears. And violent activities that mirror those of other nations—personal vengeance, mutilation, civil war, or war unrelated to the land promise—are *condemned*.[5] Israel was to remain

militarily *weak*. They were never to assemble "enough military power
to defeat the enemies." God does that.

The book of Judges begins where Joshua ends. Israel has taken
the land, but there are many Canaanites who remain. Judges 1 begins
with Israel continuing to drive out the Canaanites. As the chapter
rolls on, however, we see more and more unsuccessful attempts to
finish the conquest. The Canaanites aren't going to be driven out
quite so easily, and the rest of Judges fills in the details. The first third
of the book (chapters 1–7) describes wars waged for the purpose
of taking or retaining the land. The battles led by Othniel, Ehud,
Deborah, and Gideon are sanctioned by God; they focus on throwing off the yoke of Canaanite oppression. Judges 1–7 is therefore an
extension of the conquest.

But something changes in the story of Gideon (Judges 6–8).
Gideon starts off well by defeating the Midianites with a demilitarized, Yahweh-dependent army—only three hundred men. But
Gideon isn't satisfied with such limited objectives. He wants
revenge! Even though he reclaims the land from the Midianites,
Gideon hunts down the leaders of Midian nearly three hundred
miles *outside the Promised Land.*[6] His motivation? Personal vengeance. They killed Gideon's brothers (8:18–20), and now they will
face the wrath of Gideon. But personal vengeance has no place in
God's warfare policy. Gideon has departed from God's intention.

Furthermore, as Gideon pursues the enemy, he threatens to
torture men of an Israelite city because they won't give bread to his
soldiers (8:7). Such "psychological warfare" was popular among the
Assyrians—if you don't give me what I want, I'll butcher you—but
has no place among God's people. And Gideon isn't bluffing. After

returning from his manhunt, he drags the elders out of the city and flays their flesh with thorns.[7]

Gideon becomes a bloodthirsty warrior like the men of the surrounding nations, and nowhere does God approve his actions. Gideon hits rock bottom at the end of his life. He makes an idol out of the spoil he took from the Midianites and the jewelry of the Israelites, "and all Israel whored after it there, and it became a snare to Gideon and to his family" (Judg. 8:27). Gideon's later years are overridden with pride, power, and idolatry—not to mention quite a number of wives and concubines.

The rest of the rulers in Judges follow in Gideon's footsteps. His illegitimate son Abimelech is also a war-hungry, vengeful idolater who becomes a mighty leader in Israel after he slaughters his seventy half brothers on a single stone (Judg. 9:5). He isn't at all concerned with conquering or defending the land. He only wants to frighten people through ferocious displays of power. Later on, some of the Israelites who crowned Abimelech end up opposing him. When Abimelech gets wind of it, he goes on a violent rampage, slaughtering thousands of men and women and burning their cities to the ground—*Israelite*, not Canaanite, cities. As Abimelech is laying siege to a tower where his opposition is hiding, an unnamed woman throws a millstone out the window, crushing Abimelech's skull (v. 53). As is often the case, violence countered with violence leads to more violence. Such is the sad life of Abimelech.

The rest of Judges gets progressively worse, if you can imagine it much worse. Jephthah wages war against the Ammonites, a nation living by the border of the Promised Land.[8] It's unclear whether Jephthah's warfare reflects God's desire.[9] In any case, rather than trusting in God, Jephthah tries to manipulate God by pledging his own daughter as a child sacrifice to ensure victory.[10] As if this weren't bad enough, he ends up leading Israel into a bloody civil war where forty-two thousand Israelites are killed.

Forty-two thousand! More Israelites were killed in Jephthah's civil war than Canaanites were killed in the entire book of Judges. The Israelites are supposed to be driving out the Canaanites; instead they are slaughtering themselves.

Violence, civil war, and child sacrifice. Jephthah's Israel has become Canaanized. Yet it gets worse.

Our children's stories sometimes make Samson seem like a hero, but according to Judges 13–16, he is a violent brute whose lust for revenge and Philistine women leads him to kill thousands. God works through Samson's debauchery (14:4), but this doesn't mean He approves of it. Fornication, pride, vengeance, and violence are the character traits of Israel's deliverer. At the end of his life, he *almost* demonstrates a measure of faith by calling on God to help him kill the Philistines. But then he qualifies this plea with, "that I may be avenged on the Philistines for my two eyes" (16:28). Personal vengeance. Samson ultimately cares only for Samson.

Judges concludes on a sadistic note sung to the tune of Assyrian torture psalms. Fornication runs wild, idolatry pollutes the land, and Israel gluts itself with hellish violence: an arbitrary massacre of innocent civilians (18:27), an idolatrous priest butchering his dead concubine (19:29), and a full-scale civil war that nearly erases the tribe of Benjamin (20:1–48). The author sums it up well: "Everyone did what was right in his own eyes" (17:6; 21:25). Israel has become Canaan.

What began as a God-ordained war against the Canaanites turned into a pattern of unsanctioned and arbitrary violence. Israel's lust for power cultivated a grisly warfare policy gleaned from their Canaanite and Assyrian neighbors.

WE WANT A KING!

Israel's descent into secular militarism hits rock bottom in 1 Samuel 8. It's here that Israel explicitly demands a king, "that we also may be like all the nations" (v. 20). As I mentioned in chapter 3, kingship and warfare went hand in hand in the ancient world. To have a king meant having a warrior and an unbridled warfare policy. Even when God spoke of raising up a king (e.g., Deut. 17), He described a demilitarized kingdom: no warhorses, no chariots, and no standing army. Israel's king would hardly be recognizable by other nations. A king without military might is like a Navy SEAL who advocates nonviolence. Some say he's a walking contradiction. Others say he's redeemed.

It's in this context that we should understand Israel's demand for a king in 1 Samuel 8. The Israelites have been in the land for a few hundred years, and, as we saw from Judges, they mirror the wicked nations around them. Now they demand that Samuel "appoint for us a king to judge us *like all the nations*" (1 Sam. 8:5). They are asking to become Canaanite. Samuel warns them that such a king will enact a new warfare policy, where "he will appoint for himself commanders of thousands and commanders of fifties ... and to make his implements of war and the equipment of his chariots" (v. 12). In other words, Samuel rebukes them for wanting a warrior-king. But the people don't care. In fact, such a warrior-like, militaristic king is exactly what they're looking for: "There shall be a king over us, *that we also may be like all the nations*, and that our king may judge us and go out before us and *fight our battles*" (vv. 19–20). Instead of trusting God as their "warrior-king" (see Exod. 15:3), they want a warfare policy like the nations; they want a kingdom fully equipped with a "centralized and *militarized* government."[11] Israel's Canaanization continues.

As we saw earlier, merely having a king isn't the issue. Kingship was sanctioned by God. The issue, according to Deuteronomy 17 and here in 1 Samuel 8, is militarism: they want a military leader who will flex his muscles on the battlefield. Such misplaced trust is tantamount to idolatry, which triggers God's wrath—wrath toward Israel's thirst for military might.

WARFARE UNDER KING SAUL AND KING DAVID

God conceded to the Israelites' request by giving them Saul, their first nation-like warrior-king. Taking lessons from Gideon and Abimelech, Saul shuns Israel's Yahweh-centered, demilitarized warfare policy. Although Saul starts off well (1 Sam. 11), he slowly drifts into waging war like the surrounding nations just as Samuel had warned.[12] Saul forms a professional army,[13] wages war out of personal vengeance,[14] and while it isn't clear that he stockpiles chariots and horses, he does surround himself with an elite military entourage (1 Sam. 22:17), thus fulfilling Samuel's condemning prophecy.[15] Apparently God's protection isn't enough.

Through and through, Saul represents yet another step away from God's qualified warfare policy toward a militaristic, king-centered blank check for violence. Samuel's nightmare about having a king like the surrounding nations becomes a reality.

David is Israel's second king in the monarchy, and in many ways he is God's corrective for the wayward monarchy. He doesn't multiply horses or chariots, and he humbly submits to God. In the early stages of David's reign, God is clearly in charge of Israel's warfare. Early on, David seems to wage war *only* at God's command, as in his early battles with the Philistines (2 Sam. 5:17–25).

But something changes with David, though it's more delayed and subtle than with Saul. Power breeds violence, which breeds more violence and more power. As David continues to wage war against his enemies, he slowly—like Saul—becomes a "me-centered" warrior-king. In later battles with the Philistines, instead of God striking down David's enemies (2 Sam. 5:24), it's now "David" who "defeated the Philistines and subdued them" (8:1). In fact, 2 Samuel 8's summary of David's wars is "a delicate balance between human aggression and divine blessing."[16] God is mentioned only two times in the chapter.[17] By now David has built a professional army, including a few chariots (vv. 4, 16), and uses excessive violence toward the Moabites in battle (v. 2) even though his own great-grandmother was a Moabite. David has become less concerned with defending the land and more concerned with extending his kingdom to make a name for himself (vv. 13–14). And in 2 Samuel 10, another summary of David's wars, God's name is completely left out. The wars are no longer sanctioned by God. By 2 Samuel 11–12, David is now waging wars just like the nations—besieging a city outside the land, boasting in his kingly might, and possibly even torturing the city's inhabitants.[18] The king who once affirmed that "the LORD saves not with sword and spear" (1 Sam. 17:47) has now turned to sword and spear, instead of to God, for his military strength. Like Saul before him, David becomes a warrior-king like the kings of the surrounding nations.

Toward the end of David's life, God confronts him for taking a census. But it's not just any census—it's a *military* census: "Joab, the *commander of the army*" and "the *commanders of the army* went out from the presence of the king to number the people of Israel" (2 Sam. 24:2, 4). And when they returned, they counted "800,000 valiant men *who drew the sword*, and the men of Judah were 500,000" (v. 9). With the census, David wants to "mobilize military power."[19] And King Yahweh punishes him for it by killing seventy thousand of his people. Once again, God is a warrior against, not for, those who are Canaanized and militaristic.

Should we look approvingly on David's militarism when God opposes it? Using David's military exploits to sanction modern warfare—as some Christians do—is a haphazard use of the Bible. Just because it happened (e.g., David torturing his enemies) doesn't mean it ought to happen. Professional armies, wars unrelated to the land, and king-centered wars do not reflect God's warfare policy for Israel. God's critical assessment of David's military prowess is therefore fitting: "You have shed much blood and have waged great wars. You shall not build a house to my name, because you have shed so much blood before me on the earth" (1 Chron. 22:8; cf. 28:3).

To be clear, David was "a man after [God's] own heart" (1 Sam. 13:14). I'm not suggesting that David was wicked or that God had no purpose for him. But I am saying that David was flawed and in need of grace, just as every other character in the Bible was. And his flawed nature shows up particularly in his later approach to warfare. God used David to further His purposes, but setting David's militarism as an example for the ages was never God's intention.

INCREASING MILITARISM UNDER KING SOLOMON

Israel's march toward militarism continues with King Solomon. Though he is often presented as a good king who fell away in his old age, the Bible views Solomon's kingship much more critically. First Kings 3:3 sums it up best: "Solomon loved the LORD ... *only he sacrificed and made offerings at the high places.*" Solomon loves God, but he also has a thing for pagan gods. Solomon commits not only religious idolatry but political idolatry as well (the two go hand in hand). Contrary to God's law for the king (Deut. 17), Solomon has a massive standing army and stockpiled superior weapons beyond imagination—forty thousand stalls of warhorses, fourteen hundred chariots, and twelve thousand horsemen.[20] One could say that stockpiling superior weaponry was the cause for much peace during Solomon's reign. The same logic drove America to amass nuclear weapons during the Cold War. But the Old Testament doesn't work like this. Solomon's accumulation of warhorses and chariots blatantly violates Deuteronomy 17:16, leading Old Testament scholar Walter Brueggemann to label Solomon's reign "the quintessence of Canaanization in Israel."[21] In fact, the Bible makes clear that the peace during Solomon's reign is not due to his military might, but to God's covenant with David (1 Kings 11:11–12). Solomon's military might serves only to condemn him.

MILITARISM AFTER SOLOMON

The kings and other leaders in the next few hundred years follow in Solomon's footsteps. The wicked kings of Israel trust in military might and wage wars at a whim. Again, God sanctions specific wars to protect His living room, but the primary weapons were to be faith, obedience, and prayer rather than chariots and horses. But most of Israel's kings abandon God's supernatural warfare policy. Like Solomon, they beef up their military might—the true object of their faith—and wage war for all sorts of ungodly reasons.[22]

A few kings, such as Jehoshaphat and Hezekiah, do reinstate Israel's unconventional warfare policy and are praised by the biblical authors. Jehoshaphat's Israel, outmanned and under-gunned, watches God defeat the enemy single-handedly. Israel doesn't lift a finger. They lift only their voices to God in worship.[23] The same goes for Hezekiah when Assyria lays siege to Jerusalem.[24] But these positive examples are exceptions that prove the rule. On the whole, Israel falls deeper and deeper into a Canaanized warfare policy, in which its trust in horses and chariots replaces its trust in God.

THE PROPHETIC CONDEMNATION OF WARFARE AND VIOLENCE

The Hebrew prophets rebuke Israel for many things, one of which is the idolatry of militarism.

Hosea anticipates an age when God will shatter Israel's weapons of war and save not "by bow or by sword or by war or by horses or by horsemen" (1:7; cf. 1:5). Hosea rebukes Israel for multiplying "violence," making "a covenant with Assyria" (12:1), trusting in "the multitude of [its] warriors" (10:13), and trusting in its homeland defense instead of God (8:14). Woven throughout Hosea's book is a thick castigation for trusting in military power for national security.[25]

Likewise, Micah says that God will "cut off your horses from among you and will destroy your chariots" and "all your strongholds" (i.e., military defense).[26] Such militarism has engendered Israel's idolatrous trust. As far as the prophet is concerned, militaristic fervor is incompatible with faith in God.

Amos, too, highlights God's judgment on those who violently destroy other nations,[27] and he critiques Israel's trust in military power.[28] Like other prophets, Amos longs for a time when God will bring Edenic peace back to the world (9:11–15).

The prophets never say, "You can have a strong military as long as you still trust in God." Rather, they forbid building a strong military so that Israel's trust *can be only* in God. These prophets would have much to say to the nations today that trust in military might, stockpile superior weapons, and spend billions of dollars on national defense while much of the world lives in grinding poverty.

ISAIAH'S NONVIOLENCE

The prophet Isaiah unleashed the most scathing mantras against Israel's militarism. This is because Isaiah was a pacifist.

Okay, maybe pacifist is a bit strong. We're not sure if Isaiah believed that all violence was wrong. Still, more than any other prophet, Isaiah vehemently critiques Israel's trust in military power: horses, chariots, weapons, and defensive fortresses.[29]

In Isaiah's day, Assyria was trying to conquer the Middle East. Remember, the Assyrians were most known for "psychological warfare"—brutally torturing their enemies to incite panic across the land. They would rip out intestines, cut off testicles, and skin people alive to inspire others to give up and open the coffers. During Isaiah's ministry, they set their sights on Jerusalem. Israel was horrified to say the least. What would they do? Who would they turn to?

Isaiah lives in the middle of this predicament. In fact, Isaiah 7–39 could be considered a warfare tract for ancient Israel, addressing the question: *What should Israel do to prepare for Assyria's impending attack?*

One option is to submit to Assyria. Just give in. If the Israelites raise the white flag, maybe Assyria won't skin them alive. Another option is to make a military alliance with surrounding nations that are opposing Assyria: Egypt, Syria, Babylon, and others. Throughout Isaiah's ministry, various kings choose one of these options. King Ahaz rejects the rebel alliance and submits to Assyria, but that doesn't go so well. Assyria's demands are heavier than Ahaz expected, and though his intestines aren't ripped out (or worse!), he does have to pay a much heavier tribute than expected. Later on, King Hezekiah breaks Ahaz's treaty with Assyria and joins the rebel alliance against Assyria. But that doesn't work either. No alliance can prevent the mighty Assyrians from hacking their way through the Mediterranean world.

In both cases—Ahaz's treaty with Assyria and Hezekiah's rebel alliance against Assyria—Isaiah rebukes Israel for misplaced trust. He scolds Ahaz for giving in to Assyria and reprimands Hezekiah for trusting in Egypt's military might for protection. And beyond trusting in Assyria or Egypt, Isaiah critiques Israel for trusting in its own military strength.[30]

What's the option, then? If Israel isn't allowed to give in to Assyria, trust in Egypt, or rely on its own military, how in the world is it to survive Assyria's attack? No doubt Israel despises Isaiah's nonviolent stance, as would any military leader today. But Isaiah had a different, otherworldly military policy: trust in God. Trust in the God of the Red Sea to save.

This reminds me of the story of Tom Skinner, the New York gangster turned preacher. Skinner was the leader of the "Harlem Lords," one of the most violent gangs in the city. One day, Skinner came to faith in Jesus Christ and immediately renounced his violent ways. Shortly after, he faced his gang to tell them he could no longer be their leader. As he stood in front of the 129 men armed with guns and knives, he told them about his newfound faith in Jesus Christ and how he had to leave the gang. Standing in front of Skinner was the second in command, a man called "Mop"—so named because he loved to draw blood and put his feet in it afterward. Skinner knew he was done for. After he finished speaking, Skinner turned around and walked away, anticipating Mop's blade thrust into his back.

But Mop didn't lift a finger. "I wanted to shove my blade into your back," Mop later told Skinner, "but I couldn't move." All the other gangsters said the same thing. Shortly after, Skinner stood on a street corner and told Mop about the One who had prevented him from shanking Skinner that day. He told him about the God of Israel, Hezekiah's deliverer, and Mop bowed his head and submitted to King Jesus.[31]

Hezekiah is in a similar spot, though he isn't as passive as Skinner. He tries to reestablish the treaty with Assyria, but that doesn't work. They want blood, and blood they will get. So Hezekiah makes a military alliance with Egypt, but that doesn't work either. Assyria pummels Egypt's counterattack with ease.[32] Hezekiah then builds up his defense system, but even that doesn't work.[33] Assyria's military overpowers Hezekiah's "homeland security." So finally, the bloodthirsty, skull-toting, flesh-flaying Assyrians are at Jerusalem's doorstep, shouting out threats that the Israelites will eat their own dung if they don't give in. And there is nothing Hezekiah can do—nothing except trust in God. And so he prays:

> O LORD of hosts, God of Israel, enthroned above
> the cherubim, you are the God, you alone, of
> all the kingdoms of the earth; you have made
> heaven and earth. … So now, O LORD our God,
> save us from his hand, that all the kingdoms of
> the earth may know that you alone are the LORD.
> (Isa. 37:16, 20)

Hezekiah's last-minute turn to a God-centered, demilitarized policy works! Immediately, God sends an angelic warrior to slaughter 185,000 Assyrians. In the spirit of the exodus, God—and God alone—delivers His people. No doubt a worship service thundered across Jerusalem that evening, and they probably sang Psalm 33:

> The king is not saved by his great army;
> a warrior is not delivered by his great strength.

> The war horse is a false hope for salvation …
> Our soul waits for the LORD. (vv. 16–17, 20)

Isaiah believes that all military efforts are worthless in the face of an advancing enemy. Violence carried out by the hands of Israel's army, or by its allies, cannot create peace out of impending war. *Shalom* is created by the hand of God, not the sword of man. Yes, the angel violently slays thousands of Assyrians, but such violence is kept from the hands of God's people: "Vengeance is mine … says the Lord" (Rom. 12:19).

Isaiah's ministry marks a shift in perspective. Israel began with a limited degree of divinely sanctioned warfare. But after Joshua, the people morphed into a warmongering nation like Canaan, where Abimelech, Saul, David, and others soothed their fears with military strength. Finally, by Isaiah's day, the Israelites have so distanced themselves from trusting in God that they look to all sorts of military avenues to secure their existence—trusting in alliances and beefing up their military defense. They have lost sight of God, who promised to protect them through His might, not theirs.

Beginning with Isaiah, we see God moving increasingly away from all species of militarism. The Hebrew prophets following Isaiah prophesy about a time of peace, an age of *shalom*. They envision a kingdom shaped by Edenic harmony, a demilitarized dominion not of this world, a newly created people whose very identity will be marked by nonviolent peace.

The prophets, in other words, paint the shadow of Jesus.

SWORDS INTO PLOWSHARES

Through many oracles, visions, and dreams, the Hebrew prophets look forward to a peace-saturated kingdom that God will inaugurate through His Messiah. God's people will

> beat their swords into plowshares,
>> and their spears into pruning hooks;
> nation shall not lift up sword against nation,
>> neither shall they learn war anymore. (Isa. 2:4)

This prophecy, repeated by Micah (4:3), looks to a future time when instruments of warfare will be transformed into instruments of agricultural productivity. The people of God will learn war no more. God's qualified warfare policy of the old covenant will be abandoned under the new covenant.

Similarly, Zechariah reports God saying:

> I will cut off the chariot from Ephraim
>> and the war horse from Jerusalem;
> and the battle bow shall be cut off,
>> and he shall speak peace to the nations;
> his rule shall be from sea to sea,
>> and from the River to the ends of the earth. (9:10)

God will abolish all instruments of warfare among His people: chariots, horses, and bows. Instead of using Israel to defeat the nations, which had its place in the old covenant, God will "speak peace to the nations" through His Messiah:[34]

> For to us a child is born,
>> to us a son is given;
> and the government shall be upon his shoulder,
>> and his name shall be called ...
>> Prince of Peace.
> Of the increase of his government and of peace
>> there will be no end. (Isa. 9:6–7)

The identity of the Messiah will be one of peace.[35] And He will win this peace by absorbing violence rather than encouraging it. Again, when He comes,

> the wolf shall dwell with the lamb,
>> and the leopard shall lie down with the young
>>> goat,
> and the calf and the lion and the fattened calf together;
>> and a little child shall lead them ...
> They shall not hurt or destroy
>> in all my holy mountain. (Isa. 11:6, 9)

Peace. *Shalom*. Edenic harmony. The Messiah will usher in a kingdom nonviolently:

> He will not cry aloud or lift up his voice,
>> or make it heard in the street;
> a bruised reed he will not break,
>> and a faintly burning wick he will not quench;
>> he will faithfully bring forth justice. (Isa. 42:2–3)

The Messiah will fight for justice, but through nonviolent means.
The Messiah will *absorb violence*, not perpetuate it:

> He was crushed for our iniquities;
> upon him was the chastisement that brought us
> peace,
> and with his wounds we are healed. (Isa. 53:5)

Such blood-bought peace is a major theme in the latter part of
Isaiah[36] and is shared by other prophets as well.[37] And it's not just the
prophets who long for peace. Many biblical writers living after the
monarchy distance themselves from warfare and cultivate the messianic hope for peace.

The books of 1–2 Chronicles, for example, show a deep longing
for *shalom*.[38] Written toward the end of Israel's history, when the
glories of war are fading and a new longing for peace is widespread,
Chronicles considers nonviolence to be the ideal. War is not completely criticized.[39] Sometimes it is seen as inevitable given Israel's
unique historical and theological context. Yet the books set forth
a prophet-like longing for peace. God critiques David for being a
man of war and praises those who trust in Him instead of in military might.[40] Hezekiah's trust in God (after a brief stint of trusting
in Egypt) is set forth as a model, while Josiah's arbitrary war against
Egypt is tantamount to "opposing God" (2 Chron. 35:21). Josiah's
violence is met with violence, as he is killed in battle—a sad ending
to an otherwise good reign.

Together with the prophets, the books of 1–2 Chronicles "reveal
a late biblical tradition groping toward peace," as Old Testament

scholar Susan Niditch put it.[41] The Old Testament begins with peace set forth as the ideal. It also witnesses Israel's failure to carry out a distinctive warfare policy, as it drifts toward nation-like militarism. The prophets of Israel steer our attention back to the Genesis ideal that God will reclaim through His suffering Messiah. And the new covenant people of God, redeemed by the suffering Servant, will enthusiastically fight for peace. Violence by the hands of the redeemed will be a thing of the past, a mark of the old age, a detour from God's blood-bought procession back to Paradise.

The prophets certainly don't answer all of our questions about war and violence. (Are all forms of violence outlawed? What about Christians in the military? What about capital punishment?) We will get to these in due time. For now, it's important to see that the prophets proclaim a message that in general moves *away from violence* and *toward peace*. And this is how the Old Testament ends. Longing for peace. This longing creates the seam that stitches together the seemingly contradictory portraits of violence in the Old Testament and nonviolence in the New.

The stage is set. The journey is under way. It's time for the Messiah to bring us back to Eden.

6

THE KING AND HIS KINGDOM

JESUS'S VIOLENT WORLD

The Prince of Peace was born into a world drowning in violence. The years between the Old and New Testaments were anything but silent, as kingdom rose up against kingdom, nation warred against nation, and the Jewish people hacked their way to freedom with swords baptized in blood.

About two hundred years before Christ, the Greeks who ruled over Israel banned the practice of Judaism and slaughtered those who resisted. But the Jews wouldn't give in so easily. Led by Judas "the Maccabee" (literally, "the hammer"), zealous Jews took up the sword and threw off the yoke of their Gentile overlords, massacring thousands in their wake. A few decades later, the Maccabees reclaimed their religious and political freedom and set up a quasi-messianic kingdom through violent force. The success of Maccabean swords would shape the way Jewish people in Jesus's day would understand— and anticipate—the kingdom of God.[1]

Over time, the Maccabean heroes turned their swords on their own people. Aristobulus (Judas's grandnephew) killed his brother and starved his mother to death, all the while claiming to be king of Israel.[2] The next Jewish king, Alexander Jannaeus, formed an impressive military to defend the nation and expand its territory: one thousand cavalry, ten thousand infantry, and eight thousand mercenaries. Jannaeus fought off Greek invaders and secured

Israel's freedom. But soon power led to madness as Jannaeus terrorized his own citizens. On one occasion, he crucified eight hundred Pharisees and, according to Josephus, "butchered their wives and children before their eyes" while he "reclined amidst his concubines" and "enjoyed the spectacle." On another occasion, Jannaeus executed six thousand Jews for throwing fruit at him during a festival.[3]

Jesus's world was submerged in violence.

After eighty years of Maccabean rule, Israel's kingdom crashed to an end when the Roman general Pompey killed twelve thousand Jews while taking control of the land. Israel again was under Gentile rule, this time by the Romans. But seething unrest for freedom, fueled by Maccabean memories, fostered a violent spirit among the Jewish people. Years later, Herod the Great picked up where Jannaeus left off, killing his own mother-in-law, his favorite wife (he had many), and several of his sons, along with anyone who was even suspected of threatening his rule, including a number of babies in Bethlehem.[4] Herod's sons—the ones who weren't killed—also wielded the sword. Herod's son Archelaus slaughtered many thousands of Jews and on one occasion stuffed three thousand murdered bodies into the temple as an "offering to God."[5]

MESSIANIC FREEDOM?

This was the world Jesus entered, a world ruled by violence. Many Jews sought freedom through bloodshed. Others kept their swords close at hand, ready for a signal to rise up and conquer.

During Jesus's lifetime on earth, several messianic figures rose up to establish God's kingdom through violent revolution. Immediately after Herod the Great died, two messiah-like figures named Simon and Anthronges led independent revolts. Their "principle purpose," according to Josephus, was "to kill Romans" and claim the Jewish throne. Both movements were crushed, and Simon and Anthronges were executed. A few years later, when Jesus was about twelve years old, a warrior named Judas (not Iscariot) tried to overthrow Rome and set up God's kingdom. The insurrection—which happened a few miles away from Nazareth—gained some traction but was halted by Rome.[6] Judas's two sons, Jacob and Simon, also led violent revolts that failed, and both men were caught and crucified. Around the same time, a certain Tholomaus worked up an unsuccessful revolt, as did Theudas, who claimed to be a prophet and mustered up a sizable force. Both were executed.[7] Three decades after Jesus's death, two other messianic figures, Menahem and Simon ben Giora, led a massive revolt against Rome that also ended in failure. Menahem was caught, dragged through the streets, and "put to death by prolonged torture."[8] Simon was taken back to Rome, paraded as a trophy, and then pulled with a rope around his neck to the Forum, where he was executed.[9]

Welcome to Jesus's world.

Despite the failure of these many revolts, the earlier success of the Maccabees ensured that messianic zeal was not easily snuffed out. Hope still burned for the establishment of God's kingdom through force. Struck down but not defeated, the Jews cooked up yet another revolt a hundred years after Jesus's death. They hailed as Messiah a certain Simon bar Kochba, who led an impressive force against Rome. But the uprising was put down. Bar Kochba was killed, Jerusalem was razed to the ground, and the land of Israel was once again muddied with the blood of Jewish insurrectionists—messiahs, who sought to usher in God's kingdom by hammering their plowshares into swords.

We could go on and on about the so-called dagger men (*sicarii*) who wandered the streets of Jerusalem in stealth, thrusting blades into the ribs of their enemies. Or the Zealots, whose very identity was shaped by violently resisting evil. Suffice it to say that Jesus's world was a tinderbox ready to explode into flames, and messianic figures kept dousing it with gasoline. The reign of God became synonymous with the sword of man. A would-be Messiah who turned the other cheek and loved his enemies would not be taken seriously. Or he would be killed.[10]

It's in this context that we must understand the strange words and deeds of the peasant son of a Jewish carpenter—a rather unmessianic messianic figure.

Despite the widespread expectation of peace envisioned by the Hebrew prophets, history had gone a different direction. The Maccabean kingdom cultivated a thirst for political independence through the sword. Yet from birth to death, Jesus preached a non-Maccabean kingdom. He would bear a plowshare, not a sword, and set up God's kingdom without using violence. And He would tell His followers to do the same.

A KINGDOM HERE AND NOW

Jesus's central message was not primarily about how to get to heaven when you die, or about becoming a better person. The central message of Jesus was about the coming of God's kingdom.

This kingdom language is everywhere in the four gospels. When the gospel writers sum up Jesus's message, they say things like the following: Jesus "went throughout all Galilee ... proclaiming the gospel of the kingdom" (Matt. 4:23), or Jesus proclaims "the gospel of God, and say[s], '... the kingdom of God is at hand'" (Mark 1:14–15). Everything He says and does is in some way related to the kingdom.

Jesus's kingdom-message is rooted in the Old Testament. Simply put, "the kingdom" means *God's reign over Israel through its Messiah.* We've seen glimpses of the kingdom during the time of David, Solomon, and other kings. And we've looked at how the prophets longed for God to restore His kingdom to Israel, where the Messiah's rule would extend to the ends of the earth. This is the same kingdom that Jesus is talking about. Jesus announces that this long-anticipated reign of God over the earth is breaking into history through Him.

The kingdom is what the prophets looked forward to and what the Maccabeans and their heirs tried to establish through violence.

But Jesus's kingdom talk gets Him into hot water. The term *kingdom* isn't invented by Jesus or the New Testament writers. Most people in Jesus's day understand *kingdom* to mean the empire (kingdom) of Rome. Jewish people, as we have seen, tried to set up their own kingdom. So when Jesus talks about the kingdom, everyone already has a category to understand what He is saying. Jesus isn't inventing a term or concept unknown to people. Rather, He takes a well-known concept, guts it, and stuffs it with new meaning. What God does with the concept of *kingship* in the Old Testament (for example in Deut.17), Jesus does with *kingdom* throughout the Gospels. And one central feature of Jesus's unkingdom-like kingdom is the issue of power and violence. Whereas all other kingdoms (Roman, Jewish, or whatever) are breaking in with force and violence, Jesus will erect the kingdom of peace without using violence. Put simply: Jesus preaches a demilitarized Deuteronomy 17-like kingdom.

NOT OF THIS WORLD

Perhaps the best place to see this is in John 18:33–38, where Jesus is on trial and describes His kingdom to Pontius Pilate. "Are you the King of the Jews?" Pilate asks. But Jesus doesn't give him a straight answer, and we can imagine why. Pilate understands the concept of king to be a powerful, coercive, violent earthly ruler. Since Rome already has one of these—Caesar Tiberius—all other self-proclaimed kings are impostors or revolutionaries trying to overthrow Rome. Jesus will affirm that He is indeed a king (v. 37), but first He must redefine kingship:

> My kingdom is not of this world. If my kingdom were of this world, my servants would have been fighting, that I might not be delivered over to the Jews. But my kingdom is not from the world. (v. 36)

Jesus's statement has been subject to its own slew of interpretive violence. Some people think that the kingdom is wholly spiritual, or completely otherworldly.[11] While early Gnostics held this view,[12] few (if any) biblical scholars believe that this is what Jesus means. Others think that "not of this world" means that the kingdom is a present spiritual reality, but in the future it will be a physical reality.[13] "Christ's kingdom is spiritually active in the world today," says one writer, "and one day He will return to physically reign on the earth in millennial glory (Rev. 11:15; 20:6)." During the church age, Jesus's "Kingdom exists in the hearts of believers" and is irrelevant to the "political and military identity of Rome."[14] This view is correct in that Jesus wasn't seeking to overthrow Rome, and there is definitely some sort of "already/not yet" dimension of Jesus's kingdom. The kingdom is only partially here ("already"), and certainly there's more to come ("not yet"). However, this view still falls into the trap of taking "not of this world" to refer to some spiritual, immaterial realm. Also, as we will see, Jesus's kingdom *was* viewed as a challenge to the political and military identity of Rome. That's why He was crucified.

So what does Jesus mean by "my kingdom is not of this world"? The answer comes in Jesus's very next words: "If my kingdom were of this world, *my servants would have been fighting.*" Nonviolence is at the heart of Jesus's definition of *kingdom.* More broadly, Jesus means that His kingdom will not follow the script of all the other nation-like worldly kingdoms of history. Jesus's kingdom will enact God's reign on earth, which according to the prophets will speak peace to the nations, offer forgiveness to the undeserving, and extend love to neighbor and enemy alike. So the contrast between "of this world" and "not of this world" isn't between a material versus spiritual reign, but between a worldly way and a godly way of reigning.[15] Jesus's statement, in other words, reflects the counter-cultural spirit of Deuteronomy 17.

When Jesus uses the term *world* (as in "not of this world"), therefore, He does not mean physical creation, as if Jesus was opposed to trees, rocks, and mountains. John uses the term *world* (*kosmos*) throughout his gospel and his letters to refer to "the systems of the world" or "social construction of reality."[16] Put simply, *world* often means *the way unbelievers do things.* For instance, Jesus says that He has come to testify against the *world* that its deeds are evil (John 7:7). Or as John will say elsewhere, "Do not love the world or the things in the world" (1 John 2:15). This does not refer to the material stuff on earth, nor does it refer to people, whom Jesus and John say we are to love. The "world" refers to the worldly *systems* that run against God's way of doing things. Unjust economic systems, dehumanizing social classification, and advancing one's kingdom through violence. These are all "of the world."

GOD'S EMPIRE

The most daring word that Jesus throws at Pilate is the term *kingdom.* As I said, this was the typical Greek term used for the Roman Empire. And it's the same word that Jewish freedom fighters would use when they tried to oust Rome and set up their own empire (as the Maccabees did). *Kingdom,* therefore, cannot be reduced to individual salvation, or some immaterial religious experience. If Jesus's kingdom was restricted to individuals or the spiritual realm, He would use a different word. But He doesn't. He uses the word *kingdom.* He uses the word *empire.*[17]

Jesus seeks to set up God's empire on earth, and it will look different from Rome and the Maccabees in one crucial aspect: Jesus's empire will not come about through physical fighting. It will be a demilitarized empire where enemies are loved and offenders are forgiven.

We see that those in the crowd recognize the subversive nature of Jesus's claims when they cry out: "If you release this man, you are not Caesar's friend. Everyone who makes himself a king opposes Caesar" (John 19:12). And again the people affirm, "We have no king but

Caesar" (v. 15). The crowd plays up the political nature of Jesus's claims, which is necessary to get Him crucified—capital punishment for insurrectionists.

Now, the crowd is wrong on one level. Jesus isn't a physical threat, nor is He trying to overthrow Rome. But His kingdom will challenge Rome's ideology: its economics, social classification, treatment of the outcast, and its use of power and violence.[18] Nonviolence takes center stage as Jesus singles out physical *fighting* as the key difference between His empire and Caesar's.[19]

WE WANT A KING LIKE THE NATIONS—AGAIN

Jesus's words are rooted in the rich soil of the Old Testament. As we have seen, God intended Israel to be a kingdom quite unlike the other nations, which was why God prohibited Israel from having a king like the nations. But Saul, Ahaz, and even David fell into nation-like kingship. The failure of Israel's kings cultivated hope for a new Son of David, a Prince of Peace who would match the Deuteronomy 17 ideal, who would not trust in military might or accumulate wealth, but who would love the Lord and serve God's people. According to the prophets, this new King would "speak peace to the nations" and set up a kingdom that would reach the ends of the earth (Zech. 9:10). Jesus's "kingdom not of this world" is directly connected to God's original intention with Israel in the Old Testament. God wants to set up an alternative kingdom, one that will have a different type of king and a distinct way of living.

Jesus's nonviolent kingdom doesn't make immediate sense to His followers, however. We see this confusion in Matthew 11 when John the Baptist is thrown into prison and wonders if Jesus really is the Messiah. "Are you the one who is to come?" John asks. "Or shall we look for another?" (v. 3). John was on board for a while, but after Jesus has talked about turning your cheek, loving your enemy, and forgiving people like a Roman centurion, John starts to have his doubts. He then finds himself in prison with all the other unsuccessful revolutionaries, ready to be executed. So you can imagine John's confusion about whether Jesus's kingdom is truly drawing near. From behind bars, it looks like it's fading away.

Jesus, however, reassures John that He is indeed the One. Though He hasn't overthrown Rome, nor has He acted violently, "the blind receive their sight and the lame walk, lepers are cleansed and the deaf hear, and the dead are raised up, and the poor have good news preached to them" (Matt. 11:4–5). These are the types of things the Messiah will do, according to the prophet Isaiah.[20] And Jesus has been doing them (Matt. 8–9). He is the true King of Israel. But "from the days of John the Baptist until now," Jesus says, "the kingdom of heaven has suffered violence, and the violent take it by force" (11:12). Jesus here refers to the persecution that will accompany His kingdom ("suffered violence") and to the response others have taken toward this violence. "The violent" (the Maccabees and the Zealots) have tried to set up God's kingdom by overpowering their oppressor.[21] But not Jesus. His kingdom is not of this world. A divine kingdom doesn't need to be propped up by human swords.

The expectation of a warrior-like Messiah, stirred up by Maccabean zeal, has all but snuffed out the prophetic hope for a Prince of Peace, but Jesus is rekindling that hope. His unworldly kingdom befits the unworldly king extolled in Deuteronomy 17—a King and kingdom that are not militarized like the nations.

ARE YOU THE MESSIAH?

Have you ever noticed that Jesus frequently tells His disciples not to tell others about His identity as the Messiah? On several occasions, Jesus sternly warns His disciples *not* to tell people that He is the Messiah. This is because by the first century, the titles *messiah* and *king* were fraught with images of warfare and violence, as we have seen. Jesus, therefore, has to redefine what *messiah* and *king* mean to the ears of His Jewish followers, who are steeped in the ideology of the Maccabees. This is probably why Jesus is reluctant to call Himself the Messiah. The title is loaded with violent images fostered by the frequent messianic revolutions sought by the Jewish people.

Consider Mark 8:27–38. This a turning point in Jesus's life, when He asks Peter point blank, "Who do you say that I am?" (v. 29). And Peter answers correctly, "You are the Messiah" (usually translated "Christ," which is the Greek word for the Hebrew "Messiah"). This is the first time that the disciples rightly identify Jesus as the Messiah. But rather than celebrating, Jesus "strictly charged them to tell no one about him" (v. 30). Sounds like Jesus is stifling their evangelistic zeal. But this isn't the point. Jesus tells them not to go around heralding Him as the Messiah since people would immediately think of Jesus as a violent revolutionary when they heard this term. This is why Jesus immediately redefines the meaning of Messiah. Instead of a coercive, violent, power-hungry king, Jesus will be a suffering Servant:

> And he began to teach them that the Son of Man
> must suffer many things and be rejected by the
> elders and the chief priests and the scribes and be
> killed, and after three days rise again. (8:31)

The disciples still don't get it. Peter turns and rebukes Jesus for speaking such nonsense. Messiahs don't suffer, and they certainly aren't killed prematurely—unless they are imposters. If they are legitimate, they conquer. They fight. They do kingly things like getting rid of their Gentile oppressors and cleansing the land of sin through violent insurrection.[22] "Get behind me, Satan!" Jesus responds. "For you are not setting your mind on the things of God, but on the things of man" (Mark 8:33). In other words, Peter is still trapped in a "kingdom of this world" way of thinking. For Peter, messiahs wield power; they don't submit. That's what messiah *means* according to Peter's worldview. Jesus goes further and says that He's not the only one who will suffer. All of His would-be followers must deny themselves, pick up their crosses, and suffer—if they want to follow the Messiah. The cross and resurrection are what constitute the power of the kingdom.

The disciples are still confused, so Jesus takes three of them up to a mountain to show them "the kingdom of God after it has come with power" (Mark 9:1). The kingdom that they see is the transfigured Messiah appearing in His resurrected glory. God's kingdom will come, and it will come in power. Not human power—coercive violence, military might, or legions of fighting servants—but divine power. The kingdom will come, in other words, through the suffering, death, and resurrection of Jesus.

Welcome to Jesus's upside-down kingdom, where weakness is power, power is weakness, and suffering leads to glory.

POWERFUL WEAKNESS

Nonviolence becomes a hallmark of Jesus's kingdom. Such understanding of the kingdom, though not far from Isaiah and the prophets, is foreign to the violent first-century world of Jesus. This is why Jesus often corrects His disciples' misperception. On one occasion, Jesus and His disciples are rejected from a Samaritan village. James and John react by wanting to call down fire and nuke the entire town. Such vengeance may have fit the Maccabees or Zealots, but it has no place in Jesus's kingdom of peace. On another occasion, Jesus reminds His disciples that the Son of Man is going to be condemned, killed, mocked, flogged, spit upon, and then "after three days he will rise" (Mark 10:32–34). But James and John don't get it. So they ask Jesus if they can surround His throne in the kingdom. Jesus rebukes them like He did Peter and tells them again that the pathway to glory is suffering:

> And Jesus called them to him and said to them, "You know that those who are considered rulers of the Gentiles lord it over them, and their great ones exercise authority over them. But it shall not be so among you. But whoever would be great among you must be your servant." (Mark 10:42–43)

Like Israel in the days of Saul, the sons of Zebedee want a kingdom like the other nations. But Jesus flips the logic of kingdom and kingship. Unlike the Babylonian, Canaanite, Egyptian, and—nearer at hand—Roman kingdoms, the kingdom of God will be shaped by servitude and suffering, not human power and violence. Jesus came to serve, not be served; to suffer on behalf of many. Following Jesus in His kingdom means we do the same.

STRANGERS IN A STRANGE LAND

Jesus's not-of-this-world kingdom is shaped by nonviolence. This doesn't always stand out to us, but no Jew in the first century would have missed the radical nature of Jesus's claim. In a world where *king* and *kingdom* were synonymous with coercion, power, and violence, Jesus's upside-down kingdom stuck out like a baseball team with no bats, or a megachurch with no sound system or comfy chairs. But that's precisely the point. As God's reign on earth is enacted through nonviolence, the power of God rather than the power of humans is showcased for all to see.

The apostles frequently speak of the kingdom of God in ways similar to Jesus, as we'll see in chapter 8. Peter says that Christians are sojourners and exiles scattered throughout the world.[23] John commands Christians to live in the world but not like the world. And Paul says that our citizenship is in heaven, not on earth.[24] This means that instead of being colonies of earthly governments, we are colonies of heaven *on earth*. God's kingdom continues to spread across creation through local bodies of believers called the church.

We are called to be different, to give our allegiance to Jesus's not-of-this-world kingdom. Worldly kingdoms flex their muscles to rule the earth; Jesus kneels to wash feet. Gentiles lord it over other people; Christians become servants to everyone. Rome crucifies those who threaten its power; Jesus endures crucifixion as a pathway to resurrection glory. And He calls His disciples to bear their cross and follow Him down the bloodstained road to Calvary.

Something is wrong when the kingdom of God is indistinguishable from that of the world. Christians should contribute to the good of the nation in which they live (Jer. 29:7). But we are first and foremost citizens of Jesus's kingdom spread throughout the world. We have more in common with Christians in other nations—nations our country may war against—than we do with neighbors who share the same passport. When nations war against other nations, this critical point gets snuffed out. Take the Iraq war, for instance. Regardless of America's cause for invasion—to secure oil reserves, disarm weapons of mass destruction, get rid of a dictator—the kingdom of God has suffered horrific effects from the war. And this should cause citizens of God's kingdom to mourn. For instance, prior to 2003, there was relative freedom for the 1.5 million Iraqi Christians. But since 2003, more than half of these Christians have been tortured, killed, or exiled to other countries.[25]

It's sad when American Christians talk about "us" and "them" and use these identity markers solely in terms of different national identities. But "we"—the *kingdom of God* in America and Iraq—have suffered greatly. Citizens of God's kingdom did not win the war. We lost.

Citizens of God's kingdom, wherever we live, should pray for our leaders and submit to our governing authorities insofar as such submission doesn't conflict with the law of Christ. But through Jesus's blood, we have more in common with our fellow kingdom-citizens in Iraq, who have suffered from America's invasion, than we do with most of our nation's military, which caused the suffering. We should never let our national citizenship take priority over our heavenly citizenship.

A TENSION OVER CITIZENSHIP

Such a tension over citizenship was felt by a man named Martin on the eve of World War II. Martin was the son of a Lutheran pastor and a heroic submarine commander in World War I. After his service in the armed forces, Martin became a pastor like his father. By the time World War II was on the horizon, Martin spoke positively of his government and the need to fight the war. "When this great nation was formed," proclaimed Martin, "God gave it Christianity as its soul, and it is from these Christian roots that it has grown and developed." The Christian church, however, was divided on whether the war was just. Some said that going to war would violate Jesus's teaching. Others, including Martin, appealed to Romans 13 for biblical proof that their government had the divine mandate to punish evildoers. When the war finally broke out, Martin joined the army along with his two sons.

Regardless of whether World War II was considered a "just war," I don't think Martin should have gone to fight. His allegiance should have been toward God's kingdom, not the earthly nation where he lived. Martin should have considered the fact that those he was seeking to kill may actually have been *fellow citizens of Christ's kingdom*. And regardless of whether his country won the war, this would not advance God's kingdom on earth. Jesus sought to advance His kingdom *without fighting*, and Martin was called to further Jesus's kingdom not by fighting, but by proclaiming the good news that Jesus, not Franklin D. Roosevelt or Harry Truman or Adolf Hitler, is King.

Martin Niemöller, by the way, was a German citizen. He volunteered to serve in the Nazi army out of allegiance to his earthly nation. It's a dangerous thing when national ideology dims the lights on that city set on a hill.[26]

7

LOVE YOUR ENEMIES

THE CHARTER FOR THE KINGDOM

Jesus sought to establish a counter-cultural, counter-Maccabean, non-Roman, anti-Canaanite kingdom whose citizens would embody a not-of-this-world reign over the earth. And on one Galilean afternoon, King Jesus sat down to tell His followers what this unconventional kingdom would look like. His instructions are contained in one of the most cherished passages in the Bible: Matthew 5–7, otherwise known as the Sermon on the Mount.

Jesus's Sermon is more than a personal ethic—a way in which individuals can be better people. Rather, the Sermon is intended to reconfigure God's new community, to mold His people into a visibly different kingdom in the face of all other imposter kingdoms. Or in Jesus's own words, we are to be the "salt of the earth" and the "light of the world"—a public display of a different way (Matt. 5:13–14). The Sermon's instructions are designed to be very different, communal, visible; they attract attention, cause bewilderment, and showcase the missional heart of the King. "Let your light shine before others, so that they may see your good works and give glory to your Father who is in heaven" (v. 16).

Jesus is not just teaching people how to be better, nor is He giving them some impossible standard they'll never live up to. The Sermon, rather, is the "definitive charter for the life of the new covenant community,"[1] and through it Jesus seeks to sculpt counter-cultural masterpieces—citizens of the great King—to embody a different society and disclose a different God. We should *expect* these instructions to jar our thinking, challenge our desires, and contradict normality—the way we usually do things around here. If you're "of the world," the Sermon will seem outlandish and impractical.

It doesn't make sense, for instance, that mourners will be happy, sufferers will be glad, and meek people will rule the world, but this is exactly what Jesus says (Matt. 5:4–5, 10). We will be salt and light when we reconcile with our offenders and love the spouse we've fallen out of love with. It's all there in the Sermon. Salt and light. Such unexpected ways of doing things—a King in a manger—will draw attention to Jesus's upside-down kingdom ruled by meek, pure-in-heart peacemakers. When we are wronged, we forgive; when we have money, we give; when we don't have money, we give; when we give, we don't flaunt it; when we fast, we smile; when we need food and clothing and the bank account is dry, we don't worry like the rest of the world. Instead, we pray.

And this peculiar posture, taught and modeled by Jesus, unknown and unloved in the world, has everything to do with violence.

YOU HAVE HEARD ... BUT I SAY

Toward the beginning of the Sermon, Jesus gives six so-called antithetical (think: contrasting) statements that form the moral bedrock of Jesus's Sermon. They all go something like, "You have heard that it was said ..., but I say to you ..." These statements address murder, lust, divorce, oaths, retaliation, and how to relate to your enemies. Notice: three of these six have to do with violence—daring words, considering Jesus's violent world. Overthrowing one's enemies to set up God's kingdom on earth was the route most self-proclaimed messiahs chose. But Jesus seeks a different way. After highlighting peacemaking and suffering as identity markers of the kingdom (Matt. 5:7, 9–12), Jesus takes the issue of murder to new heights in His first antithetical statement:

> You have heard that it was said to those of old, "You shall not murder; and whoever murders will be liable to judgment." But I say to you that everyone who is angry with his brother will be liable to judgment; whoever insults his brother will be liable to the council; and whoever says, "You fool!" will be liable to the hell of fire. (vv. 21–22)

Not only are you not to murder, but the very desire that leads to murder is prohibited. In other words, by prohibiting anger, Jesus takes one more incremental step toward peace by nipping murder in the bud. Jesus goes on to rule out *verbal violence* toward the offender. The physical act of murder, the verbal act of slander, and even anger—the heartbeat of all violence—are prohibited. Jesus therefore *intensifies* the law's prohibition of murder by including a wide range of violent activities.

The next command that addresses violence deals specifically with retaliation:

> You have heard that it was said, "An eye for an eye and a tooth for a tooth." But I say to you, Do not resist the one who is evil. (vv. 38–39)

Jesus cites a familiar Old Testament statement about justice in the courts.[2] If, for instance, someone poked out your eye and you took him to court, he would receive a punishment that matched the crime. He would have his eye poked out. As barbaric as this may seem, the Old Testament law was intended to limit retribution, not celebrate it. By the first century, however, what should have been decided in the courts was settled on the streets. But Jesus doesn't direct the victim to settle it in court. Rather, He unexpectedly tells the victim, "Do not resist the one who is evil."

What in the world does "do not resist the one who is evil" mean? Can we really live this way?

Yes, we should. Indeed, we can. The Greek word for "resist" is *anthistemi*, and it often (though not always) refers specifically to violent resistance.[3] Throughout the Old Testament, for instance, *anthistemi* refers to military action: Israel *resists* its enemy in battle, and the Canaanites weren't able to *resist* Israel in the conquest.[4] In the New Testament, other words related to *anthistemi* refer to violent revolts, insurrections, and war. Josephus, the first-century Jewish historian, almost always used *anthistemi* in ways that convey some sort of violent action.[5] So when Jesus tells His followers not to resist evil people, He uses a word that suggests a violent resistance. In fact, New Testament scholar N. T. Wright translated the verse "Don't *use violence* to resist evil" to remove all ambiguity.[6] Put simply, when Jesus says, "Do not resist the one who is evil," He specifically prohibits using violence to resist evil.

OUTRAGEOUS NONRESISTANCE

Jesus then fills out His command with five different examples of what such nonresistance may look like.

But if anyone slaps you on the right cheek, turn to
him the other also.
And if anyone would sue you and take your tunic,
let him have your cloak as well.
And if anyone forces you to go one mile, go with
him two miles.
Give to the one who begs from you,
and do not refuse the one who would borrow from
you. (Matt. 5:39–42)

These five statements define what Jesus means by "do not resist
the one who is evil," and each one covers a different sphere of life.
That's actually important. Jesus takes the "do not resist evil" command and scatters it across *all of life*—and so should we.

The first situation deals with a physical attack: "But if anyone
slaps you on the right cheek, turn to him the other also" (v. 39). I
know—this doesn't make sense to me either, and this is probably
the reaction Jesus is hoping for. Now, some people think that Jesus
wasn't talking about a physical attack but more of a shameful slap in
the face. After all, Jesus specifically says that it's the *right* cheek that
was hit, and since most people were right-handed, they would strike
the right cheek with the back of the right hand. This may be the case,
though Jesus certainly doesn't spell it out that clearly. Even still, we
should notice two things.

First, if it is a shameful backhand that Jesus is talking about, this
only heightens the severity of the attack. Judaism was an "honor/
shame" culture, where shaming somebody was *more* (not less)
destructive. I point this out because some interpreters like to say that

Jesus is *only* talking about a shameful slap, not a physical attack—as if the shameful slap is less harmful. This may be true of some cultures, but not Jesus's.[7] Whether or not Jesus refers to a backhanded slap, He's certainly not talking about a minor offense.

Second, even if Matthew 5 refers to a backhanded slap, the parallel in Luke 6 clearly describes a raw slug to the face: "To one who strikes you on the cheek, offer the other also" (v. 29). Notice: there's no mention here of the *right* cheek, just the cheek.

So when Christ-followers are attacked with shame, pain, shameful pain, or whatever, they should *not* respond with violence. They are to respond with unconditional, inexplicable, shocking love that comes from being redeemed by a God who loves His enemies.

The second situation deals with a legal attack: "If anyone would sue you and take your tunic, let him have your cloak as well" (Matt. 5:40). In Judaism, if someone had an unpaid debt, the debtor would give up his cloak as collateral until the debt was paid. If the debtor couldn't pay, then the lender would take his cloak for keeps.[8] But Jesus intensifies the situation by mentioning the less-valuable "tunic" (think: undershirt) and then the "cloak" (coat). The cloak was much more valuable, if not necessary for life, since it could be used as a blanket for sleeping at night.[9] Losing your tunic isn't a big deal. Losing your cloak is a huge deal. Once again, Jesus intensifies the love that His followers are to have toward those who wrong them. If someone wants to sue you and take your bike, give him your car also. Counterintuitive! Shock your enemy by drowning him or her with generosity. No one who has watched *Les Misérables* can deny the stunning power of such radical behavior.

The third situation is even tougher. It pertains to political oppression by a foreign army: "If anyone forces you to go [*angareuo*] one mile, go with him two miles" (Matt. 5:41). Jesus doesn't mean any old journey with a random person. He's thinking of first-century Palestine, where Roman soldiers force Jews to carry their packs. This is what the Greek work *angareuo* means.[10] Think about this. The Jew carrying the soldier's gear eases the burden of his oppressor—the foreigner who invaded his homeland. Jesus says to address imperialism by loving the imperialists!

What would this look like for us? Say that al-Qaeda took over America (or wherever you live), and one of its soldiers barked at you to carry his pack. I'm not sure what I would do, but Jesus tells us what we *should* do: carry it twice as far. Ease his burden. Love your enemy. It's tough to follow Jesus while clutching on to our rights, our honor, our reputation. This kingdom stuff isn't for the fainthearted.

The fourth and fifth situations deal with unpleasant financial scenarios: "Give to the one who begs from you, and do not refuse the one who would borrow from you" (Matt. 5:42). The context of such giving is unclear, but we must remember that Jesus is still filling out what it means to not resist the evil person (v. 39). Jesus doesn't envision giving all your money to every beggar on the street. Some sort of "evil" lies behind the one asking you for your money. Maybe they don't deserve it. Maybe you don't have it. Or maybe the person is a thief who's after your stuff. Either way, Jesus says we should give money when it doesn't benefit us. Go above and beyond. Respond differently to evil. Shower the Jean Valjeans of the world with unpredictable grace. You just might turn a thief into a saint.

Jesus therefore gives a smattering of examples of what not resisting evil may look like: physical attack, social shame, legal injustice, political oppression, economic hardship. Jesus invades every sphere of our lives. He claims lordship over it all! As Abraham Kuyper famously said, "There is not a square inch in the whole domain of our human existence over which Christ, who is Sovereign over all, does not cry, 'Mine!'" He doesn't let us hold on to little compartments of life where we can respond to evil however we darn well please. Trying to find exceptions to the rule works against what Jesus is doing here. Jesus demands Calvary-shaped behavior that confounds and loves the enemy. Salt stands out in tasteless food, as does light in a dark world. And this is what the kingdom of God is to be. When the kingdom of God becomes a chameleon and reflects the worldly kingdoms, it's no longer salt and light. Jesus advocates not for balmy passivity but for *nonviolent* hyperactivity soaked in stubborn love.

NONVIOLENT HYPERACTIVITY AND STUBBORN LOVE

Such was the response of Emily Klotz toward the man who kidnapped her. Emily was out jogging one day when a man grabbed her, filled her face with pepper spray, and stuffed her into the trunk of his car. "This is my worst fear," Emily thought, "and it's happening to me right now." As the car rumbled along, Emily started to sing some old hymns she remembered from church when she was a kid. The sound must have agitated the driver, because he turned up the radio to drown out his conviction.

An hour later, the man opened the truck and Emily tried to escape. "I was able to scratch his face but he grabbed me and threw me to the ground and pinned me to the ground," Emily said. "And at that point I looked at him and I said, 'Are you working for the Devil?' and he looked at me funny and said 'No,' and I said, 'Well, God is with me.'" Emily was tossed back in the trunk and driven for another forty-five minutes. The man then parked, dragged Emily out, brought her into a house, tied her up to a bar, and brutally raped her.

Even as I describe Emily's experience, anger wells up inside of me. If there ever is a time to find a place for violent retaliation and vengeance, this is it. Logically, emotionally, physically—I see every reason to break into that house and beat the rapist to a bloody pulp.

Emily, however, chose a different route. Emily had more faith in King Jesus than in human vengeance. When she was shoved back into the car, she began to sing "Amazing Grace." Interestingly, Emily herself considers that very moment to be the time when she came to a genuine faith in the Lord Jesus Christ. After being dumped off and finding her way home, she called the cops, and the rapist was arrested and given a thirty-year sentence. But no arrest, not even a three-hundred-year sentence, could heal Emily's wounds. She suffered from seemingly incurable wounds. Yet above all, Emily wanted to follow Jesus, to *live like Jesus.*

"I felt the Lord wanted me to forgive the man who had raped me. He reminded me of Jesus on the cross when he said 'Father forgive them for they know not what they do.' So I spoke it out loud, 'I choose to forgive this man,' and I said his name, 'Father I want you to forgive him because he doesn't know what he's done and I ask you to bring him to his knees in repentance before you.'" Emily faithfully prayed for the man's salvation. She asked the Lord to help relieve her of her hatred and despair. She depended upon Christ, rather than retaliation, to be her healer.

While the man was in prison, Emily's words "Are you working for the Devil?" and her singing "Amazing Grace" gnawed at the man's broken heart. Two years into his sentence, he gave his life to Jesus, and now he witnesses to other inmates in prison. After hearing about his conversion, Emily recalled, "I jumped up and down praising God in my kitchen ... and I was so excited that my prayers had been answered."[11]

Emily resisted evil, not with a gun but with songs of praise. She responded *nonviolently* to violence, and God used her counterintuitive response to conquer both her own heart and the rapist's. She fought violence with nonviolence, and she won.

JESUS DIDN'T REALLY MEAN THAT

Now, some interpreters say that Jesus's Sermon doesn't apply to governments, only to individuals. There is certainly some truth to this. After all, Jesus doesn't preach His Sermon to the Roman Empire or the American government. However, the Sermon does apply to all citizens of God's kingdom, and it should saturate all areas of life. It would make no sense to say that the Sermon on the Mount is fine for individual Christians—even better for the church—but that it doesn't apply to Christians in the government.

Although he's one of my heroes, I had to rub my eyes when I stumbled across these words of Martin Luther, the great Protestant reformer. Luther said that when Christians went to war, they "struck right and left and killed," and by his own admission, "there was no difference between Christians and the heathen." Luther went on to say, "They did nothing contrary to this text [Matt 5:38–39]. *For they did it not as Christians*"—that's not a typo—"but as obedient members and subjects, under obligation to a secular person and authority." Since they were killing for the secular government, Luther said they had a "different rule" and are "a different person."[12]

What?

I can't understand this logic at all, and I don't think Jesus would either. Jesus—not Caesar—is Lord over every vocation. Certainly we wouldn't give the same allowance to a Christian who says, "As an individual Christian I shouldn't lust, but in my job as a lifeguard I can gaze with desire upon all the beach bodies I want. Every lifeguard does it. It's just part of my vocation." Why would we say this about retaliation and loving one's enemy? Jesus doesn't give any room for obeying some bits of the Sermon, while setting aside others if your vocation demands it. A lawyer who's a Christian shouldn't lie, a lifeguard who's a Christian shouldn't lust, and even if you were the secretary of defense, if Jesus is your King, then your King says you shouldn't retaliate, shouldn't hate your enemy, shouldn't confront evil with violence. As citizens of God's kingdom, we gladly surrender every fiber of our lives to the One who breathed the stars into being.

Matthew 5 isn't directed at secular governments, but it is binding on followers of Jesus no matter their vocation.

LOVE YOUR ENEMIES

Finally, Jesus offers not only a response to evil, but a command to go on the offensive. Take the initiative and fight against evil—fight it by loving your enemies:

> You have heard that it was said, "You shall love your
> neighbor and hate your enemy." But I say to you,
> Love your enemies and pray for those who perse-
> cute you, so that you may be sons of your Father
> who is in heaven. (Matt. 5:43–45)

Jesus takes a familiar Old Testament command ("Love your neighbor as yourself") and stretches it to its limits. The Old Testament commanded Israel to love their neighbors (i.e., fellow Jews) and to care for outsiders.[13] However, the law never explicitly commanded Israelites to love their enemies and pray for their persecutors.[14] Jesus therefore takes the law's incremental steps to the top of the mountain, and the mountaintop looks a lot like Eden. The Old Testament allowed Israel to use violence against their enemies (in some circumstances), but this wasn't the ideal. Loving your enemies is the ideal. It's no wonder that this command became the most-often-quoted verse during the first four centuries of the Christian church. For early Christians, enemy-love was the hallmark of what it meant to believe in Jesus. Oh, how things have changed.

So who is our enemy? As much as I would like to draw boundaries around enemy-love, Jesus doesn't. There's nothing in the context that limits the meaning of *enemy*.[15] The Greek word for enemy (*echthroi*) is often used in the broadest sense to include religious, political, and personal enemies.[16] Yes, Osama bin Laden was your enemy. In fact, the word *echthroi* is often used of *military enemies*[17]—remember what Jesus said about carrying the pack of a Roman solider. Also, the following verses talk about the Father's love for all people: "the just and … the unjust" (Matt. 5:45). Everyone. There is nothing in

Jesus's words that restricts the meaning of "enemy" to certain types of people.[18] Bombers in Boston to nuclear scientists in North Korea—they're all enemies.

Consider the parable of the Good Samaritan, where Jesus revisits the topic of loving your neighbor. As the story goes, a teacher of the law tries to corner Jesus by putting boundaries around who qualifies as a "neighbor." He's fine with loving the Jew living next door but wants to hate his non-neighbor. So Jesus expands the definition of neighbor to include *everyone*—even *enemies* like the Samaritans living up the road. If there ever were hostile enemies in the Jewish worldview, they were the Samaritans. The parable, then, is a creative commentary on Jesus's command to love your enemy. Unless you love your enemy, you actually don't love your neighbor. But Jesus doesn't stop there. At the end of the parable, it's not a Jew who loves his enemy, but an enemy who loves the Jew! The Samaritan—the *crème de la crème* enemy of the Jews—has excessive compassion on someone he doesn't even know, while the Jewish religious leaders walk on by.

I wonder who would stand in for the Samaritan if Jesus retold the parable today? It wouldn't be the annoying neighbor or abrasive coworker. These would fall far too short of Jesus's scathing rebuke. For Emily Klotz, it was the man who raped her. For many Americans, it may be a drug dealer, gang-leader, or terrorists who haunt them. The Samaritan would be the embodiment of the one you'd very well like to destroy. In fact, this is what James and John wanted to do to the Samaritans just prior to Jesus's parable. The Samaritans shut out Jesus and His disciples, and so James and John wanted to call down fire from heaven to nuke the entire village.[19] Many American

Christians resonate more with James and John than they do with Emily Klotz—or Jesus. When our enemy hates us, our desire for punishment often trumps Jesus's injunction to love. We want to nuke the village. But Jesus calls His followers to a different way, a subversive kingdom, which is why He ardently rebuked James and John for their vindictive anger toward their enemy.

Welcome to Jesus's upside-down kingdom.

The Sermon on the Mount constitutes Jesus's radical kingdom ethic. Heads will turn as we turn our cheeks. Our inexplicable behavior will call attention to our inexplicable God. Light will beam across our dark world as we love the spouses who don't love us back, keep our word when it hurts, judge ourselves rather than others, and—most shockingly—love our enemies who are harming us. When we are cursed, we bless. When we are hated, we love. When we are robbed, we give. And when we are struck, we don't strike back with violence. A person who chooses to love his or her enemies can have no enemies. That person is left only with neighbors.

NONVIOLENCE IN JESUS'S MINISTRY

And Jesus practices what He preaches. Throughout His ministry He never retaliates and always loves His enemies even when He is violently attacked.[20] When He is unjustly accused of treason, His accusers "spit in his face," "[strike] him" and "[slap] him" (Matt. 26:67). No retaliation; only love. Moments later, Roman soldiers spit on Him and pound His head with a stick (27:30). Still no retaliation; only forgiveness. Jesus therefore models His own command to not "resist evil … but turn the other cheek." He could call down a legion of angels to deliver Him, but He refuses to confront violence with violence (26:53). While on the cross He prays for His oppressors: "Father, forgive them, for they know not what they do" (Luke 23:34). Jesus's life is peppered with violent attacks, yet He never responds with violence. He embraces suffering, not because He is weak, not because He can't do anything about it, but because suffering is the God-ordained pathway to resurrection glory. For Jesus and for us.[21]

Now, you may think, *Yes, but the reason Jesus doesn't resist His death is because He has to die for the sin of the world.* This is correct. There is uniqueness to the atoning value of the cross. His nonresistance is a theological necessity: He has to die for the sin of the world. But that's not all that's going on. Jesus's nonviolent, nonretaliatory journey to the cross is also a *pattern* for us to imitate.

When Jesus talks about His suffering on the cross, He often commands His followers to do the same: "If anyone would come after me, let him deny himself and take up his cross and follow me" (Matt. 16:24). Jesus suffers injustice on a Roman cross to die for sin, but He also intends it to be a nonviolent pattern for us to follow. When Jesus washes His disciples' feet—even the feet of His betrayer—He tells His followers to do the same: "I have given you an example, that you also should do just as I have done to you" (John 13:15). Again, just after He predicts His crucifixion, He tells His followers, "Whoever would be first among you must be slave of all" (Mark 10:44). We are *slaves of all*. Jesus rebukes James and John for their thirst for violent retaliation (Luke 9:51–56), encourages His followers to endure patiently when violently attacked (Mark 13:9–13), and disarms Peter when he violently resists evil by hacking off the ear of a man trying to arrest Jesus. "Put your sword back into its place,"

Jesus tells Peter. "For all who take the sword will perish by the sword" (Matt. 26:52).[22]

Nonviolence is the astonishing rhythm of Christianity, the direction of the river that flows in Eden.

Jesus's words must have sunk deep into Peter's bones. Years later, Peter writes a letter to several churches in Asia and highlights Jesus's nonviolent, nonretaliatory journey to the cross *as a model for Christians to follow*. In the face of violence, injustice, insult, and abuse, Peter echoes the cadence of Jesus's Sermon:

> For God called you to do good, even if it means suffering, just as Christ suffered for you. He is your example, and you must follow in his steps.
>
> He never sinned,
>   nor ever deceived anyone.
> He did not retaliate when he was insulted,
>   nor threaten revenge when he suffered.
> He left his case in the hands of God,
>   who always judges fairly. (1 Pet. 2:21–23 NLT)

Jesus's nonviolent journey to Calvary shapes our own posture as salt and light in a violent world. And Jesus's words, coupled with His exemplary life, make an impression not only on Peter but also on the other New Testament writers. In fact, the New Testament highlights Jesus's nonviolent response to violence as a pattern to follow *more than any other aspect of His ministry.* I'll come back to this significant point in the next chapter.

In a world drowning in violence, Jesus never acts violently. Though evil runs rampant, Jesus never confronts it, nor does He allow His followers to confront it, with violence. Never.

EFFECTIVENESS OR FAITHFULNESS?

Responding nonviolently to violence can have a profound effect on your enemy. I can't help but think of Martin Luther King Jr., who used to say that the world expects people to respond to violence with violence. They know what to do with this. But they don't know what to do when people respond to violence with nonviolence. But King didn't just spin out lyrical wisdom. He practiced what he preached. On one occasion, while King was delivering a speech, a member of the American Nazi Party walked up on stage and slugged him in the face. King was knocked back but regained his composure, stood up, and dropped his arms. The man proceeded to pound King in the face until the crowd intervened and hauled the Nazi off to another room. Shortly after, King visited the Nazi in the room and reassured him that there would be no harm done to him. King said that he was not going to press charges for the attack and that he had forgiven the man. King then returned to the stage, holding a bag of ice to his face, to finish his speech.[23]

No one in the room had doubts about who won the fight. Sometimes nonviolence more effectively defeats violence. Perhaps Jesus was on to something.

But we shouldn't obey Jesus's commands about nonretaliation and enemy-love because they will always work. Sometimes they will, but sometimes we'll be shamed, beat down, tortured, and killed just like our Lord. The Bible, however, doesn't promote nonviolent behavior because of its effectiveness. Rather, we love our enemies and do good to those who hate us because that's what God does.

Faithfulness rather than *effectiveness* is our motivation. That's because Jesus grounds enemy-love in the character of God.[24] We are to love our enemy so that we might be "sons of the Most High" who is "kind to the ungrateful and the evil" and is merciful to the undeserving (Luke 6:35–36). We renounce power and become servants because "even the Son of Man came not to be served but to serve" (Mark. 10:45). We love our enemies, do good to those who hate us, bless those who curse us, extend kindness to the ungrateful, and flood evil people with mercy *not* because such behavior will always *work* at confronting injustice, but because such behavior showcases God's stubborn delight in un-delightful people. *Faithfulness* rather than perceived *effectiveness* motivates our response to evil. We are faithful conduits of God's undeserved love when we do good to those who hate us.

In a world swimming in violence, in a land where "messiah" meant militancy, Jesus never acts violently. Whenever violence is addressed, Jesus condemns it. Whenever His followers try to act violently, they are confronted. Whenever Jesus encounters people who deserve a violent punishment, Jesus loves them. And in doing so, He leaves His followers with a nonviolent example to follow. When people around the globe think that American Christians are pro-war, enamored with violence, and fascinated with military might, something is terribly wrong. No one in the first century would have made the same conclusion regarding Jesus and His followers.

Whether or not such behavior will lead to chaos, ruin our religious freedom, or allow enemies to rule our country is not our concern.

Our faith is in the King of all creation, who suffered, died, was raised from the dead, and now reigns from on high and seats us with Him at the right hand of the Father. Our life, future, security, freedom, suffering, and destiny—they're all in His hands. The reign of God on earth—Jesus's kingdom—does not need military might, thick borders, superior weapons, or economic prosperity for its advancement. What God started two thousand years ago through His crucified Son will triumph, and the gates of hell—let alone al-Qaeda—shall not prevail against it.

GOOD CITIZENS

WE, OUR, US

"So you're against our military!" protested Tom.[1]

"No," I said, "I wouldn't say that I'm *against* the military, but against militarism—putting faith in military might. And I also don't think the Bible sanctions violence to achieve the goals of God's kingdom."

"You don't support our troops, then. Right?" Tom responded.

"Well, it depends on what you mean by that, and it depends on *why* each person is serving as a soldier. If someone said he became a soldier so that he could kill Arabs, then no, I wouldn't support *that* troop."

"No," Tom said, "I wouldn't either. But what about the ones who are sacrificing themselves for our country?"

"In many ways, Tom, I'd say that I'm actually in support of these troops. I admire their commitment and their desire to sacrifice on behalf of others. I appreciate the dedication it takes to make it in the military. Most of all, they are created in God's image and therefore possess infinite worth in the eyes of their Creator. But this doesn't mean that I have to be okay with violence, nor with the larger ideology that drives a military to wage war. I admire many things about soldiers, but not their decision to use violence."

"But what about our religious freedom?" Tom replied. "Our troops are sacrificing their lives so that you can have your freedom!

In fact," Tom continued rather passionately, "your freedom of speech that allows you to have this very conversation is made possible because of our troops!"

Both Tom and I are Christians and share similar views on many things. But Tom and I disagree on how we should view America's military. For Tom, the military has its problems, but by and large it's the reason for much peace, democracy, and freedom in the world. For the most part, America's military fights for causes that are morally upright. And if it wasn't for our military, the world would be ruled by evil dictators and oppressive regimes.

"Yes, you are correct," I said. "The military does, in part, enable citizens of America to have religious freedom. But plenty of countries that don't have the same freedom, such as China, have a thriving Christian presence. Obviously God doesn't *need* religious freedom to expand His kingdom."

"Well, if it weren't for our military," Tom countered, "we wouldn't have such economic prosperity. We wouldn't be able to own houses, guns, cars, or even go to church. If our troops don't fight, other countries who are jealous of our freedom would take us over."

As you listen to Tom and me converse, you are probably either in agreement with Tom, or you are frustrated with the assumptions that Tom is bringing to the table. For now, I want to point out that the most important words in this conversation are *we*, *our*, and *us*.

It's fascinating how often citizens of God's kingdom use the plural pronoun (we/our/us) to describe their citizenship in the earthly nation where they were born. "Our troops," "our freedom," "our military." There's actually a measure of truth in Tom's point, but we must take out the plural pronouns to find it. "We"—if you're a Christian—first and foremost refers to our membership in God's kingdom, not our national identity. Passports are irrelevant in God's kingdom.

CITIZENS OF THE KING

Paul confronts Tom's use of the plural pronoun in his letter to the Philippians. The idea that "our citizenship is in heaven" is well-known, and it comes from Philippians 3:20. Interestingly, Paul coins this phrase in stark contrast to a believer's national citizenship. Paul never uses the plural pronoun to describe his Roman citizenship, and he discourages believers from doing the same. To see this, we have to back up a bit and look at the history of Philippi.

Philippi played a significant role in the history of the Roman Empire. It was founded by the Greeks but taken over by Rome in 168 BC. A hundred years later, the environs of the city became the scene for several important battles in the famous civil wars of Rome, which involved Julius Caesar and Brutus versus Octavian and Mark Antony. Octavian (later called Augustus) and Antony won, and they richly awarded the city of Philippi for its help. The reward? Roman citizenship. While only 10 percent of people living in the empire enjoyed Roman citizenship, the entire city of Philippi was awarded this prestigious honor. What is more, Octavian chose Philippi to be a city where Roman military veterans could settle down after they'd served. Armed with citizenship and military zeal, Philippi would bubble over with patriotic fervor.[2]

But allegiance to Jesus's kingdom often clashes with all earthly ones, and the Philippians feel the tension. This is why Paul commands them, "Live out your citizenship [*polistheuamai*] in a manner worthy of the gospel of Christ" (Phil. 1:27, author's translation). Some translations interpret this command as "walk in a manner worthy" rather than "live out your citizenship in a manner worthy," but the Greek word *polistheuamai* does not simply mean "walk" or "live" but has to do with citizenship.[3] Even if you don't know Greek, you can probably tell that the word *polistheuamai* has something to do with politics. The word contains the root *polis*, which means "city" and gives us words like *poli*tics and metro*polis*. *Polistheuamai* is a verb, so it means something like "act like a citizen," "be a good citizen," or "live out your citizenship" as I translated it above.

But notice what Paul is doing here. He does not encourage the believers at Philippi to be good citizens of Rome, but to live out their citizenship in allegiance to Jesus. Many in the church probably have Roman citizenship. They are tempted to find their pride and identity in Rome instead of in God's kingdom. In the same way, it's tempting for American Christians to find their pride and identity in American citizenship rather than in their heavenly one. Such allegiance to Rome (or America) makes good sense to the world but finds no support in the New Testament. Tom's use of the plural pronoun would have been incomprehensible to Paul—or Jesus.

Later on when Paul reminds the believers that their "citizenship is in *heaven*," you can hear a faint whisper of "*and not in Rome*." He's steering their patriotism away from Rome and toward Jesus.

Now, the New Testament is clear that we should honor, submit to, and pray for our governing authorities. We can celebrate the distinct culture of our country, promote the good that our nation achieves, and "seek the welfare of the city" where God has "sent you into exile" (Jer. 29:7). But always remember that you're in exile.

To be in exile means that you are displaced from your native land. You're a pilgrim, a foreigner, a resident with a foreign passport. Our identity—that which marks us out as a distinct people—is with God's kingdom, not Caesar's. Allegiance to Rome (or Iraq, or Argentina, or America, or Canada) becomes idolatrous when national identity is prioritized over our heavenly one. And when the values of our earthly citizenship conflict with Jesus's, as they sometimes do, we must give our allegiance to our Lord even if it means being unpatriotic toward Rome.

TWO KINGDOMS, SAME VOCABULARY

Citizenship in God's kingdom demands undiluted allegiance. This became especially difficult for early Christians because both kingdoms—God's and Rome's—used the same vocabulary to describe their politics. Let me explain. As Christians, we are very familiar with terms like *gospel*, *Lord*, *Savior*, *peace*, and other "Christianese" buzzwords—words that our secular culture doesn't always understand. But in the first century, these terms were not unique to Christianity. They were *also used by Rome to refer to its own king and kingdom.* We saw this when Jesus used the term *kingdom* (or *empire*) in His trial before Pilate. But this is only the beginning.

Two common titles used for the Roman emperor were lord (*kurios*) and savior (*soter*). And since the emperors were viewed as divine, they were also called son of god or in some cases just plain god. These divine lords were believed to have brought unprecedented peace to the world, which they referred to in Latin as the *Pax Romana*, or "peace of Rome." Rome was known for securing such peace and justice through warfare. And whenever Roman leaders returned home from another military victory, heralds were sent throughout the empire to announce the gospel—the good news—that Rome had been victorious.[4]

Lord, savior, son of god, god, peace, justice, and *gospel.* These were all familiar terms used to praise the Caesars of Rome. When Christians stole these titles and applied them to a Jew who was crucified as a revolutionary, they were bound to start a fight—especially in a patriotic city like Philippi. Roman military vets, who had sacrificed for the peace of Rome, would be particularly offended.

When Paul hails Jesus as Lord and Savior, we need to hear a faint first-century echo: *Caesar is not.*

Such contrast between Jesus and Caesar is seen clearly in Acts 17, when Paul heralds the gospel of Jesus in Thessalonica, a town not far from Philippi. Paul's message creates quite an uproar in the city. Not because the people are offended at the thought of a new religion, but because they understand the good news about Jesus as a direct critique of the good news of Caesar Nero. "These men who have turned the world upside down have come here also," the crowd shouts out in protest. "They are all acting against the decrees of Caesar, saying that *there is another king, Jesus*" (Acts 17:6–7). If Paul was merely preaching about a privatized religious experience, the authorities wouldn't bat an eye. But Paul announces that Jesus is Lord and Savior. And this means that Caesar is not.

Let's head back to the town of Philippi, because a similar situation must have erupted there as well. We know that the Philippians are under persecution, since Paul alludes to this throughout his letter.[5] As Paul heralds King Jesus in Phillipi, he gets into trouble with the authorities as he did in Thessalonica.[6]

And now the Philippian believers find themselves in a similar situation. Imagine that in a town like Philippi, where the Roman flag waves high and stories of military victories are swapped in the streets, there's a small group of people who believe that a crucified Jew, rather than Nero, is the true Lord, Savior, and bringer of good news, justice, and peace.

I can almost hear these Christians dealing with the same critique Tom lobbed at me: "The only reason you're able to say such things is because our soldiers fought and died for your freedom!"

So Paul tells these believers to hold strong. Stand firm. Give your allegiance to Jesus despite the criticism and suffering it may bring.[7] To challenge them, Paul points them to the cross of Jesus in Philippians 2:5–11, where he lays out one of the most theologically rich and counter-patriotic claims about Christ. Suffering, Paul says—against all forms of Roman ideology, human intuition, or military might—is the pathway to power and glory:

> Have this mind among yourselves, which is yours in Christ Jesus, who, though he was in the form of God, did not count equality with God a thing to be grasped, but emptied himself, by taking the form of a servant, being born in the likeness of men. And being found in human form, he humbled himself by becoming obedient to the point of death, even death on a cross. Therefore God has highly exalted him and bestowed on him the name that is above every name, so that at the name of Jesus every knee should bow, in heaven and on earth and under the

earth, and every tongue confess that Jesus Christ is
Lord, to the glory of God the Father.

Read this passage against the backdrop of Roman ideology.[8]
Rome embedded in the hearts of its citizens a thick narrative of power,
pride, and unparalleled military might. True *pax* comes through the
military of *Romana*—the hope of the world. Don't you forget it! But
the way of the cross slashes the narrative of Rome. Knowing that the
Philippians are suffering, Paul points them to their true Caesar, Jesus
Christ, who suffered on a cross—the ultimate symbol of Roman
power and military might. Paul plumbs the depths of paradox when
he claims that the most vulgar, shameful, obvious sign of weakness
(suffering on a Roman cross) was the means through which Jesus was
highly exalted. While Caesar Nero is revered as the exalted lord of
the earth, Paul daringly wrenches the crown from Nero and places it
where it belongs. On Jesus.

Philippians underscores the counter-patriotic claims of the gospel of Jesus. For the church to turn the world upside down, as it did
in Thessalonica, it must promote Jesus's lordship—His reign—where
weakness is power and cruciform suffering leads to glory.

CRUCIFORM SUFFERING

I love the phrase "cruciform suffering," which means "cross-shaped
suffering," because it gives theological meat to suffering. Jesus's cross
and resurrection infuse suffering with value and hope—hope that
Jesus-following sufferers will be raised from the dead; hope that God
will judge the wicked and reward the righteous; hope that believes
Jesus triumphed over evil through suffering and invited us to join

Him in victory. This is what I mean by "cruciform suffering": suffering that embraces the journey Jesus took to Calvary, who "continued entrusting himself to him who judges justly" (1 Pet. 2:23).

That last phrase is from 1 Peter—a letter saturated with cruciform suffering. First Peter is similar to Philippians. The churches addressed in both letters are struggling with their identity. How can they live out their heavenly citizenship when Rome is breathing down their necks by demanding allegiance to Caesar? Peter makes the same point Paul does: God's people give their allegiance to the Lord Jesus. And when this conflicts with their allegiance to Caesar—as it often does—the choice is simple. Obey God and not people.

From beginning to end, Peter tries to pry the church's gaze away from its earthly kingdom and onto the Lord Jesus. Peter refers to the church as "exiles," sojourners and aliens living in a strange land.[9] We are "a royal priesthood, a holy nation, a people for his own possession" (1 Pet. 2:9). All of these images underwrite Jesus's claim that His kingdom is not of this world. And the most visible form of Jesus's not-of-this-world kingdom is the radical, head-turning love of one's enemies, even (or especially) when we are suffering at their hands. Peter mentions this cruciform enemy-love no fewer than ten times in five chapters, making it the artery of the letter.

Peter commands the church sojourning in Rome's kingdom to "honor everyone," endure while suffering, revile no one when reviled, never "repay evil for evil or reviling for reviling" but bless your reviler. If you want to be like Jesus, Peter says, then you need to live as Jesus lived. You need to turn from evil, do good, seek peace and pursue it vigorously. To those who attack you verbally, respond with gentleness and respect.[10] To those who attack you physically, respond as Christ responded to His attackers (1 Pet. 2:20–22). Peter even uses military language ironically to speak of the believer's posture of weakness, not might: "arm yourselves" with the sufferings of Christ (4:1); abstain from sinful passions that "wage war against your soul" (2:11)—passions such as retaliation. The entire letter of 1 Peter gives sustained attention to what Paul says in Philippians 2. The church is to follow Jesus in His posture of weakness and suffering, because this is the pathway to glory.

Cruciform suffering takes center stage in 1 Peter 2. We looked at this passage briefly in the previous chapter, but it's worth another read:

> For to this you have been called, because Christ also suffered for you, leaving you an example, so that you might follow in his steps. He committed no sin, neither was deceit found in his mouth. When he was reviled, he did not revile in return; when he suffered, he did not threaten, but continued entrusting himself to him who judges justly. (vv. 21–23)

If it weren't for Jesus, no one would ever live this way. Jesus was attacked, beaten, and unjustly accused, but He didn't retaliate. Jesus, of course, *had* to die to atone for sin. But remember, His innocent suffering is also given as an example, and nowhere is this clearer than here in 1 Peter 2. When we are reviled and suffer unjustly, our posture should reflect Jesus. There's no need to return evil for evil, or violence for violence, since in the end God will vindicate us and judge our enemy. God—not our ability to avenge—deserves our trust.

Such trust in the Sovereign God is Peter's hallmark of suffering. "Let those who suffer according to God's will entrust their souls to a faithful Creator while doing good" (1 Pet. 4:19). And again: "Humble yourselves, therefore, under the mighty hand of God so that at the proper time he may exalt you" (5:6). The cruciform life, according to Peter, means that we imitate Jesus's nonviolent, enemy-loving posture, because ultimately His triumph is ours. "After you have suffered a little while," Peter concludes, God will "restore, confirm, strengthen, and establish you" (v. 10).

Peter has the Sermon on the Mount ingrained in his soul. And so does Paul. In Romans 12, Paul also quotes from the Sermon and stresses nonretaliation and enemy-love. After exhorting the church to "not be conformed to this world" (think: "my kingdom is not of this world"), Paul fills in what this means. "Abhor what is evil" (v. 9), "bless those who persecute you" (v. 14), "repay no one evil for evil" (v. 17), "live peaceably with all [people]" (v. 18), never seek vengeance (v. 19), love your enemy, and do good to those who hate you (v. 20). Put simply: "Do not be overcome by evil, but overcome evil with good" (v. 21). Paul's litany of commands comes fast and furious in Romans 12, and most of it has the scent of Jesus's Sermon. As with Jesus, nonviolent love is anything but passive. Rather, it is counter-culturally active in forgiving, honoring, blessing, and meeting the physical needs of those who can't stand you. As with Peter, the reason why Christians don't need to settle all wrongs in this world is that we are confident God will do so in the next. "Never avenge yourselves, but leave it to the wrath of God, for it is written, 'Vengeance is mine,

I will repay, says the Lord'" (v. 19). Our faith in the Sovereign Judge precludes any need to offer our enemies anything but cruciform love.

Cruciform love for our enemies—this is what it means to have the mind of Christ according to Philippians 2:5–11. Jesus became a servant to die for *and at the hands of* His enemies. We don't just serve the deserving but the undeserving. This is what it means to be a Christian: to follow Jesus, to live like Jesus, to have a mind like Jesus. Having the mind of Christ means embracing others— especially our enemies—in humble, reconciling, forgiving love. It means never giving up on them even when they are putting us to death.[11] Paul doesn't leave any wiggle room. He doesn't say, "Have this mind among yourselves *until* it gets too hard" or "*until* your enemy becomes particularly violent." Jesus's enemies were plenty violent (ever studied crucifixion?), and yet He was "obedient to the point of death, even death on a cross" (Phil. 2:8). I know, this sounds foolish, if not scandalous. Paul thinks so too (1 Cor. 1:18, 23).

Loving your enemy. Doing good things for evil people. Never taking vengeance. Responding to violence with nonviolent love— even if it brings suffering. These are not options, but the primary character traits of those who claim to follow a crucified God.

WHAT WOULD JESUS DO?

In the last chapter, I said that the New Testament highlights Jesus's nonviolent response to violence as a pattern to follow more than any other aspect of His ministry. We've already seen that Paul in Romans 12 draws heavily on Jesus's nonretaliation commands in the Sermon on the Mount and instructs believers in Philippians 2 to have the cruciform mind of Christ. Peter also makes enemy-love the ethical heartbeat of his first epistle. Elsewhere, Paul prohibits Christians from repaying "anyone evil for evil, but always seek to do good to one another and to everyone" (1 Thess. 5:15).

The author of Hebrews commends the church for "joyfully accept[ing] the plundering of your property, since you knew that you yourselves had a better possession and an abiding one" (Heb. 10:34). The motivation for enduring such suffering is Jesus's cross, where He "endured from sinners such hostility against himself," which according to Hebrews provides an example for believers to follow (12:1–3). Believers are to "strive for peace with *everyone*" (12:14)—not just their neighbors. The apostles, therefore, frequently appeal to Jesus's nonresistant journey to the cross as a model to emulate.

Let's put this in perspective. Paul celebrates the gift of celibacy, arguing that a celibate person can be hugely effective for the kingdom (1 Cor. 7). But Paul *does not* use Jesus's celibate life as an example to follow. He doesn't play the "what would Jesus do" card. Paul says that he could refrain from working and be supported by the ministry (9:6–12), but again he doesn't appeal to Jesus, who did the same (Luke 8:1–3). Also, Jesus was a man of prayer and often stole away time to pray, and yet Paul—in all his talk on prayer—*never* appeals to Jesus as a model for praying. This is fascinating: the "what would Jesus do" cliché is rarely echoed by the New Testament writers.

Rarely but not never. Because when it comes to enemy-love and our response to evil, the New Testament writers race to the life and teaching of Christ as the pattern for believers to imitate.[12]

The New Testament is ubiquitously clear: don't retaliate with evil for evil; do good to those who hate you; embrace your enemy with a cross-shaped, unyielding divine love. Such a rich and pervasive trajectory—from Jesus's Sermon, modeled through His life, commended to His disciples, taken up by the apostles, and demanded of the early church—shows that nonretaliation and enemy-love are not some insignificant whisper lingering on the edge of Jesus's ethical landscape. They are fundamental identity markers for citizens of God's kingdom. *If* there are exceptions to this—assassinating Hitler, for instance—these exceptions must be seen as deviating from the dominant rhythm of Christianity.

JESUS'S WAR

Jesus is still at war, but it's a spiritual one. Paul uses warfare imagery on several occasions, and when he does, he contrasts *physical* weapons of warfare with *spiritual* weapons.[13] For instance, in 2 Corinthians 10 he says:

> We are human, but we don't wage war as humans do. We use God's mighty weapons, not worldly weapons, to knock down the strongholds of human reasoning and to destroy false arguments. We destroy every proud obstacle that keeps people from knowing God. We capture their rebellious thoughts and teach them to obey Christ. (vv. 3–5 NLT)

Paul hijacks military vocabulary and turns it on its head. He says that physical weapons of warfare—swords and spears, tanks and drones—are not "God's mighty weapons" to tear down the works of Satan. Prayer, suffering, enemy-love, and the proclamation of the true gospel (not Caesar's) will do more to tear down the works of

Satan than ten thousand nuclear warheads. We are to join Jesus in His war, His spiritual war, and our weapons are not worldly like Rome's. Our weapons are divine.

Paul says the same thing in Ephesians 6:

> A final word: Be strong in the Lord and in his mighty power. Put on all of God's armor so that you will be able to stand firm against all strategies of the devil. For we are not fighting against flesh-and-blood enemies, but against evil rulers and authorities of the unseen world, against mighty powers in this dark world, and against evil spirits in the heavenly places.
>
> Therefore, put on every piece of God's armor so you will be able to resist the enemy in the time of evil. Then after the battle you will still be standing firm. (vv. 10–13 NLT)

Neither this passage nor the previous one can be taken to condemn all forms of violence. Not in themselves, at least. But what they do is elevate the methods of Jesus in conquering evil and downplay the worldly ways of fighting the Enemy. Again, Paul says that the true battle is not against Iran, North Korea, or al-Qaeda, but against the satanic forces working behind the scenes. We are not to war against human enemies, only spiritual ones. In fact, we are to love our human enemies.

When we buy into the American narrative that focuses on "flesh-and-blood enemies," we are spraying the tip of the flames, not the source of the fire. America could nuke the entire Middle East, and Satan would walk away untouched. China or Iran could conquer America, and God's kingdom wouldn't feel a thing. As long as we pray, love, suffer, and herald the good news that Jesus is King, we will continue to see the kingdom of God thunder against the kingdom of Satan. We need to make sure we're fighting in the right war with the right means.

Jesus never acted violently. He never allowed His followers to act violently. Whenever violence is held out as an option for Christians, it's always forbidden. Jesus's nonretaliatory, sacrificial love for His enemies—more than any other aspect of His life and ministry— provided His followers with a definitive identity marker of what it meant to follow God. Suffering love: it's not easy, but it is essential.

WHAT ROMANS 13 REALLY MEANS

"But what about Romans 13?" In talking to various people about this book, the question about Romans 13 was usually the first thing that came up. In fact, I recently presented the idea behind this book to a roomful of pastor-scholars, all of whom had PhDs in theology. Unanimously, they all wanted to know how Christian nonviolence squares with Romans 13.

It's fascinating (one might say disturbing) to see how each person's political context or position shapes his or her understanding of Romans 13. Christians living in North Korea or Burma tend to read Romans 13 differently than Americans do. Moreover, Adolf Hitler, Idi Amin, and other more recent "Christian" dictators have celebrated the passage as their divine ticket to execute justice on whomever they deemed enemies of the state. Not more than a generation ago,

Romans 13 was hailed as the charter for apartheid in South Africa. American Christian leaders did the same during the years of slavery and segregation. If the state mandates that blacks can't drink from the same water fountain as whites, it very well has the divine right to do so, according to certain interpretations Romans 13.

Most now would see such a view of Romans 13 as going a bit too far. But only a bit. Theologian and scholar Wayne Grudem, for instance, says that the "sword in the hand of good government is God's designated weapon to defeat evildoers" and goes on to apply this to America's wars in Iraq and Afghanistan.[14] The assumption, of course, is that America is the good government and that Iraq and Afghanistan are the bad governments. Maybe they are, but who gets to determine who is good and who is bad? Were it flipped around and Romans 13 was used to validate Afghanistan's invasion of America as punishment for horrific drone strikes on civilians or wholesale slaughter of women and children in, for instance, southern Kandahar or Haditha, most Americans would see this as a misreading of Romans 13.

Even though Romans 13 has been taken to celebrate violence, praise the government, or vindicate the just war tradition, there is nothing in this passage that contradicts what I've said thus far. Here's why.

First, Romans 13 does not speak of Rome's warfare policy against foreign nations, but of its police and judicial action toward its own citizens.[15] Paul's phrase "bear the sword" (v. 4) refers to police action within a government's jurisdiction, not warfare outside its territory. Using this text to support, for instance, America's war in Iraq goes beyond what Paul is actually saying. Romans 13 doesn't authorize a nation to police the world, let alone wage preemptive strikes against nations it considers a threat.

Second, the passage does not tell the church to "obey" governing authorities but to "submit to" such authorities.[16] Now, submission sometimes involves obedience, and obedience sometimes involves submission. There's an overlap in meaning. But it's important to note that Paul does not use one of the typical Greek words for "obey" here.[17] He deliberately uses the term *submit*. The difference is that Christians "obey" the law of Christ. They receive their moral marching orders from their King. And insofar as the laws of the state don't conflict with the law of Christ, they obey. But Christians do so out of allegiance to God, not out of an uncritical allegiance to the state. Don't revolt against the government, in other words. Honor it; pray for it; work for its good; pay the taxes that it demands.[18] New Testament scholar Paul Jewett said it well: "Submission to the governmental authorities is therefore an expression of respect not for the authorities themselves but for the crucified deity who stands behind them."[19]

Third, Paul's statement reflects a widespread truth in the Old Testament about God working through secular nations to carry out His will. For instance, the Old Testament calls many political figures "God's servant," such as Cyrus, king of Persia (Isa. 44–45); Nebuchadnezzar, king of Babylon (Jer. 27:6; 43:10); and the ruthlessly wicked nation of Assyria (Isa. 10:5), which God calls the "club of my wrath" and the "rod of my anger."[20] Please note: Cyrus and Nebuchadnezzar were pagan dictators. The phrase "God's servant," therefore, doesn't refer to Rome's happy service to Israel's God, but to God's ability to use Rome as an instrument in His hands. You can probably see where I'm going with this. Just because God uses secular—and sometimes quite evil—institutions to carry out His will does not mean that God approves of everything they do. Much of what they do—whether it be Assyria's sadistic practice of skinning civilians alive, or Rome's crucifixion of thousands of people in the first century—does not reflect the law of Christ. But God can still use such godlessness, because He channels evil to carry out His will.[21] This doesn't mean that He approves of the evil itself. In fact, all those who are ministers of God's wrath become the objects of God's wrath themselves precisely because of their violence when they were the "rod" of His anger.[22] If you want to serve as God's agent of wrath, well, you better watch your back when God's through with you.

Fourth, Romans 13 says that God uses governments to punish evildoers and reward the good. But what does this mean? Does every government always justly punish evil and reward good? Yeah, right. Rome was the same government that beheaded John the Baptist, beat Paul on several occasions, and crucified an innocent Jew named Jesus. In fact, just a few years after Paul penned Romans 13, Caesar Nero dipped Christians in tar, lit them on fire, and set them up as human illumination for his garden, all in the name of keeping peace. Romans 13 can't be a rubber stamp on all of Rome's attempts at punishing evil. Paul doesn't write Rome, or America, a blank check to do whatever it wants to do in the name of justice.

Paul's statement that Rome is "God's servant for your good" and "an avenger who carries out God's wrath on the wrongdoer" must mean that God can and does work justice through governments but that not everything governments do can be labeled just. Romans 13 does not sanitize all governing activities. Flip through Revelation 13 and

17–18 to see that the New Testament actually condemns much of what the government does.

The final point is the most significant. If you miss this point, then you won't understand what Paul is saying to the church in Romans 13. Paul says that God executes vengeance through Rome after he prohibits Christians from doing so. Compare these two statements, which are only a few verses apart:

> Beloved, never *avenge* yourselves, but leave it to the *wrath of God*, for it is written, "Vengeance is mine, I will repay, says the Lord." (12:19)

> For he is the servant of God, an *avenger* who carries out the *God's wrath* on the wrongdoer. (13:4)

Paul says that God's wrath and vengeance are carried out through Rome, and he has just commanded the church *not* to carry out such wrath and vengeance. Vengeance is God's business, not ours. We don't need to avenge evil, because God will. And one way that God will is through governing authorities. Moreover, the command to submit to governing authorities in Romans 13:1 is the last of Paul's litany of commands in Romans 12:9–21.[23] Bless those who persecute you, love your enemy, don't avenge evil, and *submit to your governing authorities.* Far from allowing Christians to kill in war, Romans 13 underscores the church's submissive posture in a violent world.

Romans 13 cannot be used to foster a militaristic spirit among Christians. Quite the opposite.

ONE KINGDOM UNDER GOD

"So are you saying," Tom said, "that Christians can't serve *in* the military?"

"Tom, that's a good question. In fact, Christians who advocate for nonviolence are divided over this issue. Some say yes, while others say no. My own answer is that Christians can pursue all vocations to further the kingdom, but they must obey their King no matter what. No vocation or earthly cause should trump our allegiance to King Jesus."

"So you *don't* think Christians should serve in the military," replied Tom.

"Actually, I think they can. But I don't think that Christians can serve as combatants in situations where they would be required to kill. I just can't reconcile this with what Jesus and the apostles said about violence in the New Testament. However, I do think Christians can serve in the military as agents of peace, healing, and reconciliation. They can serve as noncombatants."

Tom interjected, "But Romans 13 says that God ordained governments to bear the sword and punish evildoers. If God rightly uses governments to bear the sword, and Christians can serve in just governments, then it only makes sense that they could bear the sword."

"That's a great observation," I replied. "However, Romans 13 is focused on police action within a country's jurisdiction, not waging war outside its territory. Moreover, in the context of Paul's argument, he doesn't seem to envision Christians in this role. Paul *prohibited* Christians from executing vengeance in Romans 12, but then said that God executes vengeance through the state in Romans 13. In other words, Paul explicitly forbids the church in Romans 12 from doing what the government does in Romans 13. The church is only commanded to *submit to* (not partake in) the state's practice."

"That seems like a double standard to me," Tom replied. "You'll let the state do your dirty work but are too holy to do it yourself."

"Well, it may seem like that, Tom, but I'm only trying to make sense of what Paul actually says in Romans 12 and 13. And I should say that even though Paul doesn't explicitly envision Christians to be part of the sword-bearing role in Romans 13, there are other passages in the New Testament where we do see Christians in that role. And they are not told to immediately leave it."

"So," Tom said, "you don't think that Romans 13 allows Christians to bear the sword, but other passages do?"

"Perhaps," I replied. "But in all vocations, believers must obey Christ."

"Yes," Tom agreed. "I'm with you there."

I continued, "So a Christian lawyer must be honest."

"Absolutely," Tom said.

"And a Christian filmmaker isn't allowed to lust," I said.

"Of course," agreed Tom.

"So with all vocations," I continued, "Christians must be obedient to their Lord."

Then Tom tossed up the question—the question that has thrown advocates for nonviolence for a loop for as long as the debate has been raging. "Can a Christian be a cop?"

"Tom, that has been one of the most difficult questions for Christians who deal with the issue of violence. We'd better grab some coffee and hash this out."

THE WRATH OF THE LAMB

A BOOK DIPPED IN BLOOD

The book of Revelation stands out as an embarrassment to Christianity. The famed atheist Friedrich Nietzsche described the book as "the most rabid outburst of vindictiveness in all recorded history."[1] Historian James Carroll said, "In no text of the entire Bible is God's violence, and the violence of Christ himself, more power-fully on display than in the ... book of Revelation."[2] George Bernard Shaw dismissed the book as "a curious record of the visions of a drug addict."[3] Harsh words about a book inspired by God. But none of these opinions recognize the true beauty of Revelation. Revelation is a violent book, but as we will see, that violence is not dished out as much as it is absorbed.

Some interpreters see no problem with the violence in Revelation. One scholar described the second coming as a time when "Christ Himself will engage in actual, blood-shedding, life-taking warfare when He returns to set up His kingdom" and at the same time "instruct[s] His people to engage in that future warfare."[4] John MacArthur said, "Armageddon ... will actually be a slaughter" of "millions of people engaged in the Battle of Armageddon," and "it is the Lord Jesus Christ who crushes out their lives."[5] For pastor Mark Driscoll, the book of Revelation depicts Jesus as "a prize fighter with a tattoo down His leg, a sword in His hand and the commitment to make someone bleed." And Driscoll found great comfort in this.

"That is a guy I can worship. I cannot worship the hippie, diaper, halo Christ because I cannot worship a guy I can beat up."[6]

Whether Driscoll could take Jesus in a cage fight, I cannot say. Ironically, my own view of Revelation used to be close to Driscoll's. I remember teaching a class on ethics not long ago, and when we talked about the Jesus of the Gospels, I highlighted His nonviolent posture. "However," I argued, "the Jesus of Revelation will slaughter His enemies, and their blood will soak His garments." My students smiled with a sigh of relief while muttering heartfelt amens. After all, which American kid wants to worship a hippie, diaper, halo Jesus?

Unfortunately, I assumed I knew about this prizefighting Christ without actually studying the book of Revelation. I simply took it for granted that the Jesus of the Gospels was a pacifist, while the Jesus of Revelation was a UFC warrior.

Since teaching that class, I have studied Revelation and seen that although there's a lot of bloodshed, it often flows from the veins of Christ and His followers, not from His enemies. In fact, Revelation supports Christian nonviolence more aggressively than any other biblical book. Nowhere does Revelation encourage the church to act violently. Human violence is always condemned, and suffering is exalted. Now, make no mistake: Jesus will return as Judge, and He will pour out His wrath. But the thought of a tatted, buffed-out, commando Jesus hacking His enemies to pieces with sadistic pleasure is nowhere to be found in Revelation. Jesus receives authority to judge His enemies because He first suffers by their hands as a slaughtered Lamb. In Revelation, victory belongs to victims, and Lamb-like warriors conquer their enemies by *being conquered*. That's the theme of this bloody book.

READING REVELATION

Now, there is much debate over how to interpret Revelation. Since it would take too long to defend my approach, let me just state it up front. I do not think that Revelation is just a series of predictions of future events. Nor do I think that it should be read as a political cartoon, meant to depict first-century events. There's some truth to both of these views. The book does talk about the future and about the first century, but it can't be limited to one particular age. The book of Revelation, rather, lifts the curtain and exposes "the spiritual environment within which the church perennially finds itself living and struggling."[7] The wild images in the book, therefore, shouldn't be mapped onto first-century or twenty-first-century events in a direct, one-to-one correspondence—the beast is Iran, the locusts are Chinese tanks, the whore of Babylon is Lady Gaga, or whatever. Rather, the images and otherworldly scenes depict the struggle Christians face as they live within—and resist—the oppressive empires of every era. In this sense, "Babylon" is Rome of the first century, but it's also the Umayyad Empire, the Vikings, crusaders, Ottomans, Nazis, and every other Babel-like state that seeks global domination. *God* rules the earth. And in every age, His followers—the kingdom of God—find themselves struggling to live out God's rule in the midst of earthly empires.

The first readers of Revelation felt this tension. When John pens the book, he sends it to a group of house churches strung along the western region of Asia Minor. Some of these churches (Smyrna, Philadelphia) are faithful to Christ and are therefore threatened by Rome. But other churches (the other five) are faithful to *Rome* and are therefore threatened by the risen King!

Those who resisted the worldliness of Rome arouse localized persecutions[8] while those who compromise with the empire remain affluent and safe.[9] So around the year AD 90, Jesus appears to John, who has been exiled on the island of Patmos. Revelation records the vision Jesus gives John, which is designed to encourage the persecuted churches and confront the compromising churches in Asia Minor.

In short, there are two types of churches addressed in Revelation: the compromisers and the persecuted.

Now, even though Revelation is addressed to seven churches in the late first century, its message applies to churches of all ages. We can see this throughout Revelation 2–3, where every message to the churches concludes with the refrain: "He who has an ear, let him hear what the Spirit says to the churches."[10] Jesus is talking to you and me here. Whoever "has an ear" let him or her listen in on what Jesus is saying to these first-century churches.

Jesus therefore reveals to John a vision about what's *really* going on behind the scenes. Revelation reshapes our perception of earthly events around the reality of the risen Christ, the slaughtered Lamb, the King of Kings.[11] As far as the earthly eye can see, the beasts rule and the powerless saints are defeated by them. But as far as the heavenly eye can see, the saints have conquered the beasts through their suffering faithfulness. In the book of Revelation, perceived defeat is heavenly victory.

THE CLASH OF THE KINGDOMS

While some New Testament passages say that governing authorities reward good conduct and punish the bad (Rom. 13:1–7; see

1 Pet. 2:13–17), there's no such positive language in the book of Revelation. None. Rome is not described as a benevolent ruler but a savage creature empowered by the Devil himself (Rev. 13:2). The state is explicitly called a "beast," a "false prophet," and a sensuous "whore." All of these terms are collectively summed up by the term *Babylon*.

Babylon does not refer to the literal nation of Babylon across the desert but to the Roman Empire. Or in the words of Richard Bauckham, "Babylon … represents the corrupt and exploitative civilization of the city of Rome, supported by the political and military power of the empire."[12] However, even though Babylon refers *primarily* to Rome, its description fits all sorts of empires and nations that rival God's rule on earth. Babylon is a symbol for "all authorities, corporations, institutions, structures, bureaucracies, and the like."[13] If the shoe fits, then wear it.

Throughout Revelation, kingdoms clash—the kingdom of God and the kingdom(s) of Babylon. The two exist side by side, but the church gives its allegiance to one. We may have earthly passports, but we should never feel totally at home in Rome: "Come out of her, my people," shouts the angel, "lest you take part in her sins" (18:4). This clash of kingdoms is highlighted by many contrasting images.[14] The triune God (Father, Son, and Holy Spirit) confronts the dragon, the beast of the sea, and the beast of the land.[15] The city of Babylon is contrary to the New Jerusalem.[16] The harlot clothed in purple persecutes a woman clothed with the sun.[17] The throne of God conquers the throne of the beast.[18] Followers of God are marked with a seal, while followers of the dragon are marked with the number of the beast.[19] All of these contrasting images emphasize the overarching contrast between the kingdom of God and the kingdom of Babylon. And the book of Revelation reveals how the kingdom of God will *conquer* the kingdom of Babylon.

THE CONQUERING LAMB

Enter Driscoll's prizefighting Jesus. The image of the conquering warrior-Christ is largely gleaned from Revelation 19, where Jesus's clothes are dipped in blood, and He defeats His enemies with a sword. But as we will see, these images don't overturn the Jesus of the Gospels. The main problem with Driscoll's reading of Revelation 19 is that it fails to understand Revelation 1–18. Yes, Jesus will judge His enemies. But His authority to judge is attained by first being conquered by them. The suffering of Christ, His death on the cross, becomes the means by which Jesus slays the dragon. And the blood spattered on His garments comes not from His enemies—but from Himself.

The book of Revelation is all about how Jesus conquers Babylon. The word *conquer* (verb: *nikao*; noun: *nike*) conjures up images of military victory, and everyone in John's world knows this.[20] Homer's *Iliad* is filled with warriors who "conquer" in battle, in wrestling matches, or in other athletic events. Maccabean warriors "conquered" their Greek overlords in battle. Homer sang about the war-god Ares, who had fathered the "warlike Nike." Nike was the goddess of victory; her name means "conquer."[21]

John also uses the verb *nikao* throughout Revelation to describe how Jesus has "conquered" the beastly empire and set up His own kingdom.[22] But John uses the word differently: unlike the Roman rulers, Jesus conquers not with swords and spears but with a cross. The Lamb conquers *by being conquered*. In fact, whenever Jesus is the subject of the verb *nikao* in Revelation, it refers to His own death. Jesus conquers by dying.[23] This is why John's favorite image of Jesus is a "slaughtered Lamb," which he uses twenty-eight times in the book. The Lamb conquers *by* being slaughtered, *by* hanging on a cross—the very symbol of Roman power. Perhaps Driscoll could take Jesus in a cage fight. After all, he already crucified Him.[24]

This backward way of conquering is depicted in Revelation 5, where God sits on the throne, holding a scroll sealed with seven seals. John begins to weep because no one has the authority to break the seals and open the scroll. But then John hears about a "Lion of the tribe of Judah" who alone is found worthy to open the scroll. The Lion has authority to open it because He "has con-quered" (v. 5).

The Lion has conquered! No surprise here. That's what lions do. They hunt their prey, roar with thunder, and mangle their foe like a rag doll. The lion is a symbol of brute power—conquering power—and it's also the well-known Jewish image for the Messiah, the one who would come as a conquering king.[25] But when John turns to look, he doesn't see a lion. Instead, he sees a slaughtered Lamb (5:6). These two contrasting images of Lion and Lamb depict a single person—Jesus. And "the shock of this reversal discloses the central mystery of [Revelation]: God overcomes the world not through a show of force but through the suffering and death of Jesus."[26]

The messianic Lion defeats evil by becoming a slaughtered Lamb.[27]

Weakness is power, victims are victorious, and slaughtered Lambs rule the world in this upside-down book. Jesus reigns because He conquered, not in a cage fight but on a cross.[28] And through His own suffering, Jesus refashions our suffering into a conduit of divine power to continue the conquest—the conquest over Satan's kingdom in Asia Minor and Rome; Sudan and Nigeria; Iraq and Moravia.

THE CONQUERING LAMBS

"The Lamb has conquered! Let us follow Him!" This was the battle cry of a group of wild-eyed Christians known as the Moravians, who evangelized many difficult areas from the fifteenth to eighteenth century. Intoxicated with missionary zeal, the Moravians ventured to hard-to-reach places to proclaim the kingship of Christ. And they went not *despite* suffering, but *because of* it. They believed—with John—that suffering for Christ was not defeat but victory. Victory over the dragon. Victory over the beast. The Lamb conquers by suffering, and He told His followers to pick up their crosses and die. Throughout Revelation we see a group of cross-carrying proto-Moravians "who follow the Lamb wherever he goes" (14:4). And the Lamb goes to the cross.

The term *nikao* is used ten times for Jesus's followers. Most often, *nikao* refers to faithfulness unto death.[29] Christians will overcome, not by fighting, not by killing, not by powerful coercion. Swords and spears and machine guns are insufficient means for ruling the world. This is the way the kings of the earth—those empowered by Satan—conquer.[30] The followers of the Lamb conquer by means of divine power. Christians conquer by being killed (12:11).

In each letter to the seven churches of Revelation, Jesus exhorts believers to "conquer." That is, worship Jesus and not Caesar; hold fast to the testimony of Christ even if it kills you. Because if you are killed, you win. You conquer. "Be faithful unto death, and I will give you the crown of life," Jesus tells the believers at Smyrna (2:10). "The one who *conquers* will not be hurt by the second death" (v. 11). To the church at Pergamum, Jesus commends a saint named Antipas, since he was a "faithful witness, who was killed among you" (v. 13). Antipas conquered (v. 17). The ones who conquer in Thyatira will reign with Jesus (v. 26). The Sardis believers who conquer will be clothed with resurrection life (3:5). And to "the one who conquers" in Laodicea, says Jesus, "I will grant him to sit with me on my throne, as I also conquered and sat down with my Father on his throne" (v. 21). The ones who follow the Lamb to the slaughter will reign with Him in glory.

The book often thought to overturn the ethic of nonviolence is actually its greatest defender. By suffering unto death, believers participate in the suffering power of Christ. John states this plainly in several passages. In one climactic scene, a loud voice in heaven sings out:

> Now the salvation and the power and the kingdom of our God and the authority of his Christ have come, for the accuser of our brothers has been thrown down, who accuses them day and night before our God. And they have conquered him by the blood of the Lamb and by the word of their testimony, for they loved not their lives even unto death. (12:10–11)

The kingdom of God is breaking into history and toppling Satan's rule because believers "have conquered him by the blood of the Lamb and by the word of their testimony." They have joined with Jesus in His suffering death by suffering a death of their own. The end of the passage makes the connection clear: "*for* they loved not their lives even unto death." By picking up their crosses and following the Lamb wherever He goes, these martyrs participate in the Lamb's victory over satanic empires.

In another throne-room scene, John sees a large multitude of believers "standing before the throne and before the Lamb, clothed in white robes, with palm branches in their hands" (7:9). White robes in Revelation often symbolize the reward given to martyred saints (6:9–11). The same is true of palm branches, which are given to victorious athletes or military heroes—conquerors.[31] According to John's vision, such rewards are reserved for suffering lambs, the "ones coming out of the great tribulation" (i.e., they were killed) who "have washed their robes and made them white in the blood of the Lamb" (7:14).[32] Their martyrdom is the means by which they "conquered the beast and its image," as John says elsewhere (15:2). They conquered by being conquered.[33]

This is such a difficult truth for me to swallow. Don't think that because I'm writing a book on nonviolence that this stuff comes easy. I live in a culture where all forms of suffering are avoided, or at least medicated. I get a headache, and I pop a pill. I get hungry, and I immediately eat. If I feel cold, I put on one of my many coats. If I get tired, I rest. If I catch a cold, I crawl into bed, call in sick, and pop another pill. And if someone even thinks about oppressing me, watch out! I can bench press 250 pounds, and I own several guns. Step on my private property, and you may end up in the hospital or lying in chalk. My culture gives me no categories to view suffering—especially suffering at the hands of an oppressor—as victory. My culture sees suffering only as defeat, as evil. It never sees suffering as a means of victory. This is why I need to read John's vision about what's *really* going on from God's perspective to correct my American, self-serving, "I will defend my rights at all costs" mind-set. I need to follow the slaughtered Lamb wherever He goes, so that I can reign with Him in victory.

THE WRATH OF THE LAMB

But there's more. Christians who suffer unto death don't just conquer Satan. Their blood actually contributes to the judgment God pours out on worldly empires. In a highly symbolic scene, Jesus reaps a harvest of grain, which refers to the salvation of those who confess Christ (14:14–16). This is a familiar image from the Gospels, where the evangelization of the world is compared to a harvest.[34] In the very next scene (vv. 17–20), there's another harvest, only this time it's a harvest of grapes.

> So the angel swung his sickle across the earth and gathered the grape harvest of the earth and threw it into the great winepress of the wrath of God. And the winepress was trodden outside the city, and blood flowed from the winepress, as high as a horse's bridle, for 1,600 stadia. (vv. 19–20)

Some interpreters have misunderstood this passage, thinking that it refers to Jesus squishing His enemies (the grapes) until an ocean of their blood nearly causes Jesus's horse to drown. Though this works well with Driscoll's Jesus, most evangelical scholars do not

take this reading seriously. Many would say that the blood is symbolic for judgment. Jesus will judge His enemies. No doubt about
that. But He won't literally mount a mare and trample their bodies.

But let's look a little closer at those grapes. Are they God's
enemies or His saints? It's not entirely clear, but there is some good
evidence that the blood from the grapes refers to the blood of the
saints, which contributes to God's wrath over those who killed them.
In fact, whenever the image of blood occurs in Revelation, it always
refers to the blood of Jesus, His followers, or innocent people. God
never causes His enemies to bleed in Revelation—literally or symbolically.[35] And according to the scene, "the winepress was trodden
… and blood flowed" the same place where Jesus bled— "outside the
city." This is the same location where the author of Hebrews tells his
readers to suffer with Jesus—outside the city, the place where Jesus
cleansed "the people through his own blood" (Heb. 13:12–13).

Blood outside the city. It's a sacred Christian image for redemptive suffering. Outside the city is where conquerors go to conquer.[36]

So the grapes that are harvested are the martyrs of Jesus. But
why are they thrown "into the great winepress of the wrath of God"?
Because their blood turns into God's wrath poured out on their killers. The martyrs don't die *because of* God's wrath. Rather, their blood
(the wine) becomes the very wrath Babylon will drink. God is mix-
ing the wine of His wrath (Rev. 14:10), which will be poured out on
the Babylons that oppose Him (16:19).

Now, whether the blood is symbolic of judgment or symbolic of
martyrdom leading to judgment doesn't make a huge difference for
my main point. Nowhere are God's people allowed to act violently
in Revelation. In any case, this martyrdom-leading-to-wrath view

better fits with what John says over the next few chapters,[37] where the blood of the saints becomes the mixed wine of God's wrath toward His enemies:

> For they have *shed the blood of saints* and *prophets*,
>> and you have given them *blood to drink*.
> It is what they deserve! (16:6)

> God remembered Babylon the great, to make her *drain the cup of the wine of the fury of his wrath*. (16:19)

> And I saw the woman, *drunk with the blood of the saints*, the *blood of the martyrs of Jesus*. (17:6)

> Pay her back as she herself has paid back others,
>> and repay her double for her deeds;
>>> mix a double portion for her *in the cup she*
>>>> *mixed*. (18:6)

> And in her was found the *blood of prophets and of*
>> *saints*,
> and of all who have been slain on earth.
>> (18:24)

> He has judged the great prostitute …
>> and has *avenged on her the blood of his servants*.
>> (19:2)

All of these passages seem to draw out the meaning of the grape harvest in Revelation 14:17–20. God has stored up the blood of the martyrs in a massive winepress and is thrusting it down the throat of Babylon in seven bowls.[38] The persecution of the saints may lead to the salvation of the persecutors.[39] Otherwise, it contributes to their righteous judgment. In both cases, there is meaning—rich, theological meaning—in the persecution of saints.

The twentieth century witnessed more Christian martyrs than the previous nineteen centuries *combined*. And not a single one of them died arbitrarily. Every pool of blood contributed either to the salvation of their enemies or to their wrath. Not a single drop was meaningless.

WRATHFUL NONVIOLENCE

Violence makes no sense to citizens of God's kingdom. We don't fight with violence, because we have a more powerful weapon in our hands. It's called suffering. With it, we can conquer the hard hearts of our enemies. And with it, we condemn unrepentant sinners. Either way, choosing the violent option is not only unchristian, but a rather weak way to fight against evil. Why use an airsoft gun when you have an AK-47 at your disposal (to use an ironic analogy)? It's impossible for Christians to lose, to be defeated, to be *conquered*, because the Lamb has already conquered by being slaughtered. Nothing and no one can take away His crown, and therefore nothing can take away our crown. Our enemies can kick us, scourge us, beat us, and crucify us as they did to our Lord. But they cannot win. They cannot defeat the Lamb and His followers. The more they try, the more grapes are thrown into their winepress. And the Lamb will make them drink it.

The book of Revelation does not portray a vindictive, blood-thirsty God. It reveals a God who gives people the fruits of their labor. It reveals the wrathful power of the Lamb who was slain.

Now, all of this helps us to read rightly Revelation 19, the main passage about the second coming of Jesus. Some think that this is where Jesus throws His nonviolence out the window. But it all depends on what we mean by violence. Yes, Jesus returns to judge the world in righteousness. He will pour out His wrath on those who oppose Him. But such wrath is not arbitrarily dished out. God's wrath is simply handing people the cup they have mixed for themselves. "As she glorified herself and lived in luxury," cries the angel, "so give her a like measure of torment and mourning" (18:7). When Jesus returns in Revelation 19, we see Him "clothed in a robe dipped in blood" (19:13) *before* He wages war against the enemy. The blood, therefore, is probably His own. If the blood was His enemies', it would splatter on His garments *after* the fight, not before.

And when Jesus defeats the enemy, He does so with a sword. But contrary to Driscoll, the sword comes "from his mouth," not His hand (19:15, 21). Everywhere in Revelation, when the sword comes from the mouth, it refers to a word of judgment, not a literal sword.[40] Jesus doesn't run a carnival. He doesn't pull rabbits from His hat or swords from His throat. The sword is symbolic and refers to Jesus's "death-dealing pronouncement which goes forth like a sharp blade from the lips of Christ."[41] The robe dipped in His own blood (a reference to His crucifixion) gives Jesus the authority to conquer, to boldly announce His victory over His foes. Jesus doesn't need to hack His way through enemy lines like a crazed warrior. He doesn't need to do anything but declare with cosmic, cruciform authority that He has already won. The Lamb has conquered!

VIOLENCE IN REVELATION?

Nowhere in Revelation are the followers of Jesus commanded or even allowed to be violent. And even though Jesus carries out vengeance on His enemies, nowhere are His followers called to imitate this.[42] We are commanded to be faithful unto death, as Jesus was. We are never commanded to carry out vengeance on our enemies. We are everywhere commanded to accept the Lamb-like suffering that the empire may bring. It is true that believers are called "the armies of heaven" and will accompany Christ at His coming (19:14), but these armies never lift a finger, let alone a sword. Only Jesus fights, and only with His word of judgment. In an earlier scene, the saints are with Jesus when He conquers the beast in 17:14, but they don't *do* anything other than bear faithful witness to the point of death.[43]

Just like Paul says, the weapons of our warfare are not physical. We are armed with the Word of God, the testimony of Christ (Rev. 6:9; 12:11, 17). And such spiritual weaponry has the power to fight the Enemy—the *true* Enemy, the satanic Enemy who's empowering all human enemies.

Human violence is never encouraged in Revelation. In fact, violence is explicitly condemned. The satanic beast, not the godly saints, thinks that violence is the means of establishing world peace. The Roman Empire was John's primary referent behind many of the symbols in the book. And Rome sought to establish and maintain the *Pax Romana* (peace of Rome) and economic prosperity through violence. This is what the luxurious whore of Babylon riding the beast vividly portrays (17:3–4).[44] The barbarians of the north were kept at bay by the sword. The Parthian border to the east was secured by bloodshed. The *Pax Romana* was secured by violence. But for God, the end (peace) doesn't justify the means (killing). God condemns Rome, because "in her was found the blood of prophets and of saints, *and of all who have been slain on the earth*" (18:24). God condemns Rome not just for religious persecution, but for all types of killing.

SLEEPING WITH THE HARLOT?

Studying the book of Revelation has been one of the most paradigm-shifting experiences I've had in the last ten years. I've known that the Bible talks about suffering. But I've never seen how godly suffering has such significance in God's plan of redemption and judgment. This has revolutionized my thinking, because I don't like to suffer. But if Jesus's death, resurrection, and ascension mean anything, then I must let my eyes of faith rather than my pain sensors dictate how I process suffering. I must, like the Moravians, follow Jesus wherever He goes.

Oftentimes we want to overcome evil with more power, more force, more killing. But Revelation shows us the true power of suffering. Jesus dethroned Satan when He suffered. Christians defeat oppressive regimes when they suffer at their hands. Revelation snuffs out the human impulse that thinks violent oppression demands an even stronger violent response. Suffering unto death isn't just a sense-less misfortune that God will redeem but the very means by which God works to defeat evil. Christians who suffer never lose, because Christ has already won.

The book of Revelation has also challenged me to ask a very difficult question: Am I sleeping with Babylon's harlot? According to John's vision, the one participating in Babylon is a deceived, naked, dirty, demonized, drunken whore. What's scary is that you may not even know it. You may think you're serving Jesus, when all along you are feeding the beast and adding more grapes to God's winepress.

Such is the case of the churches of Pergamum and Thyatira. They hold fast to Jesus's name and do not deny the faith. And yet they participate in the idolatry and worldliness of Babylon—and if they don't repent, Jesus says that He will war against them with the sword of His mouth. The believers at Pergamum think they are sipping choice wine and don't know it has been mixed with the blood of the innocent.[45] Jesus commands them—and all believers entangled in beastly empires—to "come out of her, my people, lest you take part in her sins" (18:4). Be in the world, but not of the world, as John says elsewhere.

This is why I have a hard time with Christians who fail to untangle their faith from American nationalism. The Bible tells us to honor our country, pray for its leaders, and submit to its laws insofar as they don't conflict with God's laws. But I fear that many evangelical Christians go much further than this. America has done many good things. So did Rome. But they both do many things that contribute to the shedding of innocent blood.

Here's just one example. As I was writing this chapter, a young man named Adam Lanza walked into Sandy Hook Elementary School in Newtown, Connecticut, and gunned down twenty-six people, including twenty children. The Newtown massacre produced a wave of rage, confusion, and disgust across America. And it reached Washington, DC. Three days after the event, President Obama visited Newtown to mourn the tragedy and comfort the many friends and family whose suffering will continue for years. We will use "whatever power" is in our hands, declared Obama, to stop such massacres from happening again.

As a parent of four children, I mourned this tragedy. I fear that one day I might wake up to that phone call: "Sir, I'm sorry to tell you this, but you need to come down here because ..." Ugh. I can't imagine! My heart goes out to those who are suffering from this horrific evil.

But there's a bit of irony in Obama's outrage.

As I was googling around to find updates on the killing, I typed in "children killed in ..." and before I could tap my keyboard, I was struck by the next thing that automatically popped up. It wasn't *Connecticut*, it wasn't *Newtown*, and it wasn't *school*. The next words that popped up were *drone strikes*. I was instantly reminded of the horrors of killing children—both in America and abroad.

Drones are unmanned aerial combat vehicles. Or in layperson's terms, they are flying robots armed to the teeth with rockets and controlled by a pilot with a joystick in Missouri. They've been used in Afghanistan, Iraq, Pakistan, and elsewhere in the Middle East. The genius of drone strikes is that they can kill bad guys without any threat of losing American lives. And Obama has been a major advocate of drone strikes. In one sense, they have been a remarkable success. According to one study, since Obama took office there have been over three hundred drone strikes in the Middle East, resulting in over 2,500 deaths.

But who are these 2,500? Terrorists, no doubt! Unfortunately, this is not the case. According to one Pakistani report, 50 civilians are killed for every terrorist.[46] Another report says that of the 1,658 to 2,597 killed in drone strikes, 282 and 535 were civilians (that's between 10 and 32 percent).[47] The CIA, however, says that it has killed over 600 militants in drone strikes and not a single civilian has died.[48] Pakistani reports will most probably inflate the numbers, and the CIA will probably reduce them. But even if we take a mediating position and say that 25 civilians are killed for every terrorist—that's a lot of civilian deaths. The number that I keep seeing from several different sources—including horrifying pictures—is that there have been 168 children blown up in drone strikes since Obama took office.[49] If this happened on American soil, we'd call it terrorism. It did happen in Connecticut, and we called it murder. Yet few Americans are outraged over the killing of these innocent children in the Middle East.

"We can't tolerate this anymore," mourned Obama during his speech at Sandy Hook Elementary. "These tragedies must end. ... If there is even one step we can take to save another child, or another parent, or another town, from the grief that has visited Tucson, and Aurora, and Oak Creek, and Newtown, and communities from Columbine to Blacksburg before that—then surely we have an obligation to try."[50]

I appreciate Obama's concern, but I find it ironic. Can we extend his sympathy to the Middle East? Are the deaths of 168 incinerated children any less a tragedy than the massacre at Newtown? Or does their color, ethnicity, and religion justify their deaths? Better their kids than ours, said *Time* magazine's Joe Klein.[51]

I mourn both tragedies—the death of innocent, beautiful children in Connecticut and of the precious children in the Middle East. Both tragedies are evil. Both will be vindicated. Both will be judged. I also mourn the hypocrisy of the millions of Americans who endorse a military tactic that spares American soldiers at the cost of foreign children. "In her was found the blood ... of all who have been slain on earth," cries the angel in John's vision (Rev. 18:24). I fear that the whore of Babylon might not live across the pond.

So what should the church do? Again, pray for our leaders; honor the state; submit to the government insofar as it doesn't lead us to commit treason against our Lord. But let us not be seduced into thinking that America is the hope of the world, the keeper of peace, the symbol of all that is good. All nations have blood on their hands. And the Lamb will make them drink it.

THE EARLY CHURCH IN A VIOLENT WORLD

WHY CARE ABOUT WHAT THE EARLY CHURCH DID?

One of the most sobering things about writing a book on violence is where I'm writing from. Here I am, locked up in the confines of a Southern Californian suburb with little real threat of violence, while millions of Christians around the globe suffer from daily perils. As I write this chapter, Palestinian militia have sent over a thousand rockets sailing across the Israeli hill country toward Jerusalem. Israel has retaliated by shelling the Gaza Strip, killing more than 150 people, mostly civilians. In Syria, a civil war wages on; nearly ninety-three thousand people have been killed, including over six thousand in the suburbs of Damascus. Thousands of Christians in Nigeria continue to be butchered by Muslim extremists. Nearly half a million women (and not a few men) have suffered sexual violence in the Democratic Republic of Congo, the so-called rape capital of the world. And here I sit in the suburb of Simi Valley, where I've never awoken to a hissing air-raid siren or a crazed militia busting down my door. As one of my friends joked, "It's easy to be a pacifist in Indiana"—home of many Mennonite institutions. "Try living like that in Gaza."

This is why the voice of the early church is so important. As we will see, the first Christians didn't resort to violence, and they weren't living in Indiana. The first three hundred years of the faith were stained with brutal persecution. Rome lacked no creativity when it came to torture: swords, torches, chains, and wild animals were unleashed upon stubborn Christians unwilling to give up their confession of faith. Crucifixion continued to be practiced, though disembowelment and dismemberment were popular too. From the second century onward, Christians were thrown into the ring with ferocious gladiators, who shed blood for an audience thirsty for violence. One Christian woman named Blandina was executed under Emperor Marcus Aurelius (the old guy who dies in the beginning of the movie *Gladiator*) and showed inexplicable zeal through the entire ordeal. After being nailed to a stake, she was taken down and scourged, gnashed by wild animals, sent to the "roasting seat," then finally stuffed into a net and thrown before a bull that toyed with her a bit before mauling her to death. According to the historian Eusebius, she felt "none of the things which were happening to her, on account of her hope and firm hold upon what had been entrusted to her, and her communion with Christ."[1] Such was the fate of many enemy-loving Christians.

These believers weren't living in some monastery in a desert, nor were they shielded from violence by walls of Indianan cornfields. They were writing about warfare and violence from the terrifying trenches of the Roman world. And if they weren't put to the sword, they witnessed many who were. The prolific theologian Tertullian saw his own family members and fellow Christians tortured and killed. Origen, perhaps the most prestigious writer, was nearly tortured to death on "the rack" and saw his own father executed. Ignatius, the bishop of Antioch, was thrown to wild beasts in Rome. The famed Christian apologist Justin Martyr, was, well ... *martyred*.

Yet while Justin lived, he instructed believers to "pray on behalf of your enemies, love those who hate you," because "we who used to kill each other" now do "not fight our enemies."[2] Early Christians wrote about violence with a sword on their necks.

But some of you might wonder: Didn't these early Christians have all sorts of weird beliefs about Christianity? Why does it matter what they thought about violence?

Yes, it's true that we shouldn't agree with early Christians in everything they say. The Bible is our authority, and where members of the early church depart from the Bible, we go with the Bible. However, it would be naive to think that our beliefs come straight from the text with no historical filter. Many foundational doctrines, such as the Trinity, the deity and humanity of Christ, and even the decision over which books would make it into the New Testament were all hammered out by early-church leaders. Few of us would have formulated the doctrine of the Trinity ("God is one in essence but three in persons") by reading the Bible on a desert island. We got that from Tertullian. Christ's 100 percent deity and 100 percent humanity—a mathematical conundrum—was shaped by Athanasius. It took nearly three hundred years for early-church leaders to put together an official list of which books belong in the New Testament. So while these leaders weren't inspired and don't carry the same authority as the Bible, they do offer us an important perspective on various issues, including violence, that we can't ignore. They were ardent students of Scripture, living in a time and culture not far from the New Testament itself. Their opinions aren't authoritative but do matter, especially—and this is important—when there is *diverse, widespread* agreement on particular issues.

Here's what I mean by "diverse" and "widespread." When the church expanded in the first three hundred years, it settled down in various pockets of the Roman Empire. The church sprouted in places like Egypt and North Africa. It grew in Caesarea (Israel) and in Asia Minor (modern-day Turkey). And, of course, it was well established early on in Rome. During the years of persecution, there wasn't much dialogue across these regions. Later, after AD 313 when the church was no longer persecuted, it would hold church councils in which leaders from all over the empire would gather at cities like Nicaea or Constantinople to hammer out what would become orthodox Christian beliefs. But before AD 313, such dialogue was more difficult. Therefore, the different pockets of the church often formed their own distinct views on certain issues. The leaders in Caesarea, for instance, practiced a different set of interpretive principles than the leaders in Egypt did. Christians in Rome accepted the book of Revelation as Scripture, while believers in Syria rejected it.

While the opinions of the early church aren't authoritative, *where there is widespread agreement across different regions, we should pay special attention to what they're saying.* Such "widespread" and "diverse" agreement would *more likely* be the result of a raw reading of Scripture, rather than some influence or bias that's unique to a particular region.

So let me go ahead and let the cat out of the bag. This chapter will show that whenever early-church leaders discussed the issue, there was *widespread* and *diverse* agreement that Christians should never use violence; in particular, they should never kill. Leaders from North Africa, Egypt, Israel, Asia Minor, and Rome. They all agree. Christians should never kill. Not in self-defense. Not as capital punishment for the guilty. Not in a just war. Never.

But first, let me explain one thing about how I'm going to approach this chapter. Some readers may not know much about the early church, including its writers. So whenever I mention a name, I'll put the dates of that person's life in parentheses along with the region or city where he lived. For the sake of space, I'm not going to give many details about the context of the individual writers. But since the subject matter of the early church is a delicate one, I've included extensive documentation in the endnotes. You should know that there have been over a hundred books written in the last hundred years on the subject of early Christians and military service![3] So no matter how thorough I try to be here, I'll only scratch the surface. I trust that my documentation in the endnotes will satisfy the scrutiny of those few readers who may be well versed in this sprawling discussion.

Also, by "early church," I'm referring primarily to those Christians who lived before AD 313. This is the year when Emperor Constantine ended the persecution of Christians. In the wake of Constantine, Christianity became intertwined with the governance of the Roman Empire, and in AD 380 it became the official state religion. Needless to say, going from a persecuted religion to the only legitimate state-sponsored religion changed the church's perspective on many issues.[4] The period we're looking at (pre-Constantine) reflects a time when there was a separation of church and state.

We'll begin with an overview of the church's perspective on killing. Is killing ever okay? Then, we will dive into the specific question about Christians in the military, since this was a live issue in the early church.

IS KILLING EVER OKAY?

Early Christian writers were divided on many issues, such as the mode of baptism, the role of women in leadership, and whether Christians should observe the Sabbath. But when it came to killing, their voices seemed to be unanimous: believers are prohibited from taking human life.

Several writers said this explicitly. Origen (184–253, Alexandria and Caesarea), for instance, said that Christ "nowhere teaches that it is right for his own disciples to offer violence to anyone, however wicked. For he did not deem it in keeping with the laws such as His to allow killing of any individual whatever."[5] Tertullian (160–220, Carthage) agreed that God prohibits "every sort of man-killing."[6] Cyprian (202–258, Carthage) argued that persecuted Christians "do not in turn assail their assailants, since it is not lawful for the innocent even to kill the guilty."[7]

Athenagoras (ca. 133–190, Athens) went even further by saying that "we cannot endure to see someone be put to death, even justly."[8] The mere witnessing of someone being killed, even if he or she deserves it, is prohibited, because killing is wrong for Christians in principle. This point is crucial. It would be one thing to condemn *bad* types of killing such as murder, suicide, and abortion. And early Christians certainly do speak out against these.[9] But the statements cited above condemn every sort of killing—even of the guilty— on the principle that killing is always wrong. Or in the words of Lactantius (250–325, Asia Minor):

> When God forbids killing, he doesn't just ban mur-
> der, which is not permitted under the law even; he

is also forbidding to us to do certain things which are treated as lawful among men. A just man may not be a soldier, nor may he put anyone on a capital charge: whether you kill a man with a sword or a speech makes no difference, since killing itself is banned. In this commandment of God no exception at all should be made: killing a human being is always wrong because it is God's will for man to be a sacred creature.[10]

Lactantius summed up what seems to be a universal view among early Christian writers whenever they discuss the topic. All types of killing, not just murderous killing, are wrong for Christians.[11]

Many other early writers agreed that killing is wrong for Christians, though their statements are more implicit than explicit. Arnobius of Sicca (253–330, modern Tunisia), for instance, criticized Rome's worship of war and explained Christianity in nonviolent terms. Now, it's not clear that Arnobius wrestled with the issue of Christians in the military. But while discussing war, he characterized Christians as those who "have learned from His [Jesus's] teachings and His laws that it is not right to repay evil for evil." Christians, argued Arnobius, should rather "pour forth one's own blood rather than to stain our hands and conscience with the blood of another."[12] The widely read treatise called the *Didache* (80–120, Syria) begins with a series of moral instructions to newcomers in the faith, and the emphasis is clearly on Jesus's Sermon on the Mount (Matt. 5–7). Believers are commanded to bless those who hate them, pray for their enemies, fast for their persecutors, love those who hate them, turn the other cheek, go the extra mile, and abstain from "bodily passions," which in the context refers to revenge.

We already saw that Justin Martyr (100–165, Rome) contrasted our former violent nature with our peaceful, enemy-loving posture as Christians.[13] Jesus's command to "love your enemies" (Matt. 5:44) was quoted by ten different writers in twenty-eight different passages, making it *the* most cited passage by early Christian writers before Constantine.[14] Loving one's enemies was the ethical heartbeat of early Christianity. It's what separated Christians from everyone else, according to Tertullian.[15]

But what about military service? If Christians served in the military, which they did, were they allowed to kill?

CAN CHRISTIANS IN THE MILITARY KILL?

No. Or at least, not according to the Christian writings we possess. In fact, whenever military service was discussed, believers were never encouraged to join. There was not a single Christian writer in the first three hundred years of Christianity who said that Christians should serve in Rome's military.[16]

Tertullian, for instance, wrote an entire treatise forbidding military service among Christians.[17] Such sentiment is found throughout his other writings.[18] Origen too condemned military service whenever he addressed the subject. And Lactantius agreed, as seen in the previous quote: "A just man may not be a soldier." Now, to be clear, there *were* Christians in the military before Constantine, and I'll deal with this later. But as far as the opinion of early Christian writers goes, historian Alan Kreider was correct that "no Christian theologian before Constantine justified Christian participation in warfare."[19]

But this actually doesn't tell us too much. The main question is not whether the theologians permit military service. This much is clear. They condemn it. The question, though, is *why*? On what grounds, in other words, are Christians forbidden to join the military?

One reason is *idolatry*. The Roman military was inseparable from Roman religion; to serve one meant serving the other. It would have been virtually impossible to be a Christian soldier and *not* participate in idolatry. For instance, before embarking on a military campaign, soldiers would take part in various pagan rituals, including sacrificing sheep, bulls, and pigs to purify the army. Similar rituals dominated the postwar celebration. Throughout the legions, soldiers regularly burned incense and offered grain to local deities, and idolatrous symbols everywhere pervaded the camps.

It's not that Christian soldiers couldn't worship Jesus alongside other Roman gods. Well and good. But no soldier could worship a single deity (such as Jesus) without honoring the others. "[T]he totality of Roman army religion was an impressive system," wrote one historian. "[It] would be impossible for any Christian in the army to avoid dealing with it in one way or another."[20]

Christians were clearly forbidden to join the military on account of idolatry. This is indisputable. But idolatry wasn't the only reason military service was forbidden. Christians weren't allowed to join because, as we saw above, killing is wrong in principle. And several writers made this plain.

Lactantius, in the quote we read, said that "a just man may not be a soldier" and not because of idolatry. His reason was that "killing itself is banned" and "killing a human being is always wrong."[21] Tertullian spoke out most frequently against Christians joining the military and often appealed to idolatry as the main reason. But killing was another reason. In arguing whether "a believer can become a soldier," he unambiguously said no: "The Lord, by taking away Peter's sword"—referring to the incident in Gethsemane—"disarmed every soldier thereafter." Then, in the very next statement, Tertullian said: "We are not allowed to wear any uniform that symbolizes *a sinful act*." That "act" refers back to wielding a sword that Jesus took away. Military service is wrong because killing is wrong.[22] Origen also, in a lengthy treatise, said that Christians are not to participate in war, *even if they are just wars*.[23] His entire argument was governed by a rigorous defense of the nonviolent character of the Christian faith. Again, as Origen said earlier, Christians are prohibited from killing even the guilty.

The issue of killing was prohibited in every mention by early-church writers. Whenever the issue of military service and warfare was discussed, Christians were prohibited from participating. Nowhere in the written record in the first three hundred years of Christianity is killing ever justified. Not even for soldiers.

But let's revisit Origen's statement above about "just wars." It's interesting that Origen believed that there is such a thing as a "just war," and yet he still prohibited Christians from participating. In one of his many treatises, Origen dialogued with a pagan named Celsus, who chided Christians for not fighting alongside their Roman brothers to defend the empire. *If everyone did what you Christians do*, argued Celsus, *the whole empire would collapse*! I often hear the same logic today, only not from pagans but from Christians. In any case, Celsus's statement is interesting in itself because it implies that Christians on the whole were refraining from military service. Origen, however, disagreed with Celsus's argument. He said that Christians were indeed fighting for Rome, not with weapons of warfare but with spiritual armament: prayers, fasting, and acts of piety. Origen went on to show that Rome's own pagan priests were exempt from fighting. According to their own standards, there was a place for religious intervention apart from violence. Origen argued that Christians were doing the same. "Christians also should be fighting as priests and worshippers of God, keeping their right hands pure," wrote Origen. In fact, "we who by our prayers destroy all demons which stir up wars ... are of more help to the emperors than those who seem to be doing the fighting."[24] The power of prayer is stronger than the power of the sword.

Several early writers agreed with Origen. They saw a difference between just and unjust wars and considered it inevitable that the state would violently punish evildoers.[25] But at the same time, these writers didn't say that Christians should participate. This may sound like a double standard, but it all depends on your perspective. Paul says the same thing in Romans, where Christians are not to take vengeance (Rom. 12) even though the state can (Rom. 13). A similar point can be seen today with military chaplains. Even though they serve in the military, they aren't allowed to carry guns. As one chaplain friend of mine said with an ironic grin, "A man of the cloth has no business with an instrument of bloodshed. That's for nonclergy, the soldiers." The military itself doesn't see a double standard.

Origen and others saw wars as inevitable, yet still forbade Christians from participating.[26] Just because there may be such a thing as a "just war" does not give Christians a license to participate.[27] And the church fathers didn't see this as a contradiction. Irenaeus (125–202, modern France) argued that God uses the state to violently punish evil, yet the church is to remain nonviolent.[28] The state can punish enemies; the church must love them.

AN IVORY-TOWER MINORITY?

But is this aversion to killing and warfare really the opinion of common Christians, or just a few ivory-tower theologians whose writings have been preserved?

That's a good question, one that's been raised by several scholars. Peter Leithart, for instance, wondered whether Tertullian, Origen, and others actually represent the views of "the majority of Christians." "What were local pastors saying?" inquired Leithart. "We simply cannot know."[29] In fact, as we will see, there was a growing number of Christians serving in the military, especially in the late third century. Clearly some Christians found military service compatible with their faith.

But do we really have *no* evidence of what pastors were teaching their congregants, as Leithart suggested? At least one document suggests otherwise. The document is a "church order" known as the *Apostolic Tradition* (ca. 250–300, Rome),[30] which was an authoritative instruction manual that was probably used to guide leaders in church organization, liturgy, and various practices for Christian communities. In other words, *Apostolic Tradition* gives us some insight into life "on the ground," as it were. And in this document, the issues of killing and military service are clearly linked:

> A soldier in the sovereign's army should not kill or
> if he is ordered to kill he should refuse. If he stops,
> so be it; otherwise, he should be excluded [from the
> church]. ... One who has the power of the sword or

the head of a city and wears red, let him stop or be excluded. A catechumen or a believer, if they want to be soldiers, let them be excluded because they distance themselves from God.[31]

Several things should be noted here. First, as I mentioned, this opinion represents what at least some local pastors were teaching. It wasn't just the opinion of a few isolated intellectuals. Second, this manual says that believers cannot join the army on the grounds that killing—not just idolatry—is wrong. And if someone gets saved while in the military, he is never again to kill, even if given an order. Across the board, killing is forbidden. Third, *Apostolic Tradition* represents the views of Christians across various regions for at least two hundred years. In other words, it wasn't written from some Amish-like island of the empire. Rather, "it was copied repeatedly, and altered by local churches to adapt it to immediate needs" and "remains one of the most informative texts about the life and worship of early Christian communities," as one expert noted.[32] This widespread influence is exhibited by the fact that *Apostolic Tradition* was copied into three different languages (Arabic, Ethiopic, and Sahidic) and formed the basis of several other church manuals.[33] Leithart didn't mention the *Apostolic Tradition*, but it offers a direct answer to his question about "what local pastors were saying" about killing in war. Some, at least, condemned it.[34]

CHRISTIANS IN THE MILITARY

Even though some theologians prohibited military service on the grounds that killing is wrong, there were still some Christians in the military. In fact, we can reach all the way back to the New Testament to find soldiers who became Christians. Matthew 8 records a centurion coming to faith. Another centurion named Cornelius becomes a believer in Acts 10. A Philippian jailor comes to Christ through Paul's preaching in Acts 16. And when soldiers ask John the Baptist what they must do, he tells them to stop embezzling money but doesn't tell them to leave the military or stop acting violently (Luke 3:14). It seems then that the New Testament is quite comfortable with Christians in the military, and it doesn't explicitly prohibit soldiers from killing.

For hundreds of years, these stories about soldiers getting saved have been the main biblical arguments for just war theory, or for a Christian's right to serve in the military.[35] And there may be something to this. Even Richard Hays, a pacifist, said that these soldier passages "provide one possible legitimate basis for arguing that Christian discipleship does not necessarily preclude the exercise of violence in defense of social order or justice."[36]

But we need to be careful not to force these stories to say more than they actually do. They tell us that the gospel reaches unlikely candidates: Gentile military men, who symbolize Roman oppression. But they don't tell us what these converts did with their careers thereafter. Maybe they stayed in the military, or maybe they left. Maybe they continued to act violently, or maybe they didn't. Either way, nothing in these passages suggests that Cornelius and others are exempt from loving their enemies and turning the other cheek simply because they are in the military. Such a view must be read into, not out of, the text.

In fact, as we saw above, serving in Rome's military entails partaking in various idolatrous practices, and yet Peter doesn't address

the issue of idolatry when Cornelius gets converted. And as a centurion, Cornelius (as well as the centurion in Matt. 8) would not
only be pressured to worship foreign gods, but also be responsible for
leading various ceremonies on behalf of his cohort. As a centurion,
Cornelius would essentially function as a pagan priest! True, Peter
doesn't forbid Cornelius to use violence. But neither does he forbid
him to perform pagan duties. Because that's not the point of the
story. Acts 10 and other soldier-salvation passages highlight one basic
point: the gospel pierces the hearts of unlikely people—even Roman
military leaders.[37] These passages simply don't give us all the details
about what these soldiers did after they got saved.

After the New Testament, we don't have any record of Christians
in the military until AD 173. This is the year that the so-called
Thundering Legion was on the brink of dehydration until a group
of Christian soldiers prayed for rain—a prayer that was miraculously
answered. We're not sure how many Christians there were, why they
were in the military, or what specific military functions they served,[38]
but this incident marks the first time we hear of Christians in the
military after the New Testament.

We are aware of a growing number of Christians serving in
the military between AD 173 and 313 (Constantine's edict to end
persecution). Many of the authors who prohibited Christians from
joining the military acknowledged at the same time that there were
Christian soldiers. Tertullian, Origen, and others such as Clement
of Alexandria (150–215, Egypt) and Dionysus of Alexandria (ca.
200–265, Egypt) all acknowledged that there were Christians in
the military.[39] We're not sure how many there were, but by AD 303
there must have been a substantial number. That was the year when

Emperor Diocletian initiated a persecution of Christians and began with those in the military. This only makes sense if there were quite a few Christian soldiers.

So how do we reconcile the widespread belief that killing and military service is wrong with the fact that there were Christians who served in the military?

Let me make three observations. First, clearly the opinion of the Christians writers (Tertullian, Origen, etc.) wasn't shared by all Christians. In fact, since these writers had to *argue* that Christians shouldn't join the military, this tells us that there were some who disagreed. (They must have been arguing against somebody!) So not every Christian held the same view of killing, even though all the theologians—as far as we can tell—did. The same disconnect exists in every age. Christian writers may condemn things like materialism and divorce, and yet common Christians often indulge in both.[40] It's interesting that during World War II, 30 percent of Mennonite men went off to war as both combatants and noncombatants—despite their thick pacifistic tradition.[41] Christian theologians will say one thing, but this doesn't necessarily mean that Christians in the pew will follow.

Second, even though we read about Christians in the military, we often don't know if they were believers prior to joining or whether, like Cornelius, they got saved while in the military. Neither do we know how many Christians who got saved in the military ended up leaving, though we do read about several who did.[42] We also don't know whether Christian soldiers struggled with their occupation, or whether they had no problem with wielding the sword, let alone offering incense in pagan ceremonies. In other words, the same silence that surrounds soldiers getting saved in the New Testament also surrounds many early-church references to Christians in the military. We just don't know why, or how, or how long, they served.

Third, and somewhat related, we don't know whether Christians in the military were forced to use violence. Clearly some did. Julius "the Veteran" (d. AD 304, modern Bulgaria), for instance, boasted of serving in the army for twenty-seven years, which included "seven military campaigns." By his own confession: "[I] never hid behind anyone nor was I the inferior of any man in battle." No doubt, he must have shed some blood. Julius ended up leaving the military on the grounds that he wouldn't offer sacrifices to the gods; killing doesn't seem to have been the issue. And it's likely that there were other Christians soldiers like Julius, who didn't see a problem with killing for Rome.

However, even though Julius wielded the sword throughout his service, not everyone in Rome's military did. In fact, one expert historian said that a Roman soldier could have spent his entire career without striking a blow, except perhaps in a bar fight with his peers![43] Another historian noted that "once the soldier had been trained, he could look forward to a life which would be spent mainly in conditions of peace." He went on to say, "Many soldiers may never have been called upon to take part in a campaign."[44] Some military personnel served in what amounted to an office job.[45] Although every soldier had to be willing to fight, many never needed to. If a Christian served in the heart of the empire, for instance, he was much less likely to wield violence, compared to a soldier stationed on the edge of the empire.

Now, we have no clear evidence that Christians took only office jobs in the military. I'm showing only that Christians could have served without having to kill. Clearly some did kill. But perhaps others didn't. Maybe this is why in the *Apostolic Tradition* (that early-church manual) Christians were allowed to be soldiers as long as they didn't kill. Such allowance makes sense only if one could actually serve without killing.[46] Put simply, the presence of Christians in the military doesn't mean that they all disagreed with Tertullian that God prohibits "every sort of man-killing."

Despite the presence of Christians in the military, it is clear that no single Christian writer before Constantine sanctioned the use of violence, not even toward bad guys. Christian soldiers were not exempt (though not everyone listened). Whenever the issue of violence, killing, warfare, or joining the military was discussed, the voices of all extant early Christian writings were in agreement: Christians are never to kill.

So what happened after Constantine? Did a largely nonviolent church turn violent?

AFTER CONSTANTINE

We won't go into all the details, but it is true that Augustine (354–430, North Africa), Ambrose (330–397, Italy), and many other post-Constantinian theologians said that Christians may participate in just wars and kill under certain circumstances. However, even this position, though dominant, was not universal. Basil of Caesarea (330–379, Caesarea), for instance, said that Christians who killed in war should be excluded from taking Communion for three years.[47] Clearly, he had reservations toward bloodshed. Two different church manuals, the *Canons of Hippolytus* (336–340, Egypt) and *Testament of Our Lord* (400s, various regions), both prohibit Christian soldiers from killing—and they were used long after Constantine. Another fifth-century church order prohibits a soldier

from becoming a Christian unless he "leaves his robbery *and violence* …
otherwise, he shall be rejected."[48]

Two other leaders, Sulpicius Severus (363–425, modern France)
and Paulinus of Nola (354–431, Italy), expressed "certain hostility to
military service," and they did this "long after the danger of idolatry
had been removed."[49] In a letter to Boniface (Roman general and
governor), Augustine had to persuade him that Christians could be
soldiers: "Do not think that it is impossible for anyone to please
God while engaged in active military service."[50] If Augustine's views
were universally acknowledged, there would be no need to argue it.
Augustine himself, the so-called father of just war theory, showed less
zeal toward warfare and violence in his later years than in his earlier
writings. Whereas he used to celebrate it as part of a well-ordered
society, he later saw it as an unfortunate, though necessary, evil.[51]

Much more could be said about the post-Constantinian years.
Clearly, the dominant view among Christian writers after AD 313
was that Christians could be soldiers and that killing was allowed
under certain circumstances. But this certainly wasn't the only
position. There were at least some who were much more reluctant, maintaining the widespread pre-Constantinian position that
Christians should not kill under any circumstances.

THE BOTTOM LINE

Early-church writers, living in various parts of the empire, all agreed:
Christians should not kill. These writers didn't just condemn immoral
killing (abortion, murder, etc.), but all types of killing. Most of these
same writers didn't think Christians should serve in the military. But
even those who allowed converted soldiers to remain in the service

instructed them not to kill. This is because early Christians believed that enemy-love is the hallmark of Christianity. You can mock us. You can torture us. You can even throw us to wild beasts. But we will still love our enemies and pray for our persecutors.

And the church increased. Without the sword, the church spread. With no religious freedom, the church grew—like a mustard seed— shouldered by the stiff, persistent enemy-love of martyred saints.

The early church's view on this issue is not authoritative. Only the Bible is. Perhaps the widespread, diverse view of early Christian writers is wrong. All of them wrong. But their view should cause us to think about, perhaps question, why we believe what we believe about warfare and violence. When early Christian writers lived with a clear separation between church and state—the kingdom of Christ and the kingdom of Caesar—they didn't see killing for Rome (or killing for any reason) as compatible with enemy-love. "I do not recognize the empire of this world," said one early Christian named Speratus. "I acknowledge my Lord who is the emperor of kings and of all nations."[52] There are two kingdoms: the kingdom of Rome and the kingdom of Christ. Early Christians, like Speratus, chose the kingdom of Christ. Speratus refused to give his allegiance to Rome.

But when church and state became one, and the wars of Rome were waged under the banner of the cross, nonviolence became a minority view. I cannot help but think that this shift in perspective was due in part to the radical political and religious changes in the wake of Constantine's ascension—when nationalism became entangled with the Christian faith.

Speratus, by the way, "conquered" Rome in AD 180. That's the year he was martyred.

11

ATTACKER AT THE DOOR

But what do you do when someone breaks into your house to kill your family?

Before we answer this question, we need to revisit Calvary and linger there, pondering again that profound event where a crucified Jew turned the world inside out. Consider the cross in all its shame, foolishness, and power. Consider the call, the mandate, to take up our crosses and follow Him down the bloody road to victory, the suffering life that leads to resurrection. Only then will we be prepared to answer the attacker-at-the-door question in a way that's faithful to our King.

If you haven't been stunned by the radicalness of Jesus's ethic in Matthew 5, and by Paul's counter-intuitive demands of Romans 12, and by the shameful road we are called to walk according to 1 Peter 2; if you haven't begged God for waterfalls of grace to love your local rapist who is also your enemy and desperately needs Jesus; if you aren't perplexed at the power of martyrdom as the very means by which God conquers the Devil; if you aren't bewildered by Jesus's example and His insistence that you, too, turn the other cheek and never retaliate with evil for evil and forgive the one who's beating your face in—against all human logic, against all cultural norms, against our innate sense of justice—then the cross may not appear as scandalous as it should.

We serve a God who became a slave, a King born in a manger, a slaughtered Lamb who reigns from on high. We serve a Lord who was mocked, beaten, slapped, and whipped; who washed feet, forgave sins, and loved those who spat in His face. We worship a risen Savior, a glorified Messiah, the Son of God, who conquers evil and rules the nations. Calvary and the empty tomb are the lenses through which we must consider the attacker at the door.

Without the crucified Christ, nonviolence has little power. With Christ at the center, nonviolence conquers the world.

Several questions come up in discussions about Christians and violence. If we addressed them all, we'd have a really long book! So I've chosen to deal with just a few questions in order to work through them more thoroughly. I'll address some more in the next chapter.

Let me say up front that I don't consider my answers to these issues to be written in stone. Theologians and philosophers have wrestled with these questions for thousands of years, and I do not want to be so arrogant as to think that I have the perfect answers to them all. I don't. I'm fairly confident in some answers; others I go back and forth on. I'm on a journey. We're all on a journey. But with these questions, my goal is to be faithful to Jesus and the cruciform life He's called us to. It's not easy, and it certainly won't always make sense.

So what do you do when some guy with a gun is busting down your door and hollering that he wants to kill your family?

IN THE REAL WORLD

"You blow his head off, of course! Next question." This is how many Christians respond. And despite everything I've said in this book, there's a big part of me that wants to close my Bible, grab my shotgun, and just shoot the thug. The mere thought of someone harming my family stirs up something fierce. I can hardly describe it. But if the

Bible is God's Word, and if Jesus has been raised from the dead, then my response to this question demands that I strap on my biblical goggles to view this issue, even if it torments my intuition. My ultimate goal is to obey my Lord, not to kill people who threaten my family.

The attacker-at-the door question is often viewed as a theoretical situation in which there are two, and only two, choices: kill the killer or let him (it's always a man, right?) kill your family. Oftentimes the question is posed in such a way as to trap people committed to nonviolence into admitting that they're either inconsistent or heartless. I don't want to paint with too broad a brush, but in my experience, this question is often asked dismissively, as though the mere presentation of this one dilemma will expose the naïveté of the nonviolence position and bypass the need to do any serious biblical thinking.[1] So I'm not going to consider this question from a theoretical standpoint, because life is not theoretical. We live in the real world, where situations normally don't come down to only two options: to kill or let your family die. In real life, there are several things to consider.

First, how do you know he's going to kill your family? It's impossible to know if the attacker is 100 percent set on harming your family. In the real world, humans are moral agents who have breakable wills. The attacker is not pre-programmed to perform the worst possible evil at all cost. He's a human being made in the image of God. Even if he's screaming out, "I'm going to kill your family, and there's nothing you can do to stop me!" he could be blowing smoke so he can run off with your TV.

Second, are you 100 percent sure that God *won't* intervene? Unless God has whispered this in your ear, and you're 100 percent sure it was

God who whispered, you can't know this. I often hear Christians mock-
ingly say, "What, am I going to just sit there and pray?" But all this does
is expose that we don't believe in the power of prayer. Elijah prayed, and
the heavens were shut up for three and a half years; Hezekiah prayed,
and God intervened single-handedly to take care of 185,000 Assyrians
threatening to skin whole families alive. If the Bible means anything,
prayer is more powerful than ten thousand bullets to the head.

Third, what are the chances that your *attempt* to kill the attacker
will succeed? Realistically. Do you own a gun? Is it loaded? Are you a
good shot? Are you a better shot than your attacker? If you are such a
good shot, then why not shoot the gun out of his hand? Are you sure
that you won't miss and accidently blow off your own kid's head? In
the real world, that's a legitimate possibility, especially in the heat of
the moment.

Or what if you *thought* the attacker was trying to kill your
family, but he only wanted bread? So you fire and nick his shoulder—and *now* he's ticked. Only *now* is he going to kill your family,
even though he had no original intention of doing so. Your violent
response brought more harm on your family.

And not to open up a whole other can of worms, but most studies show that a gun kept in a home is far more likely to result in the
death of those inside the home than the death of an attacker seeking
to harm the family. No, I'm not for gun control. I own several guns,
and I'm not convinced that more laws will spare more lives. I'm only
trying to show that there are many factors involved *in the real world.*
It's not simply kill or be killed.[2]

Fourth, do you really think you could kill the attacker? Again, in
the theoretical situation, you're simply a robot who fires a weapon.

But in real life, most humans aren't hardwired to kill. My Navy SEAL friend Steve tells me that even snipers sometimes have a hard time pulling the trigger. Even when they do, they often have nightmares about killing even when it's seemingly justified. One of Steve's fellow snipers told him about a time when he shot and killed a terrorist running toward a group of US soldiers with a grenade. If some situations justify killing, this one is it. The terrorist would have died anyway! Still the sniper was tormented for many years for killing the person. And this was in war. He's a trained killer. But there's just something about killing—even "good" killing—that eats away at our humanity.

So back to your living room with the attacker at the door. Do you really think you *could* kill the man? Perhaps. But we should seriously consider the likelihood that you *wouldn't*, and therefore nonviolent attempts to restrain the attacker are much more realistic. Even if you think that killing the attacker is morally permissible, pursuing nonlethal attempts to stop the attacker might have a better chance at success.

I say all of this to show that nonviolence isn't as crazy as it's sometimes made out to be. But—and this is very important—success isn't the highest goal. Faithfulness is. So what would be the *most faithful*, Christlike response to the attacker at the door?

THE FAITHFUL RESPONSE

While this exact situation does not occur in the Bible, several related truths are clear. We know that Jesus never responded violently when threatened with evil and that His followers saw this as a pattern for Christians to follow.[3] We also know that Jesus never intervened with violence to stop the oppression of the innocent, and in first-century Palestine, there was plenty of oppression to stop. Is this an argument from silence? Not quite. On one occasion, a woman caught in adultery was about to be killed, and Jesus intervened nonviolently. He didn't resort to violence to stop the killers with stones.[4] Not an exact parallel, but it's fairly close. We also know that we are commanded to love our enemies, which would include the attacker at the door. Far from being an exception to Jesus's command, the attacker fits the role of "enemy" to a T.[5]

Suffering is the way of the cross,[6] which makes it the way of life for cross-bearing Christians. We have the hope of resurrection—our life and death in this world are only the beginning.[7] And throughout Scripture, we see God intervene to rescue people from harm when He desires to do so.[8] Through the power of prayer, we can tap into divine deliverance, as Psalm 18 so powerfully shows.

These are life-patterns, kingdom traits, the rhythm of how Christians are to live. So while Jesus doesn't directly address the attacker-at-the-door scenario, I'm not sure we need Him to. He has given us a framework of how to respond to evil. If we take all of this into consideration, it seems that the action most consistent with the New Testament is *not* to use lethal force to stop the attacker.

This doesn't mean that you shouldn't do anything. Quite the opposite. There are many different nonviolent ways to stop the attacker. These include *verbal resistance* (pleading, yelling, negotiating), *spiritual resistance* (praying, trusting God, witnessing), *sacrificial resistance* (taking the bullet), or even *physical resistance* (tackling, hitting, kicking).[9] Perhaps you're surprised that I'm describing hitting and kicking as nonviolent. But not all enforced pain is violent. It all depends on the intention. The doctor and the mugger both slash your skin with a knife, but only one is a violent act. Though some disagree, I think that one could forcefully resist without using violence. But intentionally killing the attacker would be an act of violence.

Now, perhaps as you read this, cynicism is welling up. "Yeah, right! Negotiate with the guy. Pray for him. What sort of fantasy world are you living in?" I'm living in a world ruled by Jesus. The fantasy world is one where Jesus is still in the tomb, prayer has no power, and violence is the only way to win.

Or what about showing your enemy unconditional love? In the fantasy world, this is absurd. But in the world ruled by Jesus, such love is infused with extraordinary power. There are countless stories about real-life situations where lethal force seemed like the only way to stop the attacker, and yet the victim chose to show radical love. My favorite is the story of a woman who awoke to the sound of a man coming through the window with a knife. As he approached her bed, she yelled out, "You can kill us, but first let me make you a cup of coffee." The man accepted the offer, and having slurped down his cup of joe, he decided not to kill.[10]

Now, I could go on for hundreds of pages about similar instances where nonviolence worked. But that's not the main point. Remember: *faithfulness*, not *effectiveness*. We need to respond in a way that is most faithful to Jesus, not in ways that seem to be the most effective. And if what I've said is correct, then nonviolent means of defending your family will be the most faithful.

I don't see how using lethal force to deal with your enemy resonates with the cadence of Christianity.

But is there anything in the New Testament that supports killing the attacker? Romans 13 is sometimes considered to sanction such killing. Using lethal force to defend your family is an extension of Romans 13, or so the logic goes. But we've already seen that Paul does not command the church to pick up the sword here. In fact, viewing the church as somehow an extension of the government's use of force goes against the grain of what Paul argues in Romans 12–13. If anything, Paul distances the church from the sword in Romans 12. The only command given to the church in Romans 13 is to submit to the government, not carry out divine vengeance mediated through the state. The Romans 13 argument isn't convincing.[11]

So are there no biblical grounds to use lethal force as a last resort to stop a killer?

THE LESSER OF TWO EVILS

There might be. I'm not totally convinced by this argument, but I want to lay it out as one possible option to use violence as a last resort. Again, the attacker-at-the-door scenario is a tough one, and I don't want to give the impression that I think it's easily solved. It's not. And even though I find the nonlethal response to be the most faithful to Scripture, I can see some biblical merit in using violence as a last resort as the *lesser of two evils*.[12] Let's unpack this argument.

So far, I've argued that killing is wrong and therefore killing the attacker is wrong. In other words, killing is a *moral absolute*: Christians should never do it. The same goes for all acts of obedience: fornication, greed, lying, and so on. But what happens when there is a moral conflict, when obeying one command means that you have to disobey another? The classic example, of course, is Corrie ten Boom, who lied to the Nazi authorities about hiding Jews. Lying is wrong, but when telling the truth would result in the death of innocent lives, Corrie ten Boom chose to lie as the lesser of two evils.

You may believe, as I do, that it's wrong for Christians to kill. But it's also wrong *not* to protect the innocent when you have it within your power to do so.[13] Or to use biblical terms, either you love your enemy (Matt. 5:44) or love your neighbor (22:39).[14] You have to choose one over the other, like the doctor in the emergency room who must decide whether to save the pregnant mother or her unborn child, when only one can be spared. To obey one law means disobeying another. You cannot obey both.

But aren't all laws equal? Not necessarily. Scripture affirms that some laws are higher than others—not all are of equal weight. For instance, Jesus talks about "weightier" matters of the Law (Matt. 23:23) and the "great[est] commandment" (22:36). He says that Judas committed a sin "greater" than Pilate's (John 19:11), and that one sin in particular is unforgivable, even though all others can be forgiven (Mark 3:29). Paul says that love is greater than faith and hope (1 Cor. 13:13; cf. John 15:13) and that some sins are worthy of excommunication (1 Cor. 5:1–13) or death (1 Cor. 11:30), which isn't true of other sins. John distinguishes between sin that leads to death and sins that don't lead to death (1 John 5:16–17).

Paul says that obedience to the government is actually obedience to God (Rom 13:2–3). But what happens when the government demands that you *disobey* God? When Peter and John face this exact situation, their response is "we must obey God rather than" the government (Acts 5:29; see also 4:19–20). Throughout the Old Testament, we read about various degrees of punishments for sins depending on their severity. Some sins, referred to as high-handed sins, are worthy of the death penalty, while others are not punished with the same severity.[15] Perhaps the clearest example of higher and lower laws is in Jesus's famed statement that the whole Law can be summed up in the greatest command of loving God and the second greatest of loving your neighbor (Matt. 22:36–40). Some laws, it seems, are considered higher than others.

There are other biblical examples where we seem to see a moral conflict at work. Here are just a few:

- Abraham is honored for being willing to kill his own son, even though both murder and child sacrifice are wrong. Of course, he doesn't go through with it, but the Bible considers our intentions on par with our actions (Gen. 22; Heb. 11:17–19).
- The Hebrew midwives lie to Pharaoh in order to save the lives of Hebrew babies, and they are commended for it. Saving innocent lives is the higher law (Exod. 1:15–21).
- Rahab lies to the authorities in order to save the lives of the Hebrew spies. Some say she is commended for her faith and not for her lie, but the Bible makes no such distinction—her faith is expressed through her lie. Again, saving lives is the higher law (Josh. 2:1–21; Heb. 11:31).
- David and his men take bread from the tabernacle even though they are not priests. Jesus Himself commends them for their actions. The

preservation of life overrules priestly law (1 Sam. 21:1–6; Matt. 12:1–8).

- Children are to obey their parents (Eph. 6:2), but if their parents ask them to worship idols, they are to disobey them. Not worshipping idols is the higher law; obeying parents is the lower law. When they conflict, children should obey the higher law.

So in the case of the attacker-at-the-door situation, if *not* using lethal force means that the attacker *will* kill innocent people, then saving innocent lives (higher law) by killing the attacker (disobeying a lower law) may well be the lesser of two evils. If this is true, the question then becomes, how do you know which law is the higher law? More specifically: Is loving your neighbor (your family) a higher law than loving your enemy?

This question is tougher to answer than you may think. The New Testament does place a high premium on loving your neighbor, which would include protecting your family. And throughout the Bible, the righteous are praised for coming to the aid of the oppressed. But loving our enemies is also a distinctive Christian virtue, one that separates Christianity from everybody else (Matt. 5:46–47), one that makes us perfect like the Father (5:48), one that showcases the heart of Jesus, who died for His enemies (Rom. 5:10–11).

Even if moral conflicts are real, it's not altogether clear in the hypothetical situation that loving your neighbor trumps loving your enemy. So to shoot the intruder, you would have to argue that neighborly love is higher than enemy-love, something that doesn't seem altogether clear.[16] In fact, Jesus redefines enemies as neighbors in Matthew 5. If you shoot your enemy, you've just killed your neighbor. And we're also left with that nagging truth that Jesus never endorses violence as a means of protecting the innocent. Since there's no proof that He did—and there were plenty of opportunities for Him to do so!—there's no proof that He would.

Therefore, killing the attacker as the lesser of two evils has some biblical merit, but it's not without its problems. But if you do take this route and kill your enemy, you should still explore how you can redeem the enemy-love command in this unfortunate situation. This may mean publicly mourning his death, paying for the attacker's funeral, or giving his family a generous financial gift. Perhaps you could set up a college fund for his kids, who are now without a father, even if it means that you have to get an extra job to do so. None of this will bring him back to life, but we must be salt and light so that the onlooking world sees that there's something different about us. Shooting enemies is not what we're about. We love our enemies because we were once God's enemies. We were the attacker at the door who crucified His Son, and He didn't shoot us. And even if we killed our enemy as the lesser of two evils, it's still a horrific incident. We don't cherish the death of our enemies.

WHAT ABOUT HITLER?

Even though Hitler has been dead for more than sixty years, this question often comes up in discussions.[17] The assumption seems to be that nonviolence may be effective in some cases, but with the really tough thugs, a good old-fashioned bullet to the head is the only way to deal with them. Hitler is always the case in point for this, and with the discussion of killing Hitler comes the example of Bonhoeffer.

Dietrich Bonhoeffer was a well-known German pastor, theologian, and pacifist who took part in a plot to kill Hitler. The plan failed, and Bonhoeffer was executed, but his attempt shows that even pacifists believe that in some cases killing a dictator is a necessary evil. While many Christians celebrate Bonhoeffer's attempt, Bonhoeffer himself didn't. He believed that killing Hitler was a sin. He just didn't know what else to do—call it the lesser of two evils.[18] Now, it's actually debated whether Bonhoeffer embraced a lesser-of-two-evils ethic, and his involvement in the assassination attempt is unclear.[19] But even if he was ready to pull the trigger, he was *tormented by the decision.* So I appreciate Bonhoeffer's struggle between his belief that killing is evil and his desire to stop widespread oppression. If I had been in his shoes and had the opportunity to kill Hitler, knowing what we know now about the ovens of Auschwitz, I would have had a really tough time wrestling with the issue, as Bonhoeffer did. Killing Hitler wasn't a no-brainer for Bonhoeffer, and it shouldn't be for us. We can learn a lot from Bonhoeffer.

Trying to kill Hitler may seem like an obvious way to stop such evil. In reality, though, Bonhoeffer's attempt failed and ended up strengthening Hitler's "paranoid determination to fight to the last drop of blood."[20] Therefore, the attempt to kill Hitler led to the loss of more innocent lives. Once again, we have to leave our theoretical classroom and visit the real world, where using violence to stop evil can backfire and lead to more innocent deaths.

Now, if we apply the lesser-of-two-evils approach to Hitler, one could make a case for killing him to save innocent lives. But in situations like this—dictators, evil nations—the situation is much more complex. We're not dealing with an individual attacker trying to kill your family. With Hitler and other dictators, there is a whole web of evil at work, and unraveling the many layers of wickedness can get messy. How many innocent lives will be murdered in the process?

And what makes Hitler worthy to be assassinated, while other wicked people should be spared? Is it because Hitler was responsible for killing six million Jews? What about the doctor who has aborted a hundred babies? Should we shoot him, too? Or the pilot who dropped an atomic bomb on a hundred thousand innocent civilians in Japan? How do we determine who makes the cut for our assassination list? Do we really want to start down the road of killing bad people to save good people? It certainly doesn't resonate with the rhythm of the kingdom, where loving bad people is the texture of life.

Or what about those who actively support evil dictators? Here's where it gets really messy, especially if you're a citizen of the United States. In the last sixty years, the US government has been responsible for empowering—sometimes single-handedly—several dictators around the world, including General Pinochet of Chile, the shah of Iran, Ferdinand Marcos of the Philippines, Duvalier of Haiti, General Noriega of Panama, and the brutal Mobutu Sese Seko of Zaire. America has also brought down several democratically elected leaders in Iran (1953), Guatemala (1954), Ecuador (1962, 1963), the Dominican Republic (1963), Brazil (1964), Indonesia (1965), Greece (1965–67), Chile (1973), and others. If you add up all the civilians who have been killed as a result of such US-backed evil, the number comes very close to the number of Jews killed by Hitler in the holocaust—six million.[21] Given its track record, the United States has no right to condemn Hitler while supporting many "Hitlers" behind the scenes. And if it's okay to kill a dictator, then one could make a good case that those who put him there should also be killed. But before you head off to bomb Langley, Virginia, we need to head back to Scripture and see if Jesus would have killed Hitler. There were certainly no shortages of dictator-like leaders in the first century, yet we have no record of assassination attempts by Christians.

I don't think that Christians should run around killing dictators, nor do I think the church should bomb the CIA headquarters. God has dealt with evil on the cross and will judge evil when Christ returns. And He has not commissioned Christians to carry out His judgment today.

I do think, however, that the Christian church can and should fight against such evil. Many assume that killing is the only way to confront wicked people, but this is terribly mistaken. A quick glance at the last hundred years will show that many dictators have been successfully fought—some taken down—through nonviolent means. For instance, the first Russian revolution in 1905 gained its initial traction through nonviolence. When it turned violent, its success began to wane. Germans in the Ruhr Valley resisted French invasion through nonviolent campaigns in 1925. Gandhi fought nonviolently against injustice in India.

Nonviolent action, in fact, had a good measure of success against the Nazis. We know of at least three different successful nonviolent campaigns against the Nazi persecution of Jews in Denmark, Bulgaria, and even Berlin. Remarkably, nearly every one of Bulgaria's forty-eight thousand Jews was saved from Hitler's regime—saved through nonviolence. And then there was the underground movement led by pacifists André and Magda Trocmé in the small town of Le Chambon, France. The valiant couple rallied together several people to provide safe houses for Jews. Between 1941 and 1944, more than 3,500 Jews were saved from the Nazis. Saved without violence.

But that's not all. The citizens of El Salvador removed a militant dictator in 1944 through nonviolent means. African-Americans in the South won back their civil rights through a movement based on nonviolence. Nonviolent campaigns in the Philippines ousted the American-backed dictator in 1986. Other nonviolent campaigns toppled dictators in Poland, Czechoslovakia (the Velvet Revolution of 1989), East Germany (the Revolution of the Candles), Lithuania, Liberia, Finland, Estonia, Hungry, and Bulgaria. Even the brutal genocide in the former Yugoslavia saw some success in nonviolent campaigns that nearly brought down the dictator Milosevic. But these campaigns were halted when NATO began carpet bombing the country.[22]

It's historically inaccurate to say that nonviolence can't work against extreme forms of evil. It can. And it has.

It's equally inaccurate to say that violence is the only way to deal with extreme evil. This is the route people usually take, but—sorry for the cynicism—how's that working so far? World War I ultimately brought about World War II. World War II led into the Cold War. The Cold War spawned all sorts of evil regimes and horrific conflicts. Desert Storm led to Operation Iraqi Freedom, and so on and so forth. Those who think nonviolence doesn't work (even though it often does) need to admit that violence isn't always the most successful way to deal with evil. It is not as if violence is a tried-and-true way to fight evil or establish peace. The cynical question "Can nonviolence *really* work?" has a log in its own eye.

But we're getting off track. Again, our mission as the church is to be faithful, not just effective. One could argue that Jesus's ministry wasn't very effective. Sure, many people were healed, and some ended up following Him. But at the end of His life, His chief leader denied Him, His treasurer betrayed Him, His followers deserted Him, the crowds turned against Him, and His government wrongly convicted Him of treason and nailed Him to a cross. Viewed from one angle, Jesus's entire ministry of peace was a colossal failure.

But the resurrection changed everything for Him. And the resurrection changed everything for us. We no longer view the world through the dim mist of justice and reward, but through the bright lens of resurrection, where suffering leads to glory and slaughtered lambs rule the earth. Therefore, even if we fail to bring down dictators, our rock-solid hope is that God will take care of dictators in His own way, and He will carry out perfect vengeance in the end. God can use human agents to carry out His wrath on evil even today (Rom. 13:4), but nowhere in the New Testament does God use *the church* to be an agent of wrath. We are commanded unequivocally to love our enemies and trust that God will judge the wicked in His own timing.

SHOULD A GOVERNMENT HAVE A MILITARY?

One question that often comes up whenever I talk about nonviolence is this: Do you think America should have a military? A related one is this: Should our government turn the other cheek?[23]

To answer this, we have to recognize that the New Testament is not meant to tell secular governments how to operate. Greg Boyd said it well: "God doesn't expect governments to conform to the same standard of love and nonviolence He expects of disciples of Jesus."[24] After all, people are unable to conform to God's will unless they are in Christ and have the Spirit (Rom. 8:5–16). Outside of Christ, they are dead in sin (Eph. 2:1–3), which is why Paul has no interest in judging those outside the body (1 Cor. 5:12).[25] The nations will act like the nations.

Neither does the New Testament show much interest in the politics of the day. We are to submit to the governing bodies, pray for them, and pay our taxes. But the kingdom of God is not commanded to make the kingdom of Rome more moral. Interestingly, whenever Jesus was lured into political debates, He always "transformed these kingdom-of-the-world questions into kingdom-of-God questions and turned them back on His audience (Matt. 22:15–22; Luke 12:13–15)."[26] That's because our mission is not to solve all the world's problems but to embody and proclaim the kingdom of God *as* the place where those problems are solved.

So do I think America *should* have a military? It all depends on what we mean by "should." If we mean "can," then sure. They can have a military. Or they can choose not to have a military. For citizens of God's kingdom, the question is a moot one, because militaries don't advance the kingdom of God—and neither can they stop it. The New Testament doesn't say that Rome should or shouldn't have a military. That's because the New Testament isn't concerned with advancing Rome's kingdom. Rather, it tells us how to advance God's kingdom. God doesn't command America to have a military, nor does He command it to get rid of its military.

I therefore disagree with Wayne Grudem, who thinks that "military weapons for governments are God-ordained" or that "because of the great military power of the United States, we also carry a great deal of responsibility for maintaining world peace," or even that *superior military weaponry* in the hands of a nation that protects freedom ... *is a good thing for the world*."[27] Such statements are wrongheaded, if not bizarre. World peace comes through Jesus—the One who doesn't need a military to rule the world.

Should governments turn the other cheek? Sure, that'd be great. If all governments turned the other cheek, there'd be a whole lot less violence in the world. But that's not the solution to evil in the world. Jesus is the solution to evil in the world. And trying to follow Jesus's teaching without following Jesus is ultimately bankrupt. The command to turn the other cheek is directly connected to the person and work of Christ, who turned the other cheek when attacked by sinners.

Having said this, I think there's a place for the church to hold the government to a standard of morality that may lessen evil in the world. It's part of our duty to seek the good of the city, as Jeremiah says (29:7). But our hope does not lie in enforcing our ethic upon secular governments. We can't legislate the kingdom of God into existence. We could end all wars, yet Satan would simply find another way to destroy us. He could use world peace to make us think we don't need Jesus. Our hope and victory lie in the crucified Lamb. Jesus is the solution to war and violence.

12

QUESTIONS AND OBJECTIONS

In the course of writing this book, I tried my best to listen to all the objections and questions that came up. Through blogs, tweets, conversations, Facebook, and email exchanges, I would often ask what objections people had to Christian nonviolence. I addressed some of these in chapter 11, and I will address a few more here. Some questions are biblical—certain passages seem to contradict my view—while others are more situational, like the attacker at the door. I can't address all the quandaries that may be swimming around in your head, but I'll try to answer the most salient ones I've encountered.

VIOLENT JESUS?

I've argued that Jesus never acted violently toward His oppressors, whether to spare Himself, to rescue innocent people, or to confront evil, nor did He allow His followers to do so. However, there are two passages that many believe contradict my view. The first one is the temple cleansing.

The event is recorded in all four gospels, and it's usually brought up as evidence that even Jesus acted violently on occasion.[1] As the story goes, Jesus enters the temple and drives out all the money changers. If you look at the story in Matthew, Mark, and Luke, nothing suggests that Jesus acted violently in driving them out. The gospel of John, however, seems to suggest that Jesus used violence when He tossed out the moneychangers:

> In the temple he found those who were selling oxen and sheep and pigeons, and the money-changers sitting there. And making a whip of cords, he drove them all out of the temple, with the sheep and oxen. And he poured out the coins of the money-changers and overturned their tables. (2:14–15)

I've used the ESV translation here, but it's not quite accurate. It says that Jesus made "a whip of cords" to drive "them all out of the temple" and then it says "*with* the sheep and oxen." This is where confusion sets in. The ESV implies that Jesus used the whip to drive out *the people* along with the animals. The only problem is that the word *with* is not in the Greek.[2] This may seem insignificant, but it's not. Try reading my literal translation:

> And making a whip of cords, he drove *them all* out of the temple, *the sheep and oxen.*

When you read the Greek more literally, you see that the "them all" that Jesus drove out refers to the "sheep and oxen." Jesus drove out the animals with the whip, not the people. I guess Jesus could have lacerated a few money changers along the way, but the text doesn't say this. None of the gospels say that Jesus acted with violence in the temple cleansing. So this story doesn't give us license to respond violently.

The second passage that comes up is Luke 22:

> And he said to them, "When I sent you out with
> no moneybag or knapsack or sandals, did you lack
> anything?" They said, "Nothing." He said to them,
> "But now let the one who has a moneybag take it,
> and likewise a knapsack. And let the one who has
> no sword sell his cloak and buy one. For I tell you
> that this Scripture must be fulfilled in me: 'And he
> was numbered with the transgressors.' For what is
> written about me has its fulfillment." And they said,
> "Look, Lord, here are two swords." And he said to
> them, "It is enough." (vv. 35–38)

Jesus tells them to go buy a sword, and lo and behold, two of them (probably Peter and Simon the Zealot) have swords already: "Look, Lord, here are two swords." Jesus ends the discussion with a curious phrase: "It is enough." Which raises the question: Enough for what?

I've heard some people say this passage proves that Jesus advocated for violence in self-defense. This has always struck me as odd, since two swords for eleven disciples are not enough for self-defense, especially if they go out two by two as they did before. Also, nowhere else does Jesus allow for violence in self-defense. Quite the opposite, according to Matthew 5 and Luke 6.

Just to see if I was the only one who had problems with the self-defense view, I looked at ten of the most respected commentators on Luke—many of whom definitely *aren't* pacifists—to see if I was all alone. I wasn't. Of the ten, I found only one who took the self-defense view. And he didn't give any scriptural support for this view.

There is little—if any—support from the text that Jesus all of a sudden advocates for violence in self-defense.

If self-defense isn't the point, then what does Jesus mean when He tells His disciples to buy a sword? Most scholars offered one of two interpretations. Some thought Jesus is speaking symbolically here. New Testament scholar I. Howard Marshall said that the command to buy a sword is "a call to be ready for hardship and self-sacrifice."[3] Darrell Bock of Dallas Seminary said the command to buy a sword symbolically "points to readiness and self-sufficiency, not revenge."[4] And the popular Reformed commentator William Hendriksen put it bluntly: "The term *sword* must be interpreted figuratively."[5] So when Jesus tells them to buy a sword, He is speaking figuratively about imminent persecution. According to this interpretation, when the disciples eagerly reveal that they already have two swords, they misunderstand Jesus's figurative language (this isn't the first time). When Jesus sees that His disciples misunderstand Him, He ends the dialogue with, "It is enough," which means something like "enough of this conversation."

This interpretation makes good sense in light of the context. But there's another interpretation that I think does slightly more justice to the passage.

Notice that right after Jesus says, "Buy a sword," he quotes Isaiah 53:12, which predicts that Jesus will be "numbered with the transgressors" (Luke 22:37). Then the disciples reveal that they already have two swords, to which Jesus says, "It is enough." Now, Rome crucifies only those who are a potential threat to the empire. For Jesus to be crucified, Rome has to convict Him as a potential revolutionary. And this is the point of the swords. With swords in their possession, Jesus and His disciples will be viewed as potential revolutionaries, and Jesus will therefore fulfill Isaiah 53 to be *numbered with other (revolutionary) transgressors*. If Rome doesn't have any legal grounds to incriminate Jesus, there will be no crucifixion.

This interpretation captures the meaning of Isaiah 53 and the flow of Jesus's ethical teaching. Up until Luke 22, Jesus has prohibited His followers from using violence, even in self-defense. Is Jesus now changing His mind by telling His followers to use the sword in self-defense? It seems better to take His command to buy a sword as we have suggested: Jesus is providing Rome with evidence to put Him on the cross.

So we could view Jesus's command as a figurative expression about their coming suffering or as a way of ensuring His own crucifixion. Either way, it's highly unlikely that Jesus encourages violent self-defense here. In fact, just a few verses later, Peter wields one of the two swords, and Jesus rebukes him: "No more of this!" (Luke 22:51). Peter, along with some interpreters, has misunderstood Jesus's previous command to buy a sword.

Whatever Jesus means by His command to buy a sword, it doesn't seem that He intends it to be used for violence.

VIOLENT MESSIAH?

In chapter 5, I mentioned several passages in the Old Testament that predict a peace-bringing Messiah. But we also need to take into account several other Old Testament passages that predict a violent Messiah: Psalm 2, Isaiah 11, and Psalm 110 are among the most grisly predictions. "I will make the nations your heritage" and "you shall break them with a rod of iron," writes the author of Psalm 2.

Isaiah 11 says that the Messiah will slay the wicked. These certainly don't sound like the Jesus of the Gospels, who neither wields a rod of iron nor slaughters wicked people. The question then is how, or when, are these predictions fulfilled?

The answer is twofold. First, the Messiah conquers the spiritual forces of evil in His first coming. Second, He will judge all enemies in His second coming. The violent predictions, therefore, apply to one of these two events—defeating spiritual forces (first coming) or judging all the wicked (second coming). But Jesus does not slaughter His human enemies in His first coming, and neither does He commission His followers to do so.

Take Psalm 110:1, for instance. If there ever was a picture of a violent Messiah, this is it: "Sit at my right hand, until I make your enemies your footstool." The psalm goes on to say that the Messiah "will execute judgment among the nations, filling them with corpses" and "shatter chiefs over the wide earth" (v. 6). So when did (or will) Jesus do this? Well, the New Testament often quotes Psalm 110:1 to show that Jesus defeated His *spiritual enemies*.[6] For instance, Paul quotes Psalm 110:1 in 1 Corinthians 15:24–26 to prove that Jesus conquered the spiritual forces of evil through His resurrection—a victory that will be clearly acknowledged at His second coming. Paul, in other words, quotes from this *violent messianic* text but *does not* understand it in terms of Jesus destroying human enemies.

Now, sometimes such violent Old Testament texts *are* used to depict Christ's final judgment over all enemies at this return. Isaiah 11 and Psalm 2 are both quoted throughout Revelation to describe this event.[7] But again, Revelation doesn't depict Jesus hacking His way through enemy lines but rather speaking a word of judgment that condemns His enemies to everlasting destruction.[8]

The portraits of a violent Messiah in the Old Testament are taken up and reinterpreted by New Testament authors to refer to Jesus's defeat of spiritual forces (first coming)[9] or future judgment over the wicked (second coming). And in either case, violent messianic prophecies do nothing to validate the church's use of violence.

DOES THE BIBLE ENDORSE CAPITAL PUNISHMENT?

Another question that often gets raised is whether the Bible endorses capital punishment. I don't think it does. Or at least, I think that the word *endorse* is too strong. First, let's summarize the biblical support for capital punishment.

The first time capital punishment is mentioned is in Genesis 9:5–6:

> And for your lifeblood I will require a reckoning:
> from every beast I will require it and from man.
> From his fellow man I will require a reckoning for
> the life of man.
>
> Whoever sheds the blood of man,
>   by man shall his blood be shed,
> for God made man in his own image.

We discussed this verse in chapter 2 and noted some of its ambiguity. It does seem that God allows humans to carry out the death penalty for murder. And later on in the Old Testament, the death penalty becomes a punishment for all sorts of high-handed crimes. But even in the Old Testament, the death penalty isn't absolute— there are a lot of murderers whom God doesn't sentence to death (Cain, Moses, David, etc.). The big question, however, is whether the New Testament endorses this Old Testament law.

The main New Testament passage that could be understood as endorsing capital punishment is Romans 13:4, which says that the government is

> God's servant for your good. But if you do wrong,
> be afraid, for he does not bear the sword in vain.
> For he is the servant of God, an avenger who carries
> out God's wrath on the wrongdoer.

As we saw earlier, Romans 13 does not command the government to use the sword; it acknowledges only that it does and shows that God can use secular governments to carry out His wrath. Therefore, Romans 13 does not strictly *endorse* capital punishment in the sense that governments are disobeying God if they don't institute it. If a government decided to love its enemies instead of killing them, I can't imagine Jesus saying, "No, no! Don't do that! Here, take my sword ..." But neither does Romans 13 nor the New Testament as a whole condemn the state's use of capital punishment. That's probably because the New Testament isn't an ethical guide for secular governments, but an authoritative summons to join a cruciform kingdom.

So how should the church feel about capital punishment?

If we take what Paul says in Romans 12–13 seriously, then the church should neither celebrate nor condemn the state's use of the sword.

God uses governments to carry out vengeance on evildoers. But if I were to vote on it, I'd probably vote against capital punishment, since I would rather see my enemy redeemed than killed—not to mention all the problems with the current systems of implementing the death penalty in the states where it is still legal.[10] Again, Romans 13 doesn't say that God *needs* capital punishment to judge evildoers. He can do that single-handedly. It only says that He can (and does) use the sword to judge the wicked. Regardless of what sort of punishment an evildoer receives or doesn't receive in this life, he or she will meet God's perfect justice in the end.

And from God's perspective, the wages of sin is death, which means that we all—even you—have already been convicted of capital crimes in God's courtroom and have been given the death penalty. It would be odd—some would say hypocritical—for Christians to thank God for taking *their* death penalty and then spin around to celebrate the death of someone they think is worse than them.

One Christian website uses the example of Jeffrey Dahmer as proof that some criminals need to be killed.[11] Dahmer, as you may recall, was one of the most twisted men to walk the planet. He killed, had sex with, dismembered, and then ate portions of seventeen people (in that order). Instead of getting the death penalty, Dahmer was locked up for life. And the Christian who published this website lamented Dahmer's light sentence. But what he forgot to mention is that while in prison, Dahmer came to Christ. All of the evidence points to his conversion being genuine, which means that Dahmer's death penalty was actually satisfied by Jesus. The Christian who authored the website, the one who wished Dahmer's death, will hang out with Dahmer in paradise whether he likes it or not. Won't that be an interesting conversation! Dahmer is a clear example that even the most deranged murderers can be conquered by God's grace.

Jesus endured the death penalty in the place of His enemies who deserve the death penalty—in order to give us undeserved life. We should learn to view the death penalty less politically and more theologically. When we do, it becomes tough to endorse.

SHOULD A CHRISTIAN SERVE IN THE MILITARY?

Whenever I ask this question to Christians who have served in the military, I get a mixed response. The most confident and somewhat blunt answer I've received was from my good friend and student Bob Armstrong. Everyone at my college knows Bob. That's because Bob is not your typical college student. He's eighty-five years old and has been a Christian for only six years. And Bob served as a Marine in three different wars: World War II, Korea, and Vietnam. He received a Purple Heart from Korea after a bullet ripped through his shoulder and out the other side. He's also among the few humans who have witnessed an atomic bomb explode while testing protective clothing in the deserts of Nevada. As you might suspect, the clothing didn't work, but unlike his partner, who died of stomach cancer, Bob hasn't suffered visible effects of radiation. Bob's been through a lot. And Bob knows war.

After Bob became a Christian at seventy-nine, his view of war radically changed. Bob attended the first class I ever taught at Eternity Bible College. It was a course on ethics, and we discussed Christians and warfare extensively. Here I was, a young professor talking about war to a vet who had served his country in three of them. Needless to say, I was nervous. I tried not to come down too hard against war because I assumed that he believed war was justified. But I was pleasantly shocked at his view. "War is evil. There should be no war," Bob declared in his candid style. He even protested my use of a "four views on war" book that I assigned the class. "There's only one *Christian* view on war. War is wrong."

I recently sat down with Bob over breakfast to talk about Christians in the military.[12] I asked Bob, "Do you think Christians should join the military?"

"No!" Bob blurted out. "Jesus Christ said, 'Thou shalt not kill.'"

"But," I pushed back, "what if a Christian wanted to serve his country?"

"You can serve your country in many ways, but in war you have to shoot people. And Christians shouldn't shoot people."

Bob's negative view of Christians in the military has a practical side to it. On two occasions he was used by the military as human bait to draw out enemy fire. From his experience, he doesn't think soldiers *serve* their country; he thinks soldiers are *used* by their country. But it was his newfound faith in Jesus that had the greatest effect in reconfiguring his view on war and violence. Simply put: Jesus commanded Christians not to kill.

I agree with Bob, though it's better to hear it from him than me. There's just something about the perspective of an old vet with a Purple Heart that carries more weight than that of a college professor who's read a lot of books. But if what I've said thus far is true to Scripture, then I would say that Christians should not serve as combatants in the military, because—to use Bob's words—Christians shouldn't shoot people.

However, I think Christians can serve in the military as non-combatants. I believe the kingdom of God should unleash its citizens into all areas of life to be agents of peace, healing, reconciliation, and forgiveness. What better place to do this than in the military? Cooks, nurses, doctors, psychologists, chaplains—these can be strategic positions to mediate the love of Christ in a place where it's greatly needed. I have a few Christian friends who are chaplains and psychologists in the military, and the opportunities to offer the healing power of Jesus are plentiful. And at least in these positions, they aren't required to kill. Chaplains aren't even allowed to carry a gun. If you can live like Christ in the military, then do it.

Now, to show that Christians can fight as combatants, some will point to the New Testament stories about soldiers getting saved—the centurion in Matthew 8, or Cornelius in Acts 10–11. But as I pointed out in chapter 10, these stories do not endorse their vocation, and they certainly don't sanction killing in war. All they do is show that some soldiers got saved. Nothing further is said about their vocation, and we can assume that Jesus would hold them to the same radical ethic heralded in His Sermon on the Mount.

I cannot find any biblical passage that sanctions a Christian serving as a combatant for a nation's military in a situation where he or she may take another person's life in the event of war. But I should be clear that I don't view non-Christian soldiers any differently than I do non-Christian doctors, construction workers, lawyers, or people in any other vocation. At the end of the day, all people need the love of Jesus. And Jesus loves soldiers.

SHOULD CHRISTIANS KILL IN SELF-DEFENSE?

Interestingly, many famous theologians, such as Augustine, who were okay with killing in war believed that a Christian should not kill in self-defense.[13] This view is less prevalent today. Most people assume that if someone is trying to kill you, you are justified in killing that person. But does the Bible support this?

In every instance where the New Testament portrays or discusses someone facing a personal physical threat, there is no clear allowance to use violence to defend oneself. Again, as we've seen throughout the New Testament, Christians are to follow their Lord in *not* violently resisting evil people, in turning the other check, in going the extra mile, and in never retaliating with evil for evil. These are all personal attacks. There is nothing in the New Testament that advocates self-defense, yet many passages place great value on suffering when wrongfully attacked.

If you are a Christian and somebody kills you, what do you lose, anyway? "To die," says Paul, "is gain" (Phil. 1:21). We are guaranteed resurrection life, and our attacker is given an opportunity—like Jeffrey Dahmer—to accept this gift. If an attacker kills me because I refused to use violence, thereby imitating my resurrected Lord, I cannot see how this would be a bad thing.[14]

Now, this doesn't mean I can't use physical force to restrain my attacker. Not all force is violent. Violence is "the use of physical force intending to destroy another person," and there are many ways in which I can try to restrain an attacker without resorting to violence. Although this is a tough issue and I hope I never face it, I pray that I would have the moral courage not to end the life of my enemy in order to prolong mine.

SHOULD A CHRISTIAN BE A POLICE OFFICER?

This is a tough question, one which so-called pacifists don't agree on.[15] For me, this question is especially difficult. Not only was my father in the LAPD for seventeen years, but I always said that if I hadn't become a Bible teacher I would have joined the LAPD myself. I have good friends and fellow church members who are police officers, and I have great respect for them.

To answer this question, we must begin with the commitment that if any vocation demands we do something unchristian, then we *must* obey Jesus and not our vocation. If a law firm *demanded* that its lawyers lie, then a Christian should not work for that firm. If a used-car dealer demanded that its salespeople lie about the quality of the cars, then Christians who work there should resist. And if a business owner demanded that you cheat your customers, then as a Christian you should not comply. So the question is not so much, "Can a Christian be a police officer?" but, "Can a Christian obey Jesus while serving on the police force?" We must submit all of our vocations to the lordship of Christ.

So, if carrying out your duties as a police officer demands that you disobey Jesus, then no, a Christian should not be a police officer. The big question, of course, is whether a Christian can use violence as a police officer.

No, I don't think he or she can. If violence is a sin, and if Christians shouldn't sin, then Christians shouldn't use violence as part of any vocation.

But we should point out that not all types of policing require the use of violence or lethal force. In fact, when the police force first came into existence in the early nineteenth century, officers were unarmed.[16] It wasn't until later that the police officers in America began to carry firearms. Today, police in England, Scotland, and other countries still don't carry firearms. That's because the heart of what it means to be a police officer is to keep the peace by "protecting the good and restraining evil with a minimum amount of force."[17] Killing criminals is not—or shouldn't be—the goal of the police force, even if it could possibly happen.[18]

Inasmuch as police officers seek peace, protect the innocent, and work for the good of society, certainly a Christian can take part. But what if an officer *must* kill a criminal?

Here is where the rubber meets the road. As I studied how others have dealt with this issue, I was surprised to find several well-known pacifists who said that Christians can be police officers even if a situation arises in which he or she has to kill someone. George Fox, the founder of the pacifistic Quaker movement, believed that a Christian could take part in the just use of the "sword" by the state (Rom. 13:4), which includes policing. John Howard Yoder, probably the most prolific pacifist of the twentieth century, didn't give a straightforward yes to the question, but he did say that a Christian would require "special justification" for his desire to be a cop.[19] He didn't clearly rule it out.

I agree with Fox, Yoder, and others that Christians may serve in the police force. But I don't agree that they should kill. How could I? If Christians shouldn't kill, then Christian police officers shouldn't kill. One's vocation doesn't change the ethical standard. Jesus's Sermon on the Mount transcends all vocations. So if a police officer is called upon to kill someone whom Jesus would not have him kill, then he must put away the sword and follow Jesus—even if it costs him his job. Again, if you believe that Christians should not kill, not even their enemies, then Christian police officers should not kill their enemies.[20] The only credible argument that *may* justify a Christian's use of lethal force would be that "lesser of two evils" argument I gave previously. But I have my doubts about whether this *best* reflects the cruciform life of Jesus.

George Fox and others use Romans 13 to justify a Christian's use of the sword. After all, I argued in chapter 8 that God's use of the state's sword here has to do more with policing than with soldiering (though in Roman times, the two weren't always distinguished). So one could make the following argument: God allows governments to have a police force, and God allows Christians to work for the government; therefore, God allows Christians to work for the police force and carry out God's vengeance on evildoers. This logic appears sound, except for one crucial detail, which we've discussed before: God *contrasts* the church's peaceful posture with the state's use of the sword in Romans 12–13. To say that a Christian can wield the government's sword cuts against the grain of Paul's actual argument.

But we should recognize that it's rare for a cop to actually kill someone. In 2012, there were 583 people killed by police officers in America. In the same year, however, there were over three thousand texting-while-driving-related deaths. You are five times more likely to kill someone by texting behind the wheel than a cop is while on duty. In the seventeen years that my father served in the LAPD, including the Watts riots of 1965, he was forced to kill only one person in the line of duty. This doesn't change the ethical dilemma, but it does put it in perspective. There's a good chance that you could serve as a police officer your entire life and never be faced with the ethical dilemma of killing. But if you are faced with it, you would either need to refrain from killing or argue that killing is sometimes okay as the lesser of two evils.

I wonder if being a Christian police officer could actually be an effective witness to the gospel. A Christian officer who protests unjust violence, publicly loves and forgives his or her enemy, resists retaliation or vengeance, and mediates God's grace to the innocent and oppressed could be a brighter light in a dark world than the hard-line pacifist who protests police work from the sidelines while still calling 911 when a criminal breaks into his or her house.[21] Christian police officers have a unique opportunity to be salt and light in a dark world. You've probably heard horrible stories of police brutality, racism, and other abuses of power. Christian police officers could model a better way and confront such evil where it exists—even at the risk of losing their jobs or being ostracized by their peers. I would find this commendable. We need to pursue every vocation with a view of furthering God's kingdom and carrying out the Great Commission. Being a police officer would present great challenges to this pursuit, and many Christians lack the moral strength to do so. But I find it hard to say that no Christian should ever be an officer. However, if their duties push them to disobey Jesus, then they must obey their Lord at the risk of losing their job.

I know what you're thinking. This sounds like a double standard. What's the difference between being a police officer, where you may have to kill, and serving as a military combatant? Although there's some overlap, there are also some key differences.[22] These differences aren't so much Christian as they are political, but they are still worth considering.

First, if a police officer finds himself or herself in the rare situation where he or she is forced to kill, such violence is subject to scrutiny by the authorities and sometimes by civilian review boards. The justice system is not perfect (I live in Simi Valley, the home of the Rodney King trial), but it does offer more protection against unjust killing than wartime proceedings do.

Second, in war, the line between good and evil is blurred. One nation is defending itself while the other nation is also defending itself. But in the police force, the line between the offender and the offended is often clearer.

Third, while police are trained to apprehend with minimum force necessary, soldiers are trained to kill. The very mission of the military is radically different from that of the police force—even if some police officers wrongly act like soldiers.

And fourth, violence in warfare is more broad and indiscriminate. Civilians are always killed in war, cities are always destroyed, and infrastructures are always crippled. But in policing, the killing of innocent people is extremely rare.

Again, I don't give these reasons to justify killing as a police officer, but to show only that the potential violence in policing is different in kind from the violence in war.

BACK TO THE POINT

I was hesitant to discuss such specific examples and potential exceptions. By diving into these examples and even sharing my own views,

I know that I'm opening myself up to criticism, and I run the risk of taking the focus off the heartbeat of the biblical teaching on nonviolence. I decided to include these sections, however, because theology needs to be played out in the real world. It's not enough to declare ourselves nonviolent followers of Jesus; we have to be ready to pursue the implications of that decision in every area of life. You may not agree with my stance on each of these issues, but my hope is that my thinking will help you examine these questions for yourself and will provide a model of Christian thinking for you to follow.

And this means that it's time to get back to the main point. While the exceptions are often what captivate us most, we have to remember that exceptions are, well, exceptions. These are the difficult cases that must be wrestled with, but they don't change the overall tone of Scripture, nor should they set the agenda for how we are to understand nonviolence.

So let's refocus. Let's finish this study by returning to that place where two worlds collide, where power meets suffering, where Jesus destroyed the works of Satan. Let's head back to the cross.

13

CRUCIFORM KING

Nonviolence sinks its roots deep into the narrative of a cruciform God, which stretches from a garden to a manger, a manger to a cross. It's the path we should take, because it's the path first trudged by our crucified Creator-King.

> Christ Jesus ... though he was in the form of God, did not count equality with God a thing to be grasped, but emptied himself, by taking the form of a servant, being born in the likeness of men. (Phil. 2:5–7)

When Jesus was born, Caesar Augustus had recently ushered in a time of unprecedented peace and prosperity that would make the Reagan years look like the Great Depression. Roads were built, robbers were kept at bay, the military was invincible, luxury was all around, and distant nations that would otherwise pose a threat kept to themselves. This was the *Pax Romana*—the "peace of Rome"—and Jesus was born smack dab in the middle of it.

When Jesus was around five, Augustus celebrated his twenty-fifth year as emperor, which happened to be the 750th anniversary of Rome's foundation. By now, Augustus had risen to godlike status, and the people were eager to show their affirmation. Augustus was hailed as a savior, lord, king of kings, prince of peace, son of God, the *Pontifex Maximus* or High Priest of Rome, who brought gospels and glad tidings to the people of Rome.

Meanwhile, back at the farm, or among the animals, wailed a baby born out of wedlock to a teenage girl in a small village in Judea—a backwater province nestled between the Mediterranean Sea and the desert sands. No pomp or prestige, parades or accolades. The Son of God entered human history in a whisper—through the virgin womb of a young Jewish girl. Shame, scandal, and humility clothed the birth of Christ. In the flurry of power and violence, religious pride and unprecedented economic success, the Creator of the universe descended from His glorious throne and thrust Himself into a feeding trough.

> And being found in human form, he humbled him-
> self by becoming obedient to the point of death,
> even death on a cross. (Phil 2:8)

Augustus was a tough act to follow, no doubt. So when Jesus's followers hailed Him as "Savior," "Lord," "King of Kings," "Prince of Peace," "Son of God," and "High Priest" of Israel, who brought "gospels" and "glad tidings" to the entire world, Roman folks certainly raised an eyebrow and, if need be, a sword. It made no sense to the Roman worldview that a suffering, humiliated, crucified Jew would rule the world. But He did, and He does, and He always will. Our cruciform Creator-King reclaimed His glorious throne *because* He first served and suffered. And He invites us to journey with Him to Calvary.

> Therefore God has highly exalted him and bestowed on him the name that is above every name, so that at the name of Jesus every knee should bow, in heaven and on earth and under the earth, and every tongue confess that Jesus Christ is Lord, to the glory of God the Father. (Phil. 2:9–11)

Choosing violence over nonviolence, power over suffering, vengeance over forgiveness, or temporal justice over love, disrupts this un-Roman, counter-American, not-of-this-world narrative. The nonviolent rhythms of the cross meet the melodies of this world with dissonance.

I accept the charge of being impractical. Perhaps some will think I'm weak. Maybe critics will say I'm idealistic, naive, or too heavenly minded to be of earthly good. I'll take that. But the one thing I never want to be accused of is diminishing the cross. The One who breathed stars into existence, who commands the sun and moon to do His bidding, chose humility and suffering as the stairway to His throne. The King of creation reigns. He ordains. He commands. He judges, and He loves. "Our God ... does whatever He pleases," sings the psalmist (Ps. 115:3 NASB). He "will accomplish all [His] purpose," announces the prophet (Isa. 46:10). *This God defeated evil—but not through violence.* He raised His hands, not to strike, but to be nailed to a cross. May we pick up ours to remind the world of His. May Jesus's cruciform narrative become more real than the blood in our veins, just as it has been for an untold multitude that has fought—and won—a cruciform victory. Like Erastus.

• • •

"Come on, Erastus. We're going to be late. The celebration has started!"[1]

Fear gripped Erastus's heart. He knew he had to do it, but his feet felt cemented into the marble floor as the warm Mediterranean breeze swept through his front door.

"Hang on, Gaius. Let me just grab my cloak."

"And don't forget your speech, Erastus. Remember: this is your night!"

"Oh … yes, of course," Erastus stammered as he stuffed a piece of parchment into his cloak. "Okay. Let's go."

As the two rushed to the city square, the buzz of the crowd vibrated through the alleys. Intoxicated with violence, they chanted:

"Kurios Vespasian. Kurios Vespasian. Kurios Vespasian!

"They're waiting for you, Erastus! Are you ready?"

"Um, yes. Yes, of course. I'm ready."

Celebrations ignited across the Roman world at the news of Emperor Vespasian's recent bloodbath in Jerusalem. The Jewish revolt had been crushed by Rome, and pride wafted through the Mediterranean air, especially in patriotic towns like Corinth, where Erastus was the city treasurer.

Kurios Vespasian! Kurios Vespasian!

"There it is, Erastus! Look, they built a stage for your speech. This is your night, Erastus. The favor of the gods is with you. And *kurios* Vespasian, our divine emperor, is with you. Make him proud!"

As city treasurer, Erastus was called upon by the Senate to herald the good news of Lord Vespasian's peace-bringing victory over the revolting Jews. Putting down such threats brought salvation and security to the empire. Normally, Erastus would eagerly celebrate. The only problem was that Erastus had recently renounced his belief in the Roman gods, and he no longer believed that Vespasian was his *kurios*. He had joined the community of the Way, a group otherwise known as Christians. And Erastus now worshipped a new King, a Jew from Nazareth named Yeshua whom his own government had crucified. Yeshua, the crucified Jew, was his new *Kurios*—His divine *Lord*.

"Right this way, sir." A soldier beckoned, glistening with joy. "Vespasian reigns! Make him proud, sir!"

Erastus strolled up the stage, dove into his pocket, and snatched his manuscript. He gazed over the crowd and then squinted up to the sky and whispered: "*Kurios Christos*, give me strength to follow You. May Your cross be mine. This night, I will be with You."

"Citizens of Rome," cried Erastus. "We are here to celebrate Vespasian's recent victory over the Jews in Palestine. Many people have been killed, both Romans and Jews. And Rome has reclaimed Palestine for the empire."

"*Kurios Vespasian!*" shouted the crowd. "Salvation and peace belong to Rome!"

"However," continued Erastus. "I'm here to tell you about another empire. Another *Kurios*. A better salvation and true peace."

The crowd froze.

"I stand before you as a herald of the good news that Yeshua, a Jew from the town of Nazareth in Palestine, is the true *Kurios*, the Lord of the earth. His kingdom rules over Rome, and its boundaries reach to the ends of the earth. I am a servant of this King, this Lord. He is my *Kurios*. He is *your Kurios*. I have submitted to His rule, and I can therefore not celebrate this war with you. Many innocent lives have been shed to maintain Rome's peace. But true peace is found in Yeshua."

Anger whipped through those in the agitated crowd as they gnashed their teeth. Several men rushed the stage. Soldiers drew their swords.

"Citizens of Rome. People of Corinth. I declare to you this evening that God has highly exalted Yeshua and bestowed on Him the name that is above every name, so that at the name of Yeshua every knee in this city square should bow and every tongue confess that Yeshua the Messiah is *Kurios*, to the glory of the God of heaven, our Father."

A sword slashed across Erastus's face, and he crumpled to the floor. Blood gushed out and filled the platform. Another sword hacked at his ribs, boots trampled his limbs, and soon Erastus was with his *Kurios*.

And thus Satan was dealt another blow. Erastus, citizen of Christ, had suffered—and conquered.

> And they have conquered him by the blood of the
> Lamb and by the word of their testimony, for they
> loved not their lives even unto death. (Rev. 12:11)

WHAT IS JUST WAR THEORY?

"War is evil," wrote Arthur Holmes. "Its causes are evil. … Its consequences are evil … it orphans and widows and horribly maims the innocent … it cheapens life and morality … wars that are intended to arrest violence and injustice seem only in the long run to breed further injustice and conflict. To call war anything less than evil," concluded Holmes, "would be self-deception."[1]

Arthur Holmes is not a pacifist. He's a major proponent of just war theory.

Unfortunately, some who say they believe in just war theory aren't as eager to condemn war—all war—as evil. The fact is, few people know what just war theory is or where it came from. Therefore, I have included this appendix as a basic introduction and overview of just war theory. Keep in mind that tons of books and articles have been written on just war theory, and there are many different opinions on how to interpret it. Therefore, I won't be able to chase down every strand of thinking within the debate. Instead, I will stick to the general tenets of just war theory. I will explain its history, examine the criteria that constitute the theory, and ultimately show that the moral impulse that drives just war is not far from what I've said in this book. There would be a lot less war—and certainly no celebration of war—if the church lived out the heart of what it means to be a just warrior.

WHERE DID JUST WAR THEORY COME FROM?

Just war was discussed by Greek philosophers as far back as Aristotle (384–322 BC), who was the first writer to use the phrase "just war." Many others, such as the Roman statesman Cicero (106–43 BC), debated the issue of justice in war. Therefore, the idea didn't originate in the church. It was an ethical discussion that began with non-Christian thinkers.

The first Christian leaders who discussed just war were Ambrose (AD 340–397) and his disciple Augustine (AD 354–430)—the so-called Christian father of just war theory. Interestingly, both Ambrose and Augustine believed that Jesus taught nonviolence and that Christians should not kill in self-defense. "I do not think that a Christian," wrote Ambrose, "ought to save his own life by the death of another; just as when he meets an armed robber he cannot return his blows, lest in defending his life he should stain his love toward his neighbor."[2] Augustine agreed: killing in self-defense is incompatible with loving one's neighbor. Both theologians believed that Jesus called His followers to a life of nonviolence. Yet they both believed that some wars may be justified.

So how did Ambrose and Augustine, who believed that Jesus prohibited His followers from using violence, support the idea of a just war?

"Times change," Augustine said. What Jesus commanded His followers applied to them but not to us. Augustine believed that while nonviolence was fit for the early church, it didn't work for the time when kings and rulers were Christians. (Remember, Augustine was living *after* Constantine, when church and state became one.) One just war scholar summarized Augustine's argument by saying, "What was appropriate in the time of the apostles is not appropriate in a day and age when kings and nations have succumbed to the gospel."[3] Since Augustine didn't believe that Jesus advocated fighting just wars—quite the opposite—Augustine admittedly drew upon Greco-Roman pagan thinkers to develop the theory. And thus, just war theory made its way into the church.

Throughout church history, theologians continued to develop just war theory. Francisco de Vitoria (AD 1486–1546), Hugo Grotius (AD 1583–1645), and others built upon Augustine's work. The most significant contributor, however, was the great Catholic theologian Thomas Aquinas (AD 1225–1274). Aquinas systematically hammered out many of the criteria for just war theory that are still in use today (see the next section).

But it wasn't only Christian thinkers who wrestled with the idea of a just war. Secular philosophers and ethicists took part in the discussion and shaped the just war theory that is known today. Just war, therefore, is not a distinctively Christian discussion. It didn't begin in the church, and it didn't end with the church. It is a general discussion about the morality of war that's not limited to any religion. Today, when the morality of war is discussed, it's common to find no references to Scripture or church theologians: "Justice in war is now a thoroughly secular matter."[4]

It's important to note that the phrase "just war theory" is slightly inaccurate. It gives the impression that the theory is some sort of hard-and-fast doctrine that one could adhere to. But given the diverse opinions about just war, it's better to think of it as a tradition or framework, not a fixed doctrine. Just war proponent Daniel Bell rightly concluded:

> It is not as if Augustine drew up something called a just war theory or doctrine, which was set in stone and to which the church has adhered without deviation or change ever since.
>
> Rather, Christians adopted a rudimentary vision of just war from the ancient Romans and then began a long process of developing it that has not stopped to this day.[5]

WHAT MAKES A WAR JUST?

Although there is some variation, there are seven (or sometimes eight) criteria used to evaluate the justice of a war. The first five have to do with the grounds for going to war, and the last two discuss the morality of fighting during a war.

1. Just Cause

Just cause could include two different factors. The first would be self-defense. For instance, if one country attacks another country, or if such an attack is imminent, then the nation under attack has a *just cause* to go to war (self-defense). The second would be intervention where the peace of another nation is threatened. If one nation is acting wickedly toward another nation or toward its own people (the genocide in Rwanda, for example), another nation could intervene to stop the oppression. Whether a preemptive strike could be a *just cause* is a matter of debate.

2. Right Authority

Only a legitimate government can wage war. This rules out revolutionaries, criminals, or a private militia.

3. Right Intention

Related to *just cause*, this criterion rules out unjust purposes for waging war, such as vengeance, economic gain, or imperialistic advances (i.e., expanding one's territory).

4. Reasonable Chance of Success

The expected good results of the war must outweigh the evil results. Since war should be waged to reestablish peace, the nation waging the war must have the means to achieve its goal.

5. Last Resort

All nonviolent avenues of achieving peace must be exhausted before a nation resorts to war.

6. Proportionate Means

The weaponry and the force used should be limited to what is needed to repel the aggression and secure peace. Using force beyond what is necessary to establish peace is unjust. Total or unlimited war is ruled out, and most would argue that the use of nuclear weapons is a direct violation of this criterion.

7. Noncombatant Immunity

Noncombatants (or civilians) are not to be targeted in war. This includes cities with civilians, medical personnel, POWs, or other noncombatants. However, if civilians are killed as an indirect result of an attack on a military target (i.e., the soldiers weren't *trying* to kill civilians), this would not violate the criterion.[6]

PURPOSE OF THE CRITERIA

Now, as you might imagine, these criteria have never been perfectly met, and they probably never will. "History knows of no just wars," wrote just war advocate Oliver O'Donovan.[7] The purpose of the criteria is not to sanctify war, or to be a means of labeling previous wars just or unjust. Rather, the seven criteria are intended to reduce the evil effects of war. Again, most just war supporters believe that all war is evil but that sometimes war is a regrettable necessity. The seven criteria are a "set of moral guidelines for waging war," not a scientific means of declaring war good.[8] Therefore, the idea that a Christian should fight only in "just wars" is wrongheaded. There aren't any. There never will be any. And the criteria should not be viewed as a checklist for Christians to sign off on before they enter into the military to ensure that they fight in only good wars. There are no good wars, only evil wars.

I should also point out that Scripture does not promote just war theory as we know it. The Old Testament provides rules for Israelite warfare, but those rules look quite different from the modern criteria. And since these were given to Israel under a specific covenant, they don't directly apply to all nations today. No nation is a theocracy with God as its king. The New Testament doesn't help just war advocates either. Warfare would look quite odd if warriors loved their opponents, turned the other cheek, and soothed the wounds of their enemy in the ditch as the Samaritan did.

Paul says in Romans 13, of course, that God works through secular governments to avenge evil. And this passage is often taken as clear proof for just war theory. But which criterion does it support? Taking vengeance on evil is not one of the seven. Romans 13 does not talk about last resort, proportionate means, or just cause (such as self-defense). That's because Romans 13 does not talk about war. It highlights God's sovereign ability to use secular governments to punish evildoers living within the state's jurisdiction. Paul doesn't give Rome the nod to take out a dictator in Parthia.

The Bible does not explicitly argue for just war, and most just war proponents don't say that it does. Evangelical theologian Wayne Grudem, however, is an exception. He sought to defend the just war criteria by tacking on verses to each one: Revelation 19:11 for *just cause*, Proverbs 21:2 for *right intention*, Luke 14:31 for *reasonable chance of success*.[9] While it's true that some criteria may overlap with Christian virtues—Jesus wouldn't carpet bomb civilian cities either—the biblical writers never intended to give support for just war theory. And using biblical verses in such a manner is misleading (especially if you look up the actual verses). It gives the false impression that just war is biblical and therefore Christian. It's neither.

Again, the seven criteria were formulated by Christian and non-Christian thinkers alike. Of course, Christians who contributed to just war theory (Augustine, etc.) had a biblical worldview. In this sense, the Bible is one of many sources that have helped shape the tradition. But the criteria don't directly stem from Scripture, and they aren't derived from the gospel.

If we did use the New Testament—all of it—as the ethical standard for war, which criteria would we end up with? Soldiers would be commanded to love their enemies, forgive when they are wronged, never pay back evil for evil, and never act in hatred or vengeance. They would do good to those shooting at them, and if an enemy asked them to carry his pack one mile, they would take it two. The best way to conquer your enemy would be to feed and clothe him. Even better if he kills you, since martyrdom either converts your enemy or stores up God's wrath for him, as we saw in the book of Revelation (chapter 9). Destroy your enemy by being destroyed by him. How's that for a warfare tactic?

All of this is wrongheaded, of course. Jesus didn't give Rome political advice. He commanded His followers how to live—and die. And if a believer works for the government, he or she should still follow the ethic of the Lord. If we assess just war theory strictly from the perspective of Scripture, we would find little support.

But let's leave aside Scripture for a moment and look at just war theory from the perspective of its own criteria. After all, most Christian advocates for just war agree that its foundation lies outside the Bible.

PROBLEMS WITH JUST WAR THEORY

I think there is some value to just war, and I'm glad that we have the criteria. In fact, I'll show below that the heart of the tradition (or at least one strand of it) is not far from the nonviolence I've advocated for in this book. But do these criteria effectively reduce evil in war?

The criterion of *legitimate authority* exhibits problems to my mind. What about revolution against a legitimate authority that's unjust? For instance, the government-sanctioned genocide in Rwanda was stopped when the rebel RPF (Rwandan Patriotic Front) intervened. Such intervention, however, violated the just war criterion of *legitimate authority*, even though it ended the genocide. To be fair, just war advocates have addressed this problem. Aquinas, for instance, argued that a revolution may be just if the legitimate authority is evil. Thomas Jefferson agreed: "The tree of liberty must be refreshed from time to time with the blood of patriots and tyrants. It is its natural manure." In other words, periodic revolutions can be healthy.

The only problem is this: Who gets to determine which side is evil? The Rwandan government thought it was doing quite fine; the revolutionaries were the problem. No, it was the government that was evil. No, the revolutionaries were the bad guys. And so on and so forth. Determining whether a government is evil or legitimate is a matter of perspective.

The same goes for *just cause* and *right intention*. Both nations going to war could equally justify their cause. Take 9/11 for instance. Bin Laden and his comrades struck America as a response to American presence, including military bases, throughout the Middle East and to what they perceived to be unjust attacks.[10] This is a serious violation of their culture and religion. From their perspective, 9/11 was not an evil aggression, but a response to evil aggression. Was 9/11, therefore, justified? Of course not!

Or take Desert Storm. America seemed to satisfy most of the just war criteria. They had *just cause* and *limited objectives* for going to war (freeing Kuwait). The *probability of success* was high, and it could be argued that negotiations were not going to be effective. However, two criteria were violated: many civilians were killed (*noncombatant immunity*), and the US military carpet bombed the Iraqi army as it was fleeing from Kuwait (*proportionate means*). America scored a 5 out of 7. Not bad for a batting average.

But how about Iraq? When Iraq invaded Kuwait, it was a *legitimate authority* that made the call. They believed that they had a *just cause* since Kuwait was originally part of Iraq (they were reclaiming rightful territory). They used *proportionate means*, had a *reasonable chance of success*, and the war was a *last resort* since there was no chance of negotiation. Unfortunately, *noncombatants* were killed. Thus Iraq scored a 6 out of 7.[11]

My point is not to justify bin Laden, Iraq, or America in their recent wars, but to point out that the criterion of *just cause* is unhelpfully subjective. It all depends on perspective. Without a universal moral code that all can agree upon, war becomes "just" in the eye of the beholder.

Let's take another example. Many Americans support drone strikes on Middle East soil (Pakistan, Yemen, Afghanistan, and others) even though civilians (including children) are often killed in the attacks. The logic? Terrorists plotting to kill Americans are hiding out in houses that are blown up by drones. Better to "kill them before they kill us," said Erick Erickson of Fox News.[12] The twenty-five to fifty civilians who are killed for every one terrorist are simply collateral damage.

For some, this is a *just cause* for drone strikes.

But let's reverse the situation. Say that a major drug lord was hiding out in the suburbs of Malibu, California. He's funneling heroin and cocaine back into his home country of Mexico, devastating the economy and morality of his country. Mexican lives are threatened; many have already been killed; families are torn to shreds. To stop the thug, the Mexican government sends a drone over Malibu and lights up the neighborhood where he is staying. Thirty-seven American civilians are killed, including twelve children. But they get the drug lord! And many Mexican lives are saved. Would you feel that such an attack was justified?

The point of this fictitious analogy is to show once again that what constitutes *justice* is often determined by the aggressor. Unfortunately, only one side of the analogy is fictitious. Seeing things from the other side, especially in terms of *just cause*, could foster more effort toward a nonviolent resolution.

The criterion of *last resort* is also difficult to maintain. How do you know if you have truly exhausted every possible nonviolent attempt to settle the conflict? Just war scholar Daniel Bell recognized that "this criterion is bolstered to the point that it is literally unattainable."[13] If diplomatic resolution has tried and failed fifty-nine times, how do you know a sixtieth won't work? When do we cross the line into the nebulous world of no more options?

So *last resort* can't be taken literally. Rather, the criterion should encourage the government to explore other nonviolent means of resolving the conflict. I actually agree with this criterion the most, since it's driven by a desire to resolve conflict nonviolently. I am skeptical, however, that a militarized nation like America will really pursue war only as a last resort.

I'm equally skeptical, perhaps even cynical, about the criterion *proportionate means*. Does *proportionate means* hold back the tide of evil that flows in war? Perhaps to some extent it does. It deters the use of nuclear weapons and chemical warfare. I'm certainly glad the criterion is there. But I wouldn't want to put a lot of moral stock in the criterion, thinking that it can somehow sanitize war. War is war. The goal of one nation is to defeat the enemy. It's fine to debate the ethical theories from a classroom, but soldiers on the ground will most likely resort to using whatever means possible to survive. I have little confidence that soldiers will make sure not to use excessive force when bullets are whizzing past their heads and grenades are landing nearby. Whether a man with three children at home loses half his face to a nuclear bomb or a .50-caliber cannon doesn't make a huge difference at the end of the day. War is a messy evil.

We could go through all the criteria with similar quibbles. Again, such criticisms aren't meant to undermine just war theory, but to point out that it does not offer bulletproof protection against unjust wars, even if the criteria were actually met.

The one criterion that troubles me the most—one that, to my mind, has done little to create justice in war—is *noncombatant immunity*. In war, civilians get massacred. That's just the way it is. But what I find most troubling is that the number of civilian casualties keeps getting higher. In World War I, one-fifth of all deaths were civilians. In World War II, the number rose to two-thirds. In the recent wars in Iraq and Afghanistan, the percentage has been estimated as high as 90 percent—nine civilians murdered for every combatant.[14]

"Yes," some say, "and this is why America needs to wage war, to stop such civilian casualties!" This sounds good, but the only problem is that America is not exempt.

One of my students named Parker left the military largely because of the likelihood that he would kill civilians. Of course the military says it doesn't target civilians. But according to Parker, neither does it try very hard to prevent it. "I was desensitized so that I could hate my enemy and kill them. My leaders didn't instill a moral aversion to killing civilians." Or as one drill sergeant said regarding the death of civilians: "Shit happens." Other officers joked that "if you happen to kill a civilian, just lay an AK-47 at her side so people will think she was a terrorist." When Parker was in training, he learned how to operate a .50-caliber gun that targeted mass populations and made it impossible to sort out the soldiers from the civilians. But no one seemed to care about the moral conflict. "Even in training," said Parker, "I developed a growing abhorrence to the idea of murdering civilians. While my training calloused my conscience, I had a tough time reconciling what the military was shaping me to do with how Jesus told me to live."

Now, this is only one account. I'm sure I could find other testimonies that are less troubling. But Parker's experience seems to match the statistics. America killed over one million Japanese civilians in the last few months of World War II—a war that's widely considered to be "just." Tens of thousands of German civilians were killed in a two-day bombing campaign in Dresden, which one historian called "the largest slaughter of civilians by military forces in one place at one time since the campaigns of Genghis Khan."[15] Nearly one million Korean civilians were killed by the United States between 1950 and 1953. Another three hundred thousand Vietnamese civilians and hundreds of thousands of Cambodian civilians were killed as a result of US military force during the 1960s and '70s. According to the most conservative estimate, over one hundred thousand civilians have been killed as a result of the US invasions of Iraq and Afghanistan.[16] We could add to these numbers the nearly six million civilians who have died as a result of covert CIA operations—a staggering number that former State Department official William Blum labels the "American Holocaust."[17]

That's a lot of innocent deaths. And we're supposed to be the good guys. Parker's reservations about killing civilians appear justified.

"Yes," some will say, "but all those civilian deaths were a necessary means of saving American lives." *Really?* How do we know this? Even if this were true, an ends-justifies-the-means ethic is questionable at best. It's certainly not found in Scripture. As Christians, we are to operate *on principle* of what is right and wrong, not determine what is good based on predicted outcomes.

But even if you could wiggle out some moral justification for the millions of civilians killed by the United States, the main point is that the just war criterion of *noncombatant immunity* has been largely and tragically ignored.

History knows of no just wars, and it probably never will.

JUST WAR THEORY AND NONVIOLENCE: FRIENDS OR FOES?

At the end of the day, I think the goal of just war theory is a noble one. However, many Christians, I fear, take just war to mean that war is a good thing or the best way to confront evil. Some people I talk to say they believe in just war *and not* nonviolence (or pacifism); or nonviolence *and not* just war. But this contrast reveals a misunderstanding of the heart behind just war theory (or nonviolence, for that matter). In light of what I've said in this book, and in light of what I've said in this appendix, I don't think that just war theory and nonviolence are very far apart.

Recall what Arthur Holmes said at the beginning of this appendix: war is evil. And most just war advocates agree.[18] Advocates for nonviolence also agree. War is evil. War should not be glorified or celebrated. Where the two views disagree is whether there's a place to wage war as a last resort, as the lesser of two evils. But the heart of just war is not far from nonviolence. The very fact that just war theory says that violence should be used *only* as a last resort shows that it prioritizes nonviolence as a means of resolving conflict. While nonviolence and just war are "independent methods of evaluating warfare ... they share a common presumption against the use of force as a means of settling disputes."[19]

Just war proponents and advocates for nonviolence should see each other as friends, not foes. I would love to see each view learn from the other through dialogue and debate. Such camaraderie could lessen the evil effects of war.

NOTES

CHAPTER 1: MOUNTAIN OF SKULLS

1. Carolyn Nordstrom, "Terror Warfare and the Medicine of Peace," *Medical Anthropology Quarterly* 12 (1998): 103–121.

2. Cited in Nordstrom, "Terror Warfare," 107.

3. There are many articles and blogs on the web that discuss this project. For a good, brief overview, see Amy Schwartzott, "And They Shall Beat Their Swords into Plowshares," *Peace X Peace*, September 13, 2011, http://www.peacexpeace.org/2011/09/%E2%80%9Cand-they-shall-beat-their-swords-into-plowshares%E2%80%9C/, accessed March 14, 2013.

4. According to most historians, that is. Stephen Pinker, however, has recently contested this in his *The Better Angels of Our Nature* (New York: Penguin, 2011), 193–200.

5. *Oxford English Dictionary*, OED.com, s.v. "militarism."

6. See Andrew Bacevich, *The New American Militarism* (New York: Oxford University Press, 2005); Rachel Maddow, *Drift* (New York: Crown, 2012).

7. See Bacevich, *The New American Militarism*, 122–146.

8. Hal Lindsey, *The 1980s* (King of Prussia, PA: Westgate Press, 1980), 162, 165.

9. Jerry Falwell, *Listen, America!* (New York: Bantam, 1980), 17, 82, 84, 89.

10. William Boykin, quoted in Bacevich, *The New American Militarism*, 142.

11. G. Russell Evans and C. Greg Singer, *The Church and the Sword* (Houston, TX: St. Thomas Press, 1982), 4, 32–33, 35.

12. Wayne Grudem, *Politics—According to the Bible* (Grand Rapids, MI: Zondervan, 2010), 399–400.

13. To date, there have been approximately 500 civilians, including more than 150, killed by US drone strikes in the Middle East. Some call this collateral damage; others call it a war crime. It all depends on where you live.

14. Bacevich, *The New American Militarism*, 145.

15. Bacevich, *The New American Militarism*, 146.

16. *Oxford English Dictionary*, OED.com, s.v. "violence."

17. Matt. 5:21–22; James 3:1–12

18. Glen H. Stassen and Michael L. Westmoreland-White, "Defining Violence and Nonviolence," in J. Denny Weaver and Gerald Biesecker-Mast (eds.), *Teaching Peace* (Lanham, MD: Rowman and Littlefield, 2003), 18.

19. Violence is not the same as "wrongness." According to my definition, God commits violence, and yet this doesn't mean that God commits a wrong. In the Old Testament, God even commands humans to commit violence. Again, this does not mean that God commanded humans to do something wrong.

CHAPTER 2: WAS ISRAEL A VIOLENT, GENOCIDAL, BLOODTHIRSTY NATION?

1. Richard Dawkins, *The God Delusion* (Boston: Houghton Mifflin, 2006), 31.

2. C. S. Cowles, "Radical Discontinuity," in *Show Them No Mercy*, ed. Stanley Gundry (Grand Rapids, MI: Zondervan, 2003), 28–29. For a similar perspective, see Eric Siebert, *The Violence of Scripture* (Minneapolis, MN: Fortress Press, 2012).

3. Claus Westermann, "Peace (Shalom) in the Old Testament," in *The Meaning of Peace*, ed. Perry B. Yoder and Willard M. Swartley (Elkhardt, IN: Institute of Mennonite Studies, 1992), 37–70.

4. The Hebrew word *hamas* ("violence") occurs sixty times in the Old Testament. It is almost always used of physical violence toward fellow humans (Gen. 49:5; Judg. 9:24). Sometimes the word refers to extreme wickedness where physical violence may or may not be in view (Isa 53:8; 59:6). On a few rare occasions, God is said to be the agent of violence, but this seems to be from the perspective of the one suffering and not from God (see Job 19:7; 21:27; Lam. 2:6). See I. Swart and C. Van Dam, "Hamas," in *New International Dictionary of Old Testament Theology & Exegesis*, ed. Willem A. VanGemeren (Grand Rapids, MI: Zondervan, 1997), 2.177–180.

5. Gen. 32:4, 5, 18; 33:8, 13

6. Gen. 32:13, 18, 20, 21; 33:10

7. Whether God agrees with Jacob or with Simeon and Levi is debated. Old Testament scholar Tremper Longman said that the narrator of Genesis seems to support the brothers' actions in Gen. 34 and that it's unclear how the inspired narrator thinks about Jacob's condemnation of it in Gen. 49 (personal conversation). The fact that the brothers have the last word in Gen. 34:31 seems to support this: "Should he treat our sister like a prostitute?" At the same time, Jacob's words of condemnation in Gen. 49 seem to reflect God's point of view, especially since the judgment that "I will divide them ... and scatter them" refers to *God's* judgment, not Jacob's (see Claus Westermann, *Genesis 37–50* [Minneapolis, MN: Fortress Press, 2002], 226).

8. Scholars are divided on these questions. See the discussion in Claus Westermann, *Genesis 1–11* (Minneapolis, MN: Fortress Press, 1994), 467. If Gen. 9:6 is a proverb, then it should be understood as a general principle, not an absolute command. Jesus says a similar proverb in Matt. 26:52: "For all who take the sword will perish by the sword." This is a principle, not a hard-and-fast command or promise that always, everywhere comes true. Some warriors took up the sword but didn't die by the sword. Scholars are also divided over how to translate the middle phrase in 9:6. Most translations read, "*by man* shall his blood be shed" (as in the ESV), which means that humans are to administer the death penalty for murderers. However, the Hebrew phase *ba'adam* could be translated "*for that man* his blood shall be shed" (as in the NEB), which is how the Greek Old Testament (LXX) reads. This latter translation says that God will mete out the

punishment for murderers with or without a human agent. And thus, the death penalty by human hands would not necessarily be in view. See the discussion in Victor Hamilton, *The Book of Genesis: Chapters 1–17* (NICOT; Grand Rapids, MI: Eerdmans, 1990), 315.

9. Heb. 7:1 refers to this incident as the "slaughter of the kings" and that Melchizedek "blessed him" upon his return. Hebrews still doesn't explicitly endorse Abram's violent actions. It says only that Melchizedek blessed him when he returned.

10. Paul Copan, *Is God a Moral Monster?* (Grand Rapids, MI: Baker, 2011), 95.

11. Property damage did not demand the death penalty in the Old Testament, but in other cultures it did. The Babylonian code of Hammurabi (ca. 1750 BC) sanctions the death penalty for robbery, property damage, and a whole host of other crimes where life was not harmed (e.g. Laws of Hammurabi §6–11, 21–22, 25; Chris Wright, *Old Testament Ethics for the People of God* [Downers Grove, IL: InterVarsity, 2004], 308).

12. The only reference in Old Testament law where mutilation is thought to be in view is Deut. 25:11–12. However, the reference to cutting off the woman's hand could be translated as shaving her pubic hair.

13. The phrase "incremental steps" is from Copan, *Is God a Moral Monster?*

14. There are some laws that were intended to be more absolute, however. When a law is taken up in later parts of the Old Testament, especially in Wisdom Literature, it may be less culturally bound. And, of course, if a law is taken up by Jesus or the apostles and applied to the church, it also should not be limited to the Israelite culture (for instance, the Ten Commandments, except perhaps the Sabbath law).

15. My argument in this section is in agreement with several scholars including Copan, *Is God a Moral Monster?*, 57–69; Wright, *Old Testament Ethics for the People of God*, esp. 48–75; William J. Webb, *Slaves, Women, and Homosexuals* (Downers Grove, IL: InterVarsity, 2001), 30–66.

16. Cuneiform tablets discovered at Nuzi (Iraq) document the exact same practice of a barren wife giving her slave girl to her husband as a wife. For instance: "If Gilimnimu (the bride) will not bear children, Gilimnimu shall take a woman of N/Lullu land (whence the choicest slaves were obtained) as a wife for Shennima (the bridegroom)" (cited in Tremper Longman, *How to Read Genesis* [Downers Grove: InterVarsity, 2005], 97).

17. Copan, *Is God a Moral Monster?*, 63.

18. On slavery, see Wright, *Old Testament Ethics*, 333–337; Copan, *Is God a Moral Monster?*, 124–157.

19. Laws of Hammurabi §16; Laws of Lipit-Ishtar §12; Laws of Eshunna § 49–50; Hittite Laws §24; see Copan, *Is God a Moral Monster?*, 131–132.

20. Gal. 3:15–29

21. 2 Cor. 3:7–18; cf. Heb. 8:6–13

22. 1 Cor. 9:8–12; Matt. 5–7

23. Exod. 21:28–32; 20:24–26

24. Matt. 5–7; John 1:16–18; Heb. 3:1–6

25. Copan, *Is God a Moral Monster?*, 61.

CHAPTER 3: ISRAEL'S BIZARRE WARFARE POLICY

1. Chris Wright, *Old Testament Ethics for the People of God* (Downers Grove, IL: InterVarsity, 2004), 55.

2. John Goldingay, *Old Testament Theology, Vol.3: Israel's Life* (Downers Grove, IL: InterVarsity, 2009), 511.

3. The phrase "according to their clans" is repeated throughout the land allotments (e.g. Josh. 13:15; 15:1, 20; 16:5; 17:2; cf. Num. 26:52–56).

4. God did not forbid Israel to have a king (Gen. 49:10). In fact, He even gave rules about how Israel's king should function (Deut. 17:14–20). However, the nature of kingship allowed in Israel was radically different from kingship in other ancient nations.

5. As 1 Sam. 8:12–13 makes plain.

6. Isa. 36–37; 2 Chron. 20:1–30; 2 Kings 7:1–20

7. Deut. 17:17 prohibits the king from acquiring "for himself excessive silver and gold." This refers not just to wealth but to economic power that would be used, at least in part, to build and sustain a powerful military (see Millard Lind, *Yahweh Is a Warrior* [Scottdale, PA: Herald Press, 1980], 151).

8. For illustrations of Israel's unprofessional, voluntary militia, see Judg. 5:2, 9; 7:1–8; cf. 1 Sam. 8:12.

9. Ezek. 16:26–29; 23:6–7, 12, 14–16 (Millard Lind, *Monotheism, Power, and Justice* [Elkhart, IN: Institute of Mennonite Studies, 1990], 265).

10. This becomes most clear in verse 9, where the military captains are appointed at the time of war.

11. Fruit trees were essential for the life support of the land and therefore off-limits.

12. In Judg. 7, God trims down Gideon's army to three hundred, "lest Israel boast over me [God], saying, 'My own hand has saved me'" (v. 2).

13. Every commentary I checked agrees that the prohibition of multiplying horses highlights the demilitarization of Israel's king.

14. Josh. 11:6, 9; 2 Sam. 8:4; cf. Mic. 5:10. According to 2 Sam. 8:4, David leaves one hundred horses, but nothing in the text says that God supported David's actions, and Deut. 17 warns against it.

15. Lind, *Yahweh Is a Warrior*, 84.

16. On some occasions, the enemy has a chariot-stacked army, and Israel is still told not to fear (Josh. 17:16–17; Judg. 4:3, 7, 13, 15–16). Superior weaponry is irrelevant in Israel's wars.

17. Tiglath-pileser I, cited in Jeffrey Niehaus, "Joshua and Ancient Near Eastern Warfare," *JETS* 31 (1988), 37–50.

18. The battle at Kadesh (ca. 1274 BC) between Egypt and the Hittites was believed to be the largest chariot battle in ancient history.

19. See especially Exod. 14:21; 15:6–7, 12.

20. For simplicity's sake, I'm using the general term *Israel* without distinguishing between the northern or southern kingdoms. In the Bible, however, *Israel* is often used of the northern kingdom, while *Judah* is used of the southern kingdom. Jehoshaphat is actually leading out a Judean army.

21. See Josh. 10 and 2 Chron. 32, for example.

22. There are few divinely sanctioned battles that emphasize human agency. Some, like Joshua's defeat of Ai (Josh. 8), focus on human action, but here it is God's instructions to set up an ambush, rather than the actual battle, that garners the spotlight (8:1–2). Again, in Josh. 12, there's a list of all the kings Israel defeated during the conquest (12:7–24), and God isn't mentioned. But these are minor exceptions that prove the rule: Israel's battles were Yahweh's battles, and He decided the victory apart from military might.

23. See Michael Hasel, *Military Practice and Polemic* (Berrien Springs, MI: Andrews University Press, 2005), 21–22, 38–39. I'm making a very general statement here. There are variations as to how much the gods were involved in warfare. But I have yet to find texts where a divine being has won the battle single-handedly as in Exod. 14–15 or 2 Chron. 20, while humans simply stand and watch.

24. K. Lawson Younger Jr., *Ancient Conquest Accounts* (Sheffield, UK: Sheffield Academic Press, 1990), 98.

25. This point is disputed by some scholars. Lori L. Rowlett, for instance, believes that the same dependence upon god(s) can be seen in other Near Eastern war texts (Rowlett, *Joshua and the Rhetoric of Violence* [Sheffield, UK: Sheffield Academic, 1996], 53, 71–120). After surveying all her evidence, I'm still not convinced that these ancient texts emphasize their god's power while playing up their own human weakness to the same extent that the Old Testament does.

26. Sometimes the kings of other nations gave stronger attention to their gods' miraculous involvement. But again, it's rarely (if ever) meant to highlight human weakness.

27. The point is raised by Rowlett, *Joshua and the Rhetoric of Violence*, 65–69. The phrase "moral monster" is taken from the title of Paul Copan's book.

28. Deut. 32:39; Isa. 45:6–7. See Peter Craigie, *The Problem of War in the Old Testament* (Grand Rapids, MI: Eerdmans, 1978), 42.

29. Gen. 6:6; Rom. 2:4–5; 3:25

30. This point is agreed upon by several scholars, including Paul Copan, *Is God a Moral Monster?* (Grand Rapids, MI: Baker, 2011), 159, 170–173; Richard Hess, "War in the Hebrew Bible: An Overview," Richard Hess and Elmer Martens eds.,

War in the Bible and Terrorism in the Twenty-First Century (BBRS 2; Winona Lake: Eisenbrauns, 2008), 29.

31. See Copan, *Is God a Moral Monster?*, 92–93; David Lorton, "The Treatment of Criminals in Ancient Egypt," in *The Treatment of Criminals in the Ancient Near East*, ed. Jack M. Sasson (Leiden, Netherlands: Brill, 1977), 1–64.

32. William F. Albright, *Archaeology and the Religion of Israel* (Baltimore, MD: Johns Hopkins, 1968), 77. The most gruesome accounts about Yahweh are found in Deut. 32:43; Ps. 58:11; 68:24; 110:6; Isa. 34:2; and Ezek. 32:4–6.

33. Rowlett, *Joshua and the Rhetoric of Violence*, 83; Younger Jr., *Ancient Conquest Accounts*, 191–192.

34. The phrase "spread[ing] terror in the land of the living" (or something similar) is repeated seven times in Ezek. 32 (vv. 23, 24, 25, 26, 27, 30, 32), highlighting how infuriated God was over this tactic. I used the term *hell* for simplicity, but Ezek. 32 speaks only of the netherworld in vague and poetic terms. The passage isn't intended to describe a geography of hell.

35. See Erika Belibtreu "Grisly Assyrian Record of Torture and Death," *BAR* 17 (1991), 51–61, 75.

36. Cited in Belibtreu, "Grisly Assyrian Record of Torture and Death."

37. Scholars agree that the most gruesome record of Israelite warfare is in Joshua 10:26–27, where defeated kings are hung on tress and then buried in a cave before nightfall. But if this is as bad as it gets, then the Old Testament is still much less gruesome than other ancient Near Eastern accounts mentioned above.

38. Andrew Bacevich, *The New American Militarism* (New York: Oxford University Press, 2005), 146.

CHAPTER 4: KILL EVERYTHING THAT BREATHES

1. Jack Graham, quoted in Andrew Bacevich, *The New American Militarism* (New York: Oxford University Press, 2005), 145.

2. John MacArthur, interview by Larry King, *Larry King Live*, CNN, March 11, 2003.

3. Rumsfeld's frequent use of the Bible in reference to the Iraq war is well-known. See, for instance, Robert Draper, "And He Shall Be Judged," *GQ.com*, June 2009, http://www.gq.com/news-politics/newsmakers/200905/donald-rumsfeld-administration-peers-detractors (accessed March 2013); and Daniel Nasaw, "Iraq War Briefings Headlined with Biblical Quotes, Reports US Magazine," *The Guardian*, May 18, 2009, http://www.guardian.co.uk/world/2009/may/18/rumsfeld-gq-iraq-bible-quotes-bush (accessed March 14, 2013).

4. Cited in Philip Jenkins, *Laying Down the Sword* (New York: HarperCollins, 2012), 135.

5. For an overview, see Stanley N. Gundry, ed., *Show Them No Mercy* (Grand Rapids, MI: Zondervan, 2003).

6. C. S. Cowles, "Radical Discontinuity," in *Show Them No Mercy*, 41.

7. "There is no hint anywhere in the Bible that the Israelites took the land of Canaan on the basis of a mistaken belief in God's will" (Christopher Wright, *The God I Don't Understand* [Grand Rapids, MI: Zondervan, 2008], 83).

8. Deut. 7:1–2; 20:16–18

9. This is how the Bible describes the Canaanites at least; see Lev. 18:24–25; 20:22–24; Deut. 9:5; 12:29–31; cf. Jer. 5:8. There is a debate among Old Testament scholars about the historical accuracy of the biblical description of the Canaanites. And we don't possess many Canaanite sources to crosscheck what the Bible says about their morality. The historical evidence that we do have is complex: it describes the Canaanites as a blend of wicked and relatively moral people. For the most recent discussion, see the forthcoming article by Richard S. Hess: "'Because of the Wickedness of These Nations' (Deut. 9:4–5): The Canaanites—Ethical or Not?"

10. Paul Copan, *Is God a Moral Monster?* (Grand Rapids, MI: Baker, 2011), 159.

11. Richard Dawkins, quoted in Copan, *Is God a Moral Monster?*, 163.

12. See Wright, *The God I Don't Understand*, 92; Copan, *Is God a Moral Monster?*, 163.

13. Exod. 15:14–16; Josh. 2:9–11; 5:1

14. Chris Wright, *Old Testament Ethics for the People of God* (Downers Grove, IL: InterVarsity, 2004), 476.

15. Josh. 13:1–13; 15:63; 16:10; 17:12–13; 18:3; 23:4; Judg. 1:27–36; 3:3–5

16. "Drive out": Exod. 34:24; Num. 32:21; Deut. 4:38; "dispossess": Num. 21:32; Deut. 9:1; 11:23; 18:14; 19:1.

17. Copan, *Is God a Moral Monster?*, 181.

18. Deut. 7:22; Judg. 2:20–23

19. Even when God tells Israel to "destroy" the Canaanites, the language of "destruction" doesn't have to mean total annihilation. For instance, Israel is said to be "destroy[ed]" by God when the people are driven out of the land of Canaan in years to come (Deut. 28:63; cf. Jer. 38:2, 17). Obviously, "destroy[ed]" here can't mean that they were all killed.

20. The reference to "cities" in 11:14 is ambiguous but probably refers to the cities listed in 11:1–5.

21. Judg. 1–2

22. Most evangelical Old Testament scholars advocate for the same argument I propose here (see Wright, *The God I Don't Understand*, 87–88).

23. See K. Lawson Younger Jr., *Ancient Conquest Accounts* (Sheffield, UK: Sheffield Academic Press, 1990).

24. Copan, *Is God a Moral Monster?*, 171.

25. Josh. 14:12–15; cf. 15:13–19

26. See note 19 above.

27. 1 Kings 14:24; 21:26; 2 Kings 16:3; 17:8; 21:2

28. Richard Hess, "War in the Hebrew Bible: An Overview," Richard Hess and Elmer Martens eds., *War in the Bible and Terrorism in the Twenty-First Century* (BBRS 2; Winona Lake: Eisenbrauns, 2008), 29–30; Wright, *Old Testament Ethics*, 474–475.

29. 1 Sam. 15:3; 22:19; 2 Sam. 6:19; Neh. 8:2; 2 Chron. 15:13.

30. Not to mention "Haman … the Agagite" (Esther 3:1) who is most likely an Amalekite (see 1 Sam. 15:8).

31. Chris Wright, *The God I Don't Understand*, 93.

CHAPTER 5: SWORDS INTO PLOWSHARES

1. Steve is a good friend of mine and has told me his story on several occasions.

2. Wayne Grudem, *Politics—According to the Bible* (Grand Rapids, MI: Zondervan, 2010), 388, citing Judg. 2:16–18; 1 Sam. 17; and 2 Sam. 5:17–25 as support.

3. The battles in Judg. 4 and 7 highlight the weakness of Israel and the military strength of its enemy, thus steering the spotlight from military power to where it belongs: on God.

4. Gen. 34 and 38

5. Judg. 1:6–7 records mutilation, but it's unclear whether it's divinely sanctioned.

6. Judg. 8:10–11

7. Judg. 8:16–17

8. Num. 34:11–12; Ezek. 47:18

9. The territory of the Ammonites is ambiguous, but it seems to me that Jephthah was rightfully defending what belonged to Israel.

10. It's debated whether Jephthah intended to offer child sacrifice. However, the phrase "whatever comes out from the doors of my house to meet me when I return … I will offer it up for a burnt offering" (Judg. 11:31) suggests that he had a child in mind all along (Daniel I. Block, *Judges, Ruth* [NAC 6; Nashville, TN: Broadman & Holman, 1999], 368).

11. Chris Wright, *Old Testament Ethics for the People of God* (Downers Grove, IL: InterVarsity, 2004), 229.

12. 1 Sam. 8:11–12, 20

13. 1 Sam. 14:50, 52; 17:18, 55

14. 1 Sam. 14:24, 52.

15. 1 Sam. 8:11–12

16. Walter Brueggemann, *First and Second Samuel* (Louisville, KY: John Knox, 1990), 262.

17. 2 Sam. 8:6, 14

18. The Hebrew text of 2 Sam. 12:31 says that David took the people of Rabbah and "set them under saws, sharp iron instruments, and iron axes, and made them pass through the brick kiln. And thus he did to all the cities of the sons of Ammon" (rightly translated by the NASB). Parallels in 1 Chron. 20:3, the Greek and Syriac

translations, along with Josephus (*Ant.* 7.161) agree with this reading. Many commentators reject this reading, but there is no textual reason for doing so.

19. Brueggemann, *First and Second Samuel*, 352.

20. 1 Kings 4:26; 10:26

21. Walter Brueggemann, *The Prophetic Imagination* (Minneapolis, MN: Fortress, 2001), 24. This negative assessment of Solomon's reign has been thoroughly argued by J. Daniel Hays, "Has the Narrator Come to Praise Solomon or to Bury Him? Narrative Subtlety in 1 Kings 1–11," *JSOT* 28 (2003): 149–174.

22. Most of the wars waged during the divided kingdom (1 Kings 12–2 Kings 25) are not sanctioned by God.

23. 2 Chron. 20:21–23, 27–30

24. 2 Kings 18.

25. Francis I. Anderson and David Noel Freedman, *Hosea* (The Anchor Bible Commentary; New York: Doubleday, 1980), 196.

26. Mic. 5:10–11

27. Amos 1:3, 6, 9, 11, 13; 2:1

28. Amos 2:14–16; 3:9–11; 6:13–14

29. Isa. 22:5–11; 30:1–3; 31:1–5. See M. Daniel Carroll R., "Impulses toward Peace in a Country at War: The Book of Isaiah between Realism and Hope," in Richard Hess and Elmer Martens, eds., *War in the Bible and Terrorism in the Twenty-First Century* (BBRSup 2; Winnona Lake, IN: Eisenbrauns, 2008), 59–78.

30. Isa. 2:7; 9:9–10

31. The story is recorded in John Howard Yoder, *What Would You Do?* (Scottdale, PA: Herald Press, 1983), 89–90.

32. Isa. 36:9; cf. 37:9

33. Was Hezekiah's work at building up Jerusalem's defense praised or condemned? The Bible does not present a uniform picture. Isa. 22:9–11 seems to condemn Hezekiah for not trusting God by building up his homeland security. However, 2 Chron. 32:1–8, 30, which also records Hezekiah's works, praises him for trusting in God. The issue, of course, is not that building up the walls and redirecting water in time of siege is a bad thing. The issue is where your trust lies.

34. Cf. Eph. 2:14–17

35. Some messianic prophecies describe a more militaristic warrior-king (e.g., Ps. 2, 110). I explain in chapter 12 how these are fulfilled.

36. Isa. 54:10, 13; 55:12; 66:12

37. Ezek. 34:25; 37:26; Zech. 9:9-11; 12:10

38. Susan Niditch, *War in the Hebrew Bible* (New York: Oxford University Press, 1995), 139–149.

39. 1 Chron. 22:18; 2 Chron. 13:17; 14:9–15; 26:6–15

40. 2 Chron. 12:6; 14:9–15; 16:8; 20:12; 25:7–8

41. Niditch, *War in the Hebrew Bible*, 149.

CHAPTER 6: THE KING AND HIS KINGDOM

1. For more on the Maccabean revolt, see 1 and 2 Maccabees. Political independence was gained under Simon, the older brother of Judas, in 142 BC and lasted until 63 BC. To learn about the importance of the Maccabean revolt in shaping the subsequent Jewish worldview, see N. T. Wright, *The New Testament and the People of God* (Minneapolis, MN: Fortress, 1992), 167–181.

2. Josephus, *War* 1.1.1–2.

3. On Jannaeus, see Josephus, *War* 1.4.6.

4. Matt. 2

5. On Herod the Great, see Josephus, *War* 1.30–33; for Archelaus, see *War* 2.1–2. Pompey's invasion is recorded in *War* 1.7 and reflected upon in *Pss. Sol.* 2.

6. *Ant.* 18.4–10, 23-25; Acts 5:37

7. See Acts 5:36; *Ant.* 20.5, 97–99.

8. Josephus, *War* 2.447.

9. Josephus, *War* 7.5.6.

10. I'm painting a general picture. There were some exceptions to such violence within Judaism—for instance, the Sadducees, the Essenes (for the most part), and the Pharisees of Hillel's persuasion. Some Jews, in fact, fought against oppression with nonviolent means, and they won (see Josephus, *War* 2).

11. "In recent exegesis the spiritualistic reading has almost universally been rejected" (Reimund Bieringer, "My Kingship Is Not of This World (John 18, 36): The Kingship of Jesus and Politics," in *The Myriad of Christ*, BETL 152, ed. Terrance Merrigan and Jacques Haers [Leuven, Belgium: University Press and Peeters, 2000], 162).

12. See for instance the Gnostic book the *Acts of Pilate.*

13. For an example, see George Eldon Ladd, *The Gospel of the Kingdom* (Grand Rapids, MI: Eerdmans, 1990), especially chapter 4.

14. John MacArthur, *The MacArthur New Testament Commentary: John 12–21* (Chicago: Moody, 2008), 330.

15. See Ben Witherington III, *John's Wisdom* (Louisville, KY: John Knox, 1995), 291; N. T. Wright, *John for Everyone Part 2: Chapters 11–21* (Louisville, KY: John Knox, 2004), 114–115.

16. See John 7:7; 9:39; 12:31, 47–48; 15:18–19; Bieringer, "My Kingship," 171–170.

17. Peter J. Leithart, *Between Babel and Beast* (Eugene, OR: Cascade, 2012), 166 n.4.

18. Bruce Chilton and J. I. H. McDonald rightly saw Jesus's statement about the kingdom to be "a challenge and rebuke to all worldly power-systems." They went on to say that "'my Kingdom is not of this world' is a political statement, part of the dialogue that relates to a charge of treason brought against Jesus" (Chilton and McDonald, *Jesus and the Ethics of the Kingdom* [Grand Rapids, MI: Eerdmans, 1988], 101).

19. The Greek word translated "fighting" is *agonizomai*, which in 2 Maccabees 8:16 and 13:14 unmistakably refers to violent fighting (Bieringer, "My Kingship," 172).

20. Isa. 35

21. This is a notoriously difficult verse to interpret. The first part of the verse ("has suffered violence") almost certainly refers to the persecution that followers of Jesus, like John the Baptist, will endure, as most commentators recognize (Donald A. Hagner, *Word Biblical Commentary Vol. 33a, Matthew 1–13* [Nashville, TN: Nelson, 1993], 306–307). The second part ("the violent take it by force") is more debated. I have read it to refer to violent Jews trying to set up the kingdom through violence (following W. E. Moore, "Violence to the Kingdom: Josephus and the Syrian Churches," *ExpTim* 100 [1989]: 174–77). It could also refer to potential followers of Jesus wanting Him to set up a kingdom of this world *their* way.

22. See *Psalms of Solomon* 17:22–25, 30 (although see vv. 33–34).

23. 1 Pet. 1:1; 2:11

24. Phil. 1:27; 3:19–21

25. See Leithart, *Between Babel and Beast*, 144–146.

26. The story is recounted in Daniel M. Bell, *Just War as Christian Discipleship* (Grand Rapids, MI: Brazos, 2009), 16–17.

CHAPTER 7: LOVE YOUR ENEMIES

1. Richard Hays, *The Moral Vision of the New Testament* (Edinburgh: T&T Clark, 2004), 321.

2. Exod. 21:24; Lev. 24:20; Deut. 19:21

3. Some interpretations say that Jesus isn't talking about violence here. They say that not "resisting evil" only prohibits taking the "evil person" to court (e.g. David Daube, *The New Testament and Rabbinic Judaism* [London: Athlone, 1956], 259). But this interpretation is unconvincing for reasons stated in my discussion of Matt. 5.

4. For example, Lev. 26:37 and Josh. 23:9. By looking at the use of a Greek word in the Old Testament, I'm referring to the Septuagint (LXX), the Greek translation of the Hebrew Old Testament.

5. The word is used in the Old Testament (or LXX) forty-four out of seventy-seven times to refer to some sort of *violent* resistance (e.g., Lev. 26:37; Deut. 7:24; 9:2; 11:25; Josh. 1:5; 7:13; 23:9; Judg. 2:14; 6:4; 11:82; 2 Chron. 13:7). Josephus uses the term fifteen out of seventeen times to refer to violence. The New Testament often uses the word to refer to *spiritual* warfare rather than *physical* warfare—but warfare nonetheless. "Take up the whole armor of God," Paul says, "that you may be able to *resist* in the evil day" (Eph. 6:13, author's translation), though other related words are used explicitly for violent resistance. In Acts 5:37, "Judas the Galilean *rose up* [*aphistemi*]" and started a revolt. In Acts 17:5, the Jews "*attacked* [*ephistem*] the house of Jason," and again in Acts 18:12 "the Jews made a united *attack* [*katephistemi*]!" In Acts 16:22, "the *crowd joined in attacking* [*sunephistemi*]."

Hebrews 12:4 describes the church as not having *"resisted [antikathistemi]* to the point of shedding your blood." See further Walter Wink, "Beyond Just War and Pacifism: Jesus's Nonviolent Way," *Review and Expositor* 89 (1992), 197–214: (198–199).

6. N. T. Wright, *The Kingdom New Testament: A Contemporary Translation* (New York: HarperOne, 2011), 9.

7. In Jewish tradition, for instance, if one man smacked another, "he pays him two hundred zuz," but "if it is with the back of the hand, he pays him four hundred zuz" (Mishnah *Baba Qamma* 8:6).

8. See Exod. 22:26; Deut. 24:10–13

9. Deut. 24:13

10. We see this played out during Jesus's crucifixion when Simon of Cyrene was "forced … to carry" (*angareuo*) the cross of Christ (see Matt. 27:32 NIV).

11. The story can be read at Rob Hull, "Emily Klotz: Forgiving the Unforgivable," *700 Club*, CBN.com, https://www.cbn.com/700club/features/amazing/RH44_emily_klotz.aspx (accessed March 16, 2013).

12. Martin Luther, *Commentary on the Sermon on the Mount* (Philadelphia: The Lutheran Publication Society, 1892), 196.

13. Lev. 19:18, 34; Deut. 10:18–19; cf. Lev. 19:13, 15, 17; 23:22; Deut. 24:17, 19–21

14. In fact, several passages come close to encouraging hating one's enemy (e.g., Ps. 139:19–22).

15. Richard Horsely, for instance, said that Jesus's words apply only to internal Jewish disputes that were frequent in villages of Palestine. "Enemy" here doesn't include political enemies or enemies of the state. Richard Horsley, "Ethics and Exegesis: 'Love Your Enemies' and the Doctrine of Non-violence," *Journal of the American Academy of Religion* 54 (spring 1986): 3–31.

16. This is seen by the fact that Jesus moves from the singular ("hate your *enemy*") to the plural ("but I say … love your *enemies*"), which highlights the all-inclusive nature of the command.

17. Deut. 20:1; Luke 19:43

18. Hays, *The Moral Vision of the New Testament*, 328. Grant Osborne pointed to the change "from the singular 'enemy' to the plural 'enemies,' stressing the universal nature of the command, and (2) the use of the present imperative, stressing the ongoing need of such an attitude" (Grant R. Osborne and Clinton E. Arnold, *Matthew* [Grand Rapids, MI: Zondervan, 2010], 212).

19. Luke 9:51–56

20. Matt. 26:47–56 (with parallels); also Rev. 13:10; Matt. 27:25; Luke 16:25

21. Matt. 16:21–23; 17:22–23; 20:17–19

22. Some have understood Jesus's rebuke to Peter as supporting submission to authorities, not promoting a general nonviolent posture toward evil. After all, they were being arrested, not jumped in an alley. While there's some truth to this, I

think that both nonviolence and submission to authorities are in view. Whenever New Testament writers appeal to Jesus's nonresistance to Rome, they do not make a point about submitting to the authorities but about suffering unjustly (e.g., 1 Pet. 2:21–25; 4:12–19).

23. This story is retold in David Garrow, *Bearing the Cross* (New York: Harper Collins, 1986).

24. In Matthew, this is clear with the sixth antithesis only, but in Luke, both nonretaliation and love of enemies are governed by how they mediate divine love toward one's enemies.

CHAPTER 8: GOOD CITIZENS

1. "Tom" is a composite character made up from many different people with whom I've talked about these issues.

2. For the background of Philippi, see Gordon Fee, *Paul's Letter to the Philippians* (NICNT) (Grand Rapids, MI: Eerdmans, 1995).

3. Fee, *Paul's Letter to the Philippians*, 161–62.

4. There are many good books that discuss the Roman imperial background to the New Testament. For a recent overview, see Scot McKnight, Joseph B. Modica, and Andy Crouch (eds.), *Jesus Is Lord, Caesar Is Not* (Downers Grove, IL: IVP Academic, 2013).

5. E.g., Phil. 1:28–30; 3:18–19

6. Acts 16:19–24, 35–40; cf. Phil. 1:28–30

7. Phil. 2:12–18; cf. 2:25–30

8. See N. T. Wright, *The Climax of the Covenant* (Minneapolis, MN: Fortress, 1993), 56–98.

9. 1 Pet. 1:1; 2:11

10. 1 Pet. 3:15; 4:14

11. "Father, forgive them, for they know not what they do" (Luke 23:34; cf. Acts 7:60).

12. The same point has been made by John Howard Yoder, *The Politics of Jesus* (Grand Rapids, MI: Eerdmans, 1994), 112–131.

13. See Tremper Longman III and Daniel G. Reid, *God Is a Warrior* (Grand Rapids, MI: Zondervan, 1995).

14. Wayne Grudem, *Politics—According to the Bible* (Grand Rapids, MI: Zondervan, 2010), 403.

15. Roman police officers were often referred to as "sword bearers" (Egypt; Philo *Special Laws*, 2.92–95; 3.159–63), cited in Douglas Moo, *The Epistle to the Romans* (NICNT) (Grand Rapids, MI: Eerdmans, 1996), 802. By extension, bearing the sword could refer to Rome's military putting down a revolt within the empire. The sword may include the idea of capital punishment, as it does in Acts 12:2. But in this context, it probably refers more generally to God using the government to punish wrongdoing.

16. The Greek word is *hupotassesthai* ("to submit"). This word occurs throughout the Old Testament (LXX), and in only one case is obedience the main idea (Dan. 6:13, Theodotion's Greek version). The New Testament uses the term thirty times, and in most cases, obedience is not the main idea (C. E. B. Cranfield, *Romans 9–16* [New York: T&T Clark, 2004], 660–63). *Submission* is used to describe the posture of the younger toward an elder (1 Pet. 5:5), a wife toward her husband (Eph. 5:22; Col. 3:18), a slave toward his master (1 Pet. 2:18), Christians toward their leaders (1 Cor. 16:16), and other situations where the one doing the submitting occupies a lesser place of authority (not value).

17. The New Testament has three Greek words that are used for "obedience" (*peitharkein*, *peithesthai*, and *upakouein*), none of which Paul uses here (see Cranfield, *Romans 9–16*, 660–63). However, see Titus 3:1.

18. The concern Paul has for Christians to pay taxes is a concern that they won't revolt against Rome (Romans 13:2—the verb for "resist" here is *antitasso*, which means "to range in battle against"). The reason Paul and Jesus command Christians to pay taxes isn't because we *support* the state. Rather, it's because *not paying taxes* is a *direct act of war and revolution* (think: "No Taxation without Representation" and the Boston Tea Party) especially in the first-century context (e.g., Josephus, *Wars of the Jews*, 2.8.1 or *Antiquities of the Jews*, 18.1.6).

19. Robert Jewett, Eldon Jay Epp, and Roy David Kotansky, *Romans* (Minneapolis, MN: Fortress, 2007), 790.

20. See too Prov. 8:15–16. The book of Daniel makes the same point (Dan. 2:21, 37–38; 4:17, 25, 32; 5:21; 8:11).

21. Gen. 50:20; Judg. 14:4

22. E.g., Isa. 10:7–19; Hab. 2:8, 10, 12, 17

23. There's no transition in Rom. 13:1.

CHAPTER 9: THE WRATH OF THE LAMB

1. Friedrich Nietzsche, quoted in Richard Hays, *The Moral Vision of the New Testament* (Edinburgh: T&T Clark, 2004), 169.

2. James Carroll, *Jerusalem, Jerusalem* (New York: Houghton Mifflin Harcourt, 2011), 45.

3. Shaw's comment is well-known and cited in many sources.

4. Bill Barrick, "The Christian and War," *TMSJ* 11 (2000), 225.

5. John MacArthur, *Revelation 12–22* (Chicago: Moody, 2000), 117, 118.

6. Mark Driscoll, "7 Big Questions: 7 Leaders on Where the Church Is Headed," *Relevant*, Issue 24, Jan/Feb 2007, http://web.archive.org/web/20071013102203/http://relevantmagazine.com/god_article.php?id=7418 (accessed March 23, 2013).

7. Hays, *The Moral Vision of the New Testament*, 173.

8. Rev. 2:9–10, 13; 3:8–10

9. Rev. 2:20; 3:17

10. Rev. 2:7, 11, 17, 26–29; 3:5–6, 12–13, 21–22

11. Richard Bauckham, *Climax of Prophecy* (London: T&T Clark, 2000), 234.

12. Richard Bauckham, *The Theology of the Book of Revelation* (Cambridge: Cambridge University Press, 1993), 89.

13. Bruce Metzger, *Breaking the Code* (Nashville, TN: Abingdon Press, 1993), 88.

14. See Bauckham, *The Theology of the Book of Revelation*, 93–94; Kraybill, "What about the Warrior Jesus?," Tripp York and Justin Bronson Barringer, eds., *A Faith Not Worth Fighting For* (Eugene, OR: Cascade, 2012), 201.

15. Rev. 4–5 and 12–14

16. Rev 18; 21–22

17. Rev. 12:1; 17:4; 18:16

18. Rev. 4–5; 16:10; 20:11

19. Rev. 7:3–4; 13:16–18; 14:1

20. E.g., Rev. 11:7; 12:7–8, 17; 13:7 (Bauckham, *The Theology of the Book of Revelation*, 69).

21. E.g., Homer, *Iliad*, 3.138, 255; 23.702; Homeric Hymn to Ares; 1 Macc. 3:19; 2 Macc. 10:38

22. The word *conquer* is used twice of Christ (Rev. 5:5; 17:14), twice of the beast (11:7; 13:7), and ten times of the saints (2:7, 11, 17, 26; 3:5, 12, 21; 12:11; 15:2; 21:7). Lastly, in 6:2 it is debated whether it refers to Christ. The many reasons against its referring to Christ are convincing (see G. B. Caird, *The Revelation of St. John the Divine* [New York: Harper & Row, 1966], 80–81).

23. Cf. John 16:33; Col. 2:15; Rom. 8:37; 2 Cor. 2:14

24. See Greg Boyd's take on Driscoll: "Revelation and the Violent 'Prize Fighting' Jesus," ReKnew, September 28, 2010, http://reknew.org/2010/09/revelation-and-the-violent-prize-fighting-jesus/.

25. Gen. 49:9–10; cf. 1 Macc. 3:4

26. Hays, *The Moral Vision of the New Testament*, 174.

27. Bauckham, *The Theology of the Book of Revelation*, 74; Gorman, *Reading Revelation Responsibly*, 108–112.

28. Rev. 3:21; 12:10–12; 17:14; 19:13, 20; cf. John 12:31; 1 Cor. 1:18–25; Col. 2:15

29. E.g., Rev. 12:11; 15:2; 21:7

30. Rev. 11:7; 13:2, 7

31. Gordon Fee, *Revelation* (Eugene, OR: Wipf & Stock Publishers, 2010), 111–112; Caird, *Revelation of St. John*, 101; David Aune, *Word Biblical Commentary, Vol. 52B: Revelation 6–16* (Nashville, TN: Nelson, 1998), 468–470; N. T. Wright, *Revelation for Everyone* (Louisville, KY: Westminster John Knox Press, 2011), 74.

32. Wright, *Revelation for Everyone*, 70; Aune, *Revelation 6–16*, 474.

33. Rev. 11:7; 13:7

34. Matt. 9:36–38; Luke 10:2; cf. Mark 4:29

35. Blood of Christ (Rev. 1:5; 5:9; 7:14; 12:11; 16:6; 19:13); blood of the saints (6:10; 14:20; 16:6; 17:6; 18:24; blood of the innocent (18:24). Seas and rivers also turn to blood throughout Revelation (6:12; 8:7, 8; 11:6; 16:3, 4). Nowhere does "blood" in Revelation refer to the blood of Jesus's slaughtered enemies.

36. See Wright, *Revelation for Everyone*, 134–135.

37. Those who agree with my reading include Caird, *Revelation of St. John*, 192–94; Wright, *Revelation for Everyone*, 133–135; and Peter J. Leithart, *Between Babel and Beast: America and Empires in Biblical Perspective* (Eugene, OR: Cascade, 2012), 45–47. Those who identify the blood with Jesus's enemies include G. K. Beale, *NIGTC: The Book of Revelation* (Grand Rapids, MI: Eerdmans, 1998), 782–83; Alan F. Johnson, *The Expositor's Bible Commentary with the New International Version: Revelation* (Grand Rapids, MI: Zondervan, 1996), 543.

38. Rev. 15:7; 16:1, 19

39. This is what the grain harvest seems to suggest. See Bauckham, *The Theology of the Book of Revelation*, 94–98.

40. Rev. 1:16; 2:12, 16; cf. John 12:48; 2 Thess. 2:8; Heb. 4:12

41. Robert H. Mounce, *The Book of Revelation* (NICNT) (Grand Rapids, MI: Eerdmans, 1997), 346; cf. 2 Thess. 2:8; *Pss. Sol.* 17:39; *1 En.* 62:2.

42. Rev. 6:16; 19:21; cf. 2 Thess. 1:6–9; 2:8

43. Cf. Rev. 1:9; 12:11, 17; 13:10; 14:12–13. The only passage that could be taken to refer to saints physically fighting against their enemies is Rev. 2:26–27. Here, Jesus promises that "the one who conquers … will rule *them* [the nations] with a rod of iron, as when earthen pots are broken in pieces." Jesus here quotes from Ps. 2, one of many Old Testament passages that depict a conquering Messiah. But how will He (and His followers) conquer? The rest of Revelation tells us. The basic point of Rev. 2, then, is that believers will rule with Jesus in His kingdom, as often stated in the New Testament (2 Tim. 2:12; Eph. 2:6–7). The image of "ruling" the nations shows how the *hopes* of Ps. 2 are fulfilled by the judicial word of Christ, just as the *hopes* for a militaristic messianic conqueror are fulfilled unexpectedly in a slain Lamb.

44. Bauckham, *Climax of Prophecy*, 349; See also Wright, *Revelation for Everyone*, 152.

45. Rev. 18:24; cf. 2:18–23

46. David Kilcullen and Andrew McDonald, "Death from Above, Outrage Down Below," *New York Times*, May 16, 2009, http://www.nytimes.com/2009/05/17/opinion/17exum.html?_r=3&.

47. Chris Woods and Christina Lamb, "Obama Terror Drones: CIA Tactics in Pakistan Include Targeting Rescuers and Funerals," *The Bureau of Investigative Journalism*, February 4, 2012, http://www.thebureauinvestigates.com/2012/02/04/obama-terror-drones-cia-tactics-in-pakistan-include-targeting-rescuers-and-funerals/.

48. Scott Shane, "C.I.A. Is Disputed on Civilian Toll in Drone Strikes," *New York Times*, August 11, 2011, http://www.nytimes.com/2011/08/12/world/asia/12drones.html?_r=1.

49. This number is confirmed by several diverse reports. See for instance, Rob Crilly, "168 Children Killed in Drone Strikes in Pakistan Since Start of Campaign," *Telegraph*, August 11, 2011, http://www.telegraph.co.uk/news/worldnews/asia/pakistan/8695679/168-children-killed-in-drone-strikes-in-pakistan-since-start-of-campaign.html.

50. Christina Bellantoni and Terence Burlij, "Obama: Nation Must Answer 'Hard Questions,'" *PBS NewsHour: The Rundown*, December 17, 2012, http://www.pbs.org/newshour/rundown/2012/12/obama-in-connecticut-nation-must-answer-hard-questions.html.

51. Glenn Greenwald, "Joe Klein's Sociopathic Defense of Drone Killings of Children," *Telegraph*, October 23, 2012, http://www.guardian.co.uk/commentisfree/2012/oct/23/klein-drones-morning-joe.

CHAPTER 10: THE EARLY CHURCH IN A VIOLENT WORLD

1. Eusebius, *Hist. Eccl.* V.1.41–55. For a general description of Roman torture practices in the first century, see Seneca, *Ep.* 14.4–6, and the brief overview in George Kalantzis, *Caesar and the Lamb* (Eugene, OR: Cascade, 2012), 25–34.

2. Justin Martyr, *First Apology* 1.14.3; 1.39; Kalantzis, *Caesar and the Lamb*, 54–55.

3. Some of the most extensive works on the subject include C. J. Cadoux, *Early Christian Attitudes to War* (London: Headley, 1919; reprint, New York: Seabury, 1982); Adolf von Harnack, *Militia Christi*, trans. David M. Gracie (Philadelphia: Fortress, 1981); Louis J. Swift, *The Early Fathers on War and Military Service* (Wilmington, DE: Michael Glazier, 1983). For this chapter, I'll interact with the more recent works by John Helgeland, "Christians and the Roman Army A.D. 173–337," *Church History* 43.2 (1974): 149–63, 200; Peter J. Leithart, *Defending Constantine* (Downers Grove, IL: InterVarsity, 2010); Ronald J. Sider (ed.), *The Early Church on Killing* (Grand Rapids, MI: Baker Academic, 2012); Kalantzis, *Caesar and the Lamb*.

4. Exactly how much changed is debated. And I agree with Peter Leithart, who in his fine book *Defending Constantine* argued that there is a lot of misunderstanding about this "Constantinian shift."

5. Origen, *Against Celsus* 3.7 (from Sider).

6. Tertullian, *Spec.* 2.

7. Cyprian, Letter 56.

8. *Plea on behalf of Christians (or Legatio)*, 35. He defended himself against the charge of cannibalism by saying that to cannibalize they would have to first kill.

9. See Sider, *Early Church on Killing*.

10. Lactantius, *Divine Institutes*, 6.20.15–17, quoted in Kalantzis, *Caesar and the Lamb*, 53.

11. After Constantine's conversion, Lactantius seemed to change his view considerably.

12. Arnobius, *Against the Pagans*, 1.6.

13. See especially Justin Martyr, *First Apology* 1.14.3; 1.15.9; 1.16.4; 1.39.3.

14. *Didache* 1.2; *Second Clement* 13; Justin Martyr, *First Apology* 14–16, *Trypho* 85, 96; Irenaeus, *Against Heresies* 2.32, 3.18, 4.13; Athenagoras, *Plea* 1, 11; Clement of Alexandria, *Educator* 3.12, *Exhortation* 10, *Miscellanies* 4.8; Tertullian, *Apology* 31, 37, *Spectacles* 16, *Patience* 6, 8, *Marcion* 4.16, *Scapula* 1; Origen, *Celsus* 7.58–61, 8.35, *Commentary on John*; Cyprian, *Jews* 3.49, *Patience* 16; Lactantius, *Divine Institutes* 5.10.

15. Tertullian, *Scap.* 1.3.

16. There are some disputed passages, however. Tertullian, for instance, acknowledged that there were Christians everywhere in the empire, including the "fortresses" and "the very camps," pointing to Christians in the military (*Apol.* 37). But does this mean that he was okay with this? Not necessarily. In the same passage, Tertullian argued that Christians love their enemies, don't retaliate, and "willingly yield ourselves to the sword." And elsewhere in his writings, Tertullian condemned "every sort of man-killing," as we have seen. So it seems that Tertullian was here acknowledging the presence of Christians in the military without necessarily sanctioning violence. The same goes for his statement in *Apol.* 42: "We sail with you, *and fight with you*, and till the ground with you." While some see this as Tertullian's support of Christians in the military (e.g., Helgeland, "Christians and the Roman Army," 151), this seems to go beyond what Tertullian said. He acknowledged only that there were Christians in the military, but was silent on whether he approved or disapproved of this. Elsewhere, he clearly condemned it. The same went for Clement of Alexandria, who in several treatises acknowledged that Christians are in the military (*Exhortation to the Greeks*, 10; cf. *Educator*, 2.12–13). In his *Exhortation to the Greeks*, 10, he even told Christians in the military to "listen to the commander, who orders what is right." But who did he refer to as "the commander"? This could refer to the military commander, or it could refer to Christ—*the Commander*—as he wrote elsewhere (cf. *Educator*, 1.8). Either way, Clement went on to remind these Christians to obey God's commandments: "'Thou shalt not kill' and 'Thou shalt love thy neighbor as thyself; to him who strikes thee on the cheek, present also the other'" (*Exhortation*, 10). In one treatise, Clement distinguished between just and unjust killing in war (*Resurrection*, 16). But he was not talking about *Christians* here. Finally, some have taken Origen's distinction between just and unjust wars as proof that Christians can fight in just wars. But as seen in other authors above, whenever Origen made this distinction, he was talking about non-Christians, not Christians (*Celsus*, 2.30; 4.9; 7.26; see

David Hunter, "Decade of Research on Early Christians and Military Service," *Religious Studies Review* 18, no. 2 (1992): 87–94, [88]). Origen never said that it was okay for Christians to fight in Rome's wars, no matter how just they may be.

17. Tertullian, *The Crown.*

18. Tertullian, *On Idolatry.*

19. Alan Kreider, "Military Service in the Church Orders," *Journal of Religious Ethics* 31 (2003): 415–42 (431).

20. John Helgeland, Robert J. Daly, and J. Patout Burns, *Christians and the Military* (Minneapolis: Fortress, 1985), 54, cited in Kalantzis, *Caesar and the Lamb*, 50–51.

21. Lactantius, *Divine Institutes*, 6.20.15–17, quoted in Kalantzis, *Caesar and the Lamb*, 53.

22. David Hunter, who is not a pacifist, says that "it seems likely that aversion to killing was included in Tertullian's comment" ("Decade of Research on Early Christians and Military Service," 88).

23. Origen, *Against Celsum* 8.73; see also 4.82; 7.26; similarly, Arnobius, *Pagans* 1.6; 2.1. Origen even said that it's okay to kill a tyrant but didn't allow Christians to do the killing (*Against Celsum*, 1.1).

24. Origen, *Against Celsum* 8.73.

25. E.g., Cyprian, *Mort.* 2; Ireneus *Adv. Hers.* 5.24; Adamantius, *Dialogue on the True Faith* 1.10.

26. See the discussion in Hunter, "Decade of Research on Early Christians and Military Service," 88; Kalantzis, *Caesar and the Lamb*, 42–43, 54–55.

27. In *Against Celsus* 2.30, Origen affirmed that some wars are necessary, yet explicitly forbade Christians from participating, since Jesus did not permit them "to take vengeance even upon their enemies."

28. Irenaeus, *Adv. Hers.* 5.24; cf. 2.32; 4.34.

29. Leithart, *Defending Constantine*, 261.

30. For more information about this document, see Paul F. Bradshaw et al. *The Apostolic Tradition* (Minneapolis, MN: Fortress, 2002).

31. *Apos. Trad.* c 16. I've quoted from the Arabic version. The Sahidic version is similar, and the Ethiopic version is even stricter, banning not just soldiers who kill, but all soldiers in the military: "They are not to accept soldiers of an official." All three versions prohibit a Christian from joining the military. For the different versions, see Bradshaw et al., *Apostolic Tradition*, 88–90; cf. Kreider, "Military Service in the Church Orders," 419.

32. Kreider, "Military Service in the Church Orders," 20.

33. *Canons of Hippolytus, Testament of Our Lord*, and *Apostolic Constitutions*. The first two reflect the nonviolent teaching of *Apostolic Tradition*, while the latter document diverges from it.

34. See Kreider, "Military Service in the Church Orders," 431.

35. This argument can be seen as early as Augustine.

36. Richard Hays, *The Moral Vision of the New Testament*, 335–336; however, he went on to say that "their military background is no more commended by these stories than are the occupations of other converts, such as tax collectors and prostitutes" (340).

37. Kalantzis, *Caesar and the Lamb*, 66–68.

38. "In fact, much of Roman military service consisted of what might be called police and civil service functions—firefighting, mail delivery, accounting, messenger services, general administration, custody of prisoners, public transport and road maintenance, and so forth" (Daniel M. Bell Jr., *Just War as Christian Discipleship* [Grand Rapids, MI: Brazos, 2009], 25).

39. Clement of Alexandria, *Exhortation* 10; *Educator* 2.12; *Miscellanies* 4.14; Tertullian, *Apology* 42; esp. *Apology* 37; *Crown* 1.11; Dionysius of Alexandria, quoted in Eusebius's *Ecclesiastical History*, 7.11; Origen, *Commentary on 1 Corinthians* on 1 Cor. 9:11.

40. Sider, *Early Church on Killing*, 194.

41. Kreider, "Military Service," 433.

42. Herbert Musurillo, ed. and trans., *Acts of Christian Martyrs*, Oxford Early Christian Texts (Oxford: Clarendon Press, 1972).

43. Ramsay MacMullen, *Enemies of the Roman Order* (Cambridge, MA: Harvard University Press, 1966), 255–68; idem., *Solder*, p. v.

44. G. R. Watson, *The Roman Soldier* (Ithaca, NY: Cornell University Press, 1985), 143.

45. See note 38 above.

46. Tertullian seemed to assume this when he instructed converted soldiers to refrain from killing, to love their neighbor, and to turn the other cheek (*Exhortation to the Greeks*, 10.100; 10.108).

47. Basil of Caesarea, *Ep. 188.13*.

48. From a variant of the *Apostolic Constitution* known as the Alexandrine Sinodos, quoted in Kreider, "Military Service in the Church Orders," 429.

49. Hunter, "A Decade of Research on Early Christians and Military Service," 89; Swift, *The Early Fathers on War and Military Service*, 149–54.

50. Augustine, *Letter 189*, http://www.newadvent.org/fathers/1102189.htm.

51. Augustine still advocated for the need for just wars throughout all his writings. But in his later writings, he saw war as a horrible necessity, rather than something to be celebrated. See R. A. Markus, "Saint Augustine's Views on the 'Just War,'" in *The Church and War*, vol. 20., ed. W. J. Sheils, Studies in Church History (Oxford: Published for the Ecclesiastical History Society by Basil Blackwell, 1983), 1–13.

52. This story can be found in "The Passion of the Scillitan Martyrs," Early Christian Writings, http://www.earlychristianwritings.com/scillitan.html.

CHAPTER 11: ATTACKER AT THE DOOR

1. See John Howard Yoder *What Would You Do?* (Scottdale, PA: Herald Press, 1992).

2. The guns that I own are far away from bullets and out of reach from anyone in my home. The gun-control debate will rage on, and again I'm not convinced that gun control is the answer. In any case, having a loaded firearm (or one with bullets nearby), which is necessary to kill the attacker at the door, carries other risks that aren't often considered in our attacker-at-the-door scenario.

3. 1 Pet. 2:21; 1 John 2:6; 3:16–17

4. John 8:1–11. This passage may not be original, but most scholars agree that it probably happened.

5. Matt. 5:43–48; Luke 6:27–29, 32–33, 35–36

6. Mark 10:42–45; 1 Pet. 2:21; Phil. 2:5–8; 3:10; 2 Cor. 4:8–12

7. Phil. 3:11, 21; Rom. 8:23; 1 Cor. 15:22–23

8. Dan. 3:19–29; 6:16–22, 27; Acts 5:17–25; 12:1–19; 16:22–26

9. With aggressive *physical resistance*, however, we should consider whether this behavior might incite a more violent response from the attacker. In any case, I do think that one could physically resist without violently resisting, which seems to be the point of Matt. 5:38–39. After all, stopping the attacker could give you an opportunity to love him.

10. Yoder, *What Would You Do?*, 82.

11. Exodus 22:2–3 says that if you kill a thief at night, you're not guilty, but if you kill him during the day, you are guilty of murder. But why? It could be that killing at night was accidental and therefore there's no guilt. Or it could mean that the intruder breaking in at night was trying to attack your family, not just take your stuff. Why else would he break into your house at night when everyone is home? If he broke in during the day, it's because he didn't expect anyone to be there. He was just a burglar, not a threat to your family. Although the text doesn't say clearly why killing at night is allowed, the latter option is probably best: killing your enemy to protect your family is allowed under the old covenant.

12. This ethical approach is called "conflicting absolutism." There is a similar ethical approach called "graded absolutism," which says that we shouldn't do the *lesser of two evils* but *obey the higher law*. There are many similarities in these approaches, but graded absolutism says that Christians should never "do evil." Therefore, when someone disobeys the lower law in order to obey the higher law, he or she is not doing evil, not even the lesser evil. The conflict has made obedience to the higher law the *only* good that one should do. Now, in my discussion, I'll maintain the framework of "conflicting absolutism" but use the verbiage of the "lesser of two evils" because that phrase is much more familiar.

13. E.g., Job 29:12–17

14. I already see a problem with this distinction, though. Didn't Jesus call our enemy *our neighbor* (Luke 10:29–37)? If you kill your enemy, then you've also killed your neighbor.

15. Compare Num. 15:30 and Lev. 4:2–3.

16. Note the parallelism between "love your neighbor and hate your enemy" and Jesus's improvement: "love your enemy and pray for those persecuting you" (Matt. 5:43–44).

17. Robert Brimlow has written a full-length book on the issue: *What about Hitler?* (Grand Rapids, MI: Brazos, 2006). A short summary can be found in his essay "What About Hitler?" in Tripp York and Justin Bronson Barringer, eds., *A Faith Not Worth Fighting For* (Eugene, OR: Cascade, 2012), 44–59.

18. On Bonhoeffer and Hitler, see Robert Brimlow, *What about Hitler?*

19. See, for instance, the lecture by Mark Thiessen Nation: "Dietrich Bonhoeffer the Assassin? Challenging a Myth, Recovering Costly Grace," *Eastern Mennonite University Podcast*, February 23, 2011, http://emu.edu/now/podcast/2011/02/23/dietrich-bonhoeffer-the-assassin-challenging-a-myth-recovering-costly-grace-mark-thiessen-nation/. The material can also be found in Nation's forthcoming book.

20. Yoder, *What Would You Do?*, 14. Eric Metaxes, in his biography on Bonhoeffer, quoted Hitler's response to the failed assassination attempt: "'It was Providence that spared me,' Hitler declared. 'This proves I'm on the right track. I feel that this is the confirmation of all my work'" (*Bonhoeffer* [Nashville, TN: Nelson, 2010], 481).

21. Stephen Kinzer, *Overthrow* (New York: Henry Holt, 2007); Peter J. Leithart, *Between Babel and Beast* (Eugene, OR: Cascade, 2012), 120–129.

22. All of these are well documented. For a more detailed overview, see Peter Ackerman and Jack DuVall, *A Force More Powerful* (Basingstoke, UK: Palgrave, 2001), as well as its accompanying video; Gene Sharp, *From Dictatorship to Democracy* (London: Serpent's Tail, 2012); Mark Kurlansky, *Nonviolence* (New York: Modern Library, 2008); Glen H. Stassen and Michael L. Westmoreland-White, "Defining Violence and Nonviolence," in J. Denny Weaver and Gerald Biesecker-Mast (eds.), *Teaching Peace* (Lanham, MD: Rowman and Littlefield, 2003), 23–34.

23. See Gregory A. Boyd, "Does God Expect Nations to Turn the Other Cheek?" in *A Faith Not Worth Fighting For*, 107–124.

24. Boyd, "Does God Expect," 116.

25. Boyd, "Does God Expect," 116.

26. Boyd, "Does God Expect," 117.

27. These statements and others are scattered throughout the chapter on national defense in Wayne Grudem, *Politics—According to the Bible* (Grand Rapids, MI: Zondervan, 2010).

CHAPTER 12: QUESTIONS AND OBJECTIONS

1. Matt. 21:12–13; Mark 11:15–16; Luke 19:45–46; John 2:14–16

2. The Greek word for "them all" is *pantas*. This is a masculine plural pronoun that is being modified by both "the sheep" (neuter plural noun) and "the oxen" (masculine

plural noun). We know this since all of these words are in the accusative case. (The accusative case indicates that something is the direct object of the main verb.) Since "the sheep and the oxen" are being lumped together as a collective whole, then they are referred to by one masculine plural pronoun even though "sheep" is neuter plural and "oxen" is masculine plural. Thus, "the sheep and the oxen" are functioning as adjectives in the sentence since they are modifying the pronoun "them all." Further, "the sheep and oxen" make up what grammarians call an appositional epexegetical construction, where additional words further "exegete" (i.e., explain) the previous word(s) or sentence. The meaning of this kind of construction is best brought out by using "namely" or "that is to say" right before the epexegetical statement. Consequently, for absolute clarity it can be translated: "And making a whip of cords, he drove them all out of the temple, that is to say, all the sheep and oxen."

3. I. Howard Marshall, *The Gospel of Luke* (NIGTC) (Grand Rapids, MI: Eerdmans, 1978), 825.

4. Darrell L. Bock, *Luke 9:51–24:53* (ECNT) (Grand Rapids, MI: Baker, 1996), 747.

5. William Hendriksen, *New Testament Commentary: Luke* (Grand Rapids, MI: Baker, 1978), 976.

6. Acts 2:33; 5:31; 7:55–56; cf. Mark 12:35–37

7. Rev. 2:12, 16; 12:5; 19:15

8. Rev. 19:15, 21; cf. John 12:48. Notice also how Isa. 11:4 says that the Messiah's judgment is "with the rod of his *mouth*, and with the *breath* of his *lips*."

9. Consider, for instance, the way Acts 4:25–28 interprets Ps. 2.

10. See http://www.witnesstoinnocence.org and Tim Junkin's book *Bloodsworth* (Chapel Hill, NC: Algonquin, 2004).

11. Bob Enyart, "God and the Death Penalty," *Theology Online*, http://www.theologyonline.com/DEATH.HTML (accessed March 6, 2013).

12. My conversation with Bob Armstrong has been recounted here with his permission.

13. E.g., Augustine, Ambrose, and Aquinas. Aquinas, however, believed that killing in self-defense is justifiable if the one being attacked did not *intend* to kill the attacker.

14. Some would say that your kids would suffer if you are killed. This may be true, but it's impossible to foresee this. First, if I'm right that Jesus doesn't permit killing in self-defense, then my kids would witness their father obey Jesus rather than disobey. Perhaps my kids would be more motivated to love Jesus having seen such love exemplified by their father. Second, no one knows how God can redeem the situation. It's pop psychology, not the Bible, that says that this situation will necessarily hinder the faith of my kids. It very well could strengthen it.

15. Tobias Winright surveyed four different views among pacifists regarding the police force ("From Police Officers to Peace Officers," in *The Wisdom of the Cross*, eds. Stanley Hauerwas et al. [Grand Rapids, MI: Eerdmans 1999], 84–114).

16. A police force separate from the military came into being in 1829 in Britain and in 1834 in the US.

17. James Reimer, "Christians and the Use of Force," *Canadian Mennonite,* August 30, 1999.

18. Lowell Ewert, a Mennonite, points out that 80 percent of police work involves domestic disputes, social work, accidents, fires, lightning strikes, hurricanes, tornadoes, or nonviolent restraint of people who pose a threat to themselves and society ("Law and Its Enforcement: A Substitute for Violence—A Response to the Gospel and the Glock," *Conrad Grebel Review,* 26.2 [Spring 2008]: 74). Even the most committed pacifist would resonate with these activities.

19. John Howard Yoder, *The Christian Witness to the State* (Scottdale, PA: Herald Press, 2002).

20. According to a Supreme Court decision in 1985 (*Tennessee v. Garner*), a police officer may shoot only to defend herself or himself, or to save another person from "grievous bodily injury" (Winright, "From Police Officers to Peace Officers," 96). In other words, cops legally can't kill a fleeing felon unless somebody's life is in danger. As I said above, however, I don't think a Christian is justified in killing out of self-defense, and if I'm correct, then a Christian cop should not do so even if the state sanctions it.

21. Some Christian pacifists would not actually call the cops, or would only do so under certain circumstances; see Andy Alexis-Baker, "The Gospel or a Glock? Mennonites and the Police," *Conrad Grebel Review* 25. 2 (Spring 2007): 23–49.

22. See Winright, "From Police Officers to Peace Officers," 84–114; Yoder, *The Christian Witness to the State.*

CHAPTER 13: CRUCIFORM KING

1. This story is based on Rom. 16:23 and the book of Revelation. It's not historical, but it very well could have been.

APPENDIX: WHAT IS JUST WAR THEORY?

1. Arthur Holmes, "The Just War," in Robert G. Clouse (ed.), *War* (Downers Grove, IL: InterVarsity, 1986), 117–135 (117).

2. Ambrose, quoted in Daniel M. Bell Jr., *Just War as Christian Discipleship* (Grand Rapids, MI: Brazos, 2009), 27.

3. Bell, *Just War,* 28.

4. Bell, *Just War,* 62.

5. Bell, *Just War,* 71.

6. Taken from Holmes, "The Just War." Michael Walzer argued that noncombatants may be targeted in cases where extreme evil (such as Hitler) needs to be stopped (*Just and Unjust Wars* [New York: Basic, 2006]).

7. Oliver O'Donovan, *The Just War Revisited* (Cambridge, MA: Cambridge University Press, 2003), 13.

8. Alexander Moseley, "Just War Theory," *Internet Encyclopedia of Philosophy*, http://www.iep.utm.edu/justwar/ (accessed February 23, 2013).

9. Wayne Grudem, *Politics—According to the Bible* (Grand Rapids, MI: Zondervan, 2010), 389.

10. See Vinoth Ramachandra, *Subverting Global Myths* (Downers Grove, IL: IVP Academic, 2008), 18–23, 29–31.

11. See Thomas Trzyna, *Blessed Are the Pacifists* (Scottdale: Herald Press, 2006), 82-83.

12. Erick Erickson, "Skip the Drone Debate, Just Kill the Terrorists Before They Kill Us," *FoxNews.com*, February 6, 2013, http://www.foxnews.com/opinion/2013/02/06/skip-drone-debate-just-kill-terrorists-before-kill-us/.

13. Bell, *Just War*, 91.

14. Mark Kurlansky, *Nonviolence* (London: Vintage, 2007), 145.

15. Walter Russell Mead, *Special Providence* (New York: Routledge, 2002), 219.

16. For a brief overview with bibliography, see Leithart, *Babel and Beast*, 129–134. In all of these stats, I've rounded the numbers down.

17. William Blum, *Killing Hope* (Monroe, ME: Common Courage Press, 1995). See also Steve Kangas, "The Origins of the Overclass," http://www.huppi.com/kangaroo/L-overclass.html.

18. Yoder, *War of the Lamb*, 86. Daniel Bell refused to call all war evil, though he acknowledged that many just war supporters do.

19. U.S. National Conference of Catholic Bishops, *The Challenge of Peace* (Washington DC: United States Catholic Conference, 1983), par. 120–121, cited in Yoder, *War of the Lamb*, 87.